PENGUIN HANDBOOK

PH89

MADAME PRUNIER'S FISH COOK BOOK

In 1872 Alfred Prunier and his wife opened a modest restaurant in the Rue Duphot, Paris, which soon attracted a discriminating clientèle. Their son Émile succeeded them in 1901, and under him the Maison Prunier continued to prosper, becoming famous for 'everything coming from the sea'. The premises in the Rue Duphot were enlarged twice, and in 1925 Émile opened a second restaurant in the Étoile district, at 16 Avenue Victor Hugo, which was an immediate success. Soon after this Simone, Émile's daughter, succeeded him, at the age of twenty-two. She had married Jean Barnagaud, one of her father's colleagues, and it was on her initiative that the London Prunier's in St James's was opened in 1935. She is its present managing director, and this book was compiled under her directions. Her husband is responsible for the two establishments in Paris, their son, Claude, manages the restaurant in the Avenue Victor Hugo, and their daughter Françoise (the artist 'Toune') illustrates the famous Prunier menus.

Cover design by Bruce Robertson
Photograph by Ian Yeomans

MADAME PRUNIER'S
FISH COOK BOOK

*

LES POISSONS, COQUILLAGES,
CRUSTACÉS ET LEUR PRÉPARATION CULINAIRE
BY MICHEL BOUZY
SELECTED, TRANSLATED, AND EDITED,
WITH AN INTRODUCTION AND NOTES, BY
Ambrose Heath

*

WITH A FOREWORD BY
Madame S. B. Prunier
LINE ILLUSTRATIONS BY
Mathurin Meheut

PENGUIN BOOKS

Penguin Books Ltd, Harmondsworth, Middlesex
U.S.A.: Penguin Books Inc., 3300 Clipper Mill Road, Baltimore 11, Md.
AUSTRALIA: Penguin Books Pty Ltd, 762 Whitehorse Road
Mitcham, Victoria

—

First published by Hurst & Blackett 1938
Published in Penguin Handbooks 1963

—

Copyright © Hurst & Blackett, 1938

—

Made and printed in Great Britain by
Spottiswoode, Ballantyne and Co. Ltd,
London and Colchester
Set in Monotype Fournier

CONTENTS

*

EDITOR'S INTRODUCTION

*

WHEN Madame Prunier asked me to edit and translate this book, I was not only greatly flattered, but very excited. It is not often the lot of what I may perhaps call a professional gastronomer to come across a really thrilling cookery book, but here was one at last. I read it with the avidity of a novice, and with the approval of an adept!

It is a remarkable book, and one that should take its place among the classics of the kitchen, I hope. Fish books are few and far between, and here is one that puts all the rest I have seen to shame. It is naturally not absolutely encyclopedic, but there are enough recipes in it to keep all the cooks in England busy for some time to come before they have tried them all.

It is an odd thing that to an island race, used perhaps to eating fish more than most other European nations, a French-woman should have come to teach us how to prepare it, but perhaps not so odd after all, since it was a woman bearing a name which is a household word in Europe for fish. Emboldened perhaps by the revival of interest in food which has been taking place during the last few years, Madame Prunier opened her restaurant in London, and immediately set about teaching us what we could do with the fish that all our shores shower upon us. And she hit the spirit of the time by beginning to popularize the cheaper sorts of fish, herring, mackerel, gurnard, skate – fish which we had been used to look at askance. And she accomplished what was almost a miracle by inducing fashionable diners-out to ask for herrings, and like them, too!

Although this book contains many recipes that are rare and elaborate, it is the simplicity of most of them that I should like to stress. I know that it is often very difficult to get cooks to take the trouble they should, and when the cooking devolves upon the housewife herself, she may find that she has not as much time as she could wish; but when I read the book for the first time, and afterwards when I was engaged in the business of editing it, I could not help feeling how strangely easy and inexpensive most of the dishes

7

are, in spite of an occasional rather awe-inspiring name or two!

If readers will look closely into this, instead of being a little nervous of unfamiliar nomenclature, they will, I believe, come to the same conclusion. There is one other comment that I should like to make, and that is, that the chapters on the actual business of cooking, and preparing the auxiliary dishes too, should be carefully read before any further step is taken. Words and phrases which are unfamiliar at first sight will lose all their terrors if their meaning is understood right away.

It has been a very great pleasure to me to compile this book, and I almost wish I had it all to do over again. It seems to me to be attuned to our modern culinary ideas, and I am sure that many tables will be brightened by its contents.

AMBROSE HEATH

Longstock
May 1938

FOREWORD

BY MADAME S. B. PRUNIER

I TAKE great pleasure in presenting to English readers a new edition of my fish cookery book. It has been completely revised and is augmented by fresh recipes which my late chef and collaborator, Maurice Cochois, and I have made popular. This encourages me to hope that it will have even greater success than its predecessor, which was in constant demand from its publication in 1938, in spite of the rationing restrictions of the war years. I should also like to thank again my editor and translator, Ambrose Heath, whose culinary and gastronomical knowledge have made him such an excellent interpreter.

The favour with which my book has been received in America and on the Continent, as well as in England, is possibly due to the fact that it has the unusual distinction of being devoted almost entirely to the cooking of fish and shellfish. Moreover, it is not limited to those species which come in the luxury category, but deals with those that are – so erroneously – known as 'common'. I firmly believe that all fish are equally good if they reach the table fresh, well cooked, and tastefully served, and if my recipes persuade my readers to ask their fishmongers for cod, hake, sea bream, herring, skate, rock salmon, gurnard, and the rest, I shall be well pleased.

It may seem surprising that a Frenchwoman should say this, but my father, Émile Prunier, who was a leading fishery expert as well as a great restaurateur, fought this same prejudice, which both harms the industry itself and robs our tables of a delicious variety of dishes. Just before he died, some thirty years ago, he explained to his chef and collaborator, Michel Bouzy, and to me how he would like to encourage people to eat more fish, especially of the commoner kinds, and to collate the results of his long years of experience in a book. Although this plan was never carried out, in 1929 Michel Bouzy published *Les Poissons, Coquillages et Crustacés*, mainly selected from Prunier recipes, and this formed the basis of the first edition of the present work.

The French book was dedicated to my father's memory, and when a christening luncheon was given in its honour I was present as godmother and Maître Auguste Escoffier was godfather. The bill of fare is reproduced opposite.

At the christening of my own book in London, in 1938, the menu was entirely made up of fish dishes, and for readers' interest is also given overleaf.

In conclusion I would like to stress that this book offers scope in its variety of dishes for cooks of all degrees of experience. For the beginner there are recipes of the utmost simplicity; for the *cordon bleu* there is something more elaborate; and the *blasé* will find the original and unusual. All are alike, however, in being extremely good to eat, and I hope that they may do their part in tempting my readers to take full advantage of the wealth of fish brought to these shores.

S. B. PRUNIER

72 St James's Street
London SW 1
June 1955

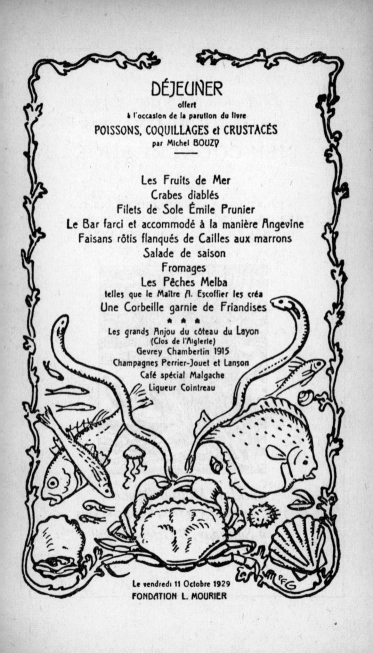

DÉJEUNER

offert

à l'occasion de la parution du livre

POISSONS, COQUILLAGES et CRUSTACÉS

par Michel BOUZY

—

Les Fruits de Mer

Crabes diablés

Filets de Sole Émile Prunier

Le Bar farci et accommodé à la manière Angevine

Faisans rôtis flanqués de Cailles aux marrons

Salade de saison

Fromages

Les Pêches Melba

telles que le Maître A. Escoffier les créa

Une Corbeille garnie de Friandises

▲ ▲ ▲

Les grands Anjou du côteau du Layon
(Clos de l'Aiglerie)

Gevrey Chambertin 1915

Champagnes Perrier-Jouet et Lanson

Café spécial Malgache

Liqueur Cointreau

Le vendredi 11 Octobre 1929

FONDATION L. MOURIER

Celebration of Christening of
MADAME PRUNIER'S
FISH COOKERY BOOK

Sponsors:

VIOLET THE LADY MELCHETT, D.B.E.
THE HON. MRS MALCOLM BOWES-LYON AND
COLONEL THE HON. ANGUS MCDONNELL,
C.B., B.M.G.

held at Maison Prunier
72 ST JAMES'S STREET, LONDON, SW1
on Saturday, 8 October 1938

MENU

*

Les Belles Huîtres de France

*

Le Consommé de Homard au Xérès

ET LE MESNIL NATURE 1937

*

Le Soufflé de Sole St James

ET LE MONTRACHET 1933

*

La Lotte Villageoise

ET LE CHÂTEAU CHEVAL BLANC 1906

*

La Pâté de Barbue et la Salade Châtelaine

ET LE CHAMBERTIN 1923

*

La Bombe Trois Maisons { *à la Madeleine à l'Étoile à St James's Street*

ET L'AYALA 1926

*

Les Fruits

Les Belles Huîtres de France

LES MARENNES. Green oysters from Marennes, a district on the River Seudre near Bordeaux.
LES BELONS. White oysters very much like Natives, from the Belon River, Brittany.

Consommé de Homard

Cook the lobster with vegetables, clarify. Finish with dry sherry and fine Julienne of lobster.

Soufflé de Sole St James

Make a soufflé mixture with the flesh of the sole. Bind the flavour well with the essence of scollops and truffles and finish by adding whipped whites of eggs. Line the mould with the soufflé. Put in layers in the mould the pieces of sole, scollops and shrimps until the top is reached. Cook gently for 25 minutes.

Lotte Villageoise

Remove the nerves of the fish. Prick the fish to garnish it. Stew the fish on a layer of chopped vegetables. Singe with calvados and finish 'à la crème'. Serve with fresh vegetables cooked in butter.

Pâté de Barbue

Macerate the brill fillets in champagne and condiments. Make a fine fish stuffing and a purée of fresh mushrooms seasoned with the essence of shallots and 'sarriette'. Put in layers in a deep mould and cook gently. When cold cut it in slices and cover with jelly of brill 'au champagne'.

Salade Châtelaine

Garnish with lettuce, hearts of artichokes and a vinaigrette of French beans and tarragon.

Bombe Trois Taisons

Flavour with rum St James and surround with small madeleines. Decorate with stars made of nougat.

L'art d'accommoder le poisson mis à la portée des familles.

Ce livre plein d'intérêt, écrit par un maître en la matière, M. Bouzy, le réputé chef de cuisine de la maison Prunier, comble une réelle lacune. En publiant dans ce recueil nombre de savoureuses et très délicates recettes, aisées à exécuter chez soi, l'auteur s'est acquis des droits à la reconnaissance de toutes les ménagères.

Nul doute que ce nouveau Né ne rencontre dès son apparition auprès du public averti et gourmet, tous les succès qu'il mérite.

A. Escoffier
Officier de la Légion d'Honneur

NOTE TO THE ORIGINAL
FRENCH EDITION

*

THE products of the seas and rivers, by their qualities and infinite variety, deserve an important place in the business of our nourishment, and they have always tempted the inventive genius of cooks greedy for beautiful and savoury dishes.

There exist at the present time thousands of recipes for preparing fish and shellfish from the sea. Many cooks and many housewives will be astonished by this, for only a few recipes are known to them, and except in certain coastal districts where special dishes have been born, our best hostesses usually have to choose between two or three recipes, of which they are already tired.

Up to the present time (1929) fish had been insufficiently understood, and its value almost unknown. Its cheapness when compared with meat offered a pretext for its nutritive properties being instinctively scorned. It has happened that the present crisis of the high cost of living has created new problems for solution, and it is thanks to these that the products of the sea have begun to take, during the last few years, the place they deserve. A campaign has been launched in honour of fish, and its nutritive and health-giving properties have been acclaimed by famous specialists on the subject. Besides all this, the actual processes of fishing and transport have assured every town good provision of fish, the variety and freshness of which leave nothing to be desired.

It only remains to popularize the methods of preparing it for the table, and fish at last will have its due.

The recipes which follow, though numerous, are only a part of the recipes in existence. They have been chosen very carefully, after thirty years' experience: they have been documented minutely; well-known chefs have been consulted; various savoury preparations have been borrowed from the coastal provinces of France, as well as picturesque dishes from foreign lands.

Thanks to their simplicity, they can be recommended to beginners in the kitchen who, if they follow our advice, will be able to give the impression of interest and knowledge. They are recommended above all to hostesses and housewives, so as to give them some economical and nourishing dishes which will bring a pleasant originality into the daily round. As for their parties, they will be able to surprise their guests by a meal in which a well-prepared and prettily presented dish of fish will leave them the memory of a feast and intrigue them by its preparation.

INTRODUCTION BY THE AUTHOR OF THE ORIGINAL FRENCH EDITION

*

GREAT efforts have been made in France to increase the consumption of fish, especially by the working classes, and to further these efforts it has been thought advisable to popularize by books the innumerable fish recipes that exist.

Very few authors have specially treated this aspect of the culinary art. Those large treatises which are written for professionals devote only a chapter to it, as do those intended for the small kitchen. But the subject is so complex that it is impossible to describe in so small a space the more usual recipes for fish. Besides, these recipes follow the general law of progress; they are modified according to times and tastes, and new ones are created which it is useful to make known.

In my position at the head of the kitchens of a restaurant which has gained an almost world-wide reputation, by the centralization in Paris of the best that comes from our seas and by its special dishes of fish and shellfish, assisted by lengthy practical experience, I have felt it my duty to collect in a book some of the recipes which are prepared daily in this restaurant, and many others as well; and I have written them down according to my own methods, which I hope my professional colleagues and the housewives will appreciate. But above all it is on the advice of famous gastronomes and with the encouragement of celebrated chefs that I have undertaken this task: and it is almost under their guarantee of a favourable reception, of which I myself am confident, that the greatest of them all, the great Escoffier, has agreed to write the Preface.

MICHEL BOUZY
(*Chef des Cuisines de la Maison Prunier*)

August 1929

CHAPTER ONE

*

Elementary Rules for Cooking Fish

IN a country where fish is hardly ever served in any other way than boiled, fried, or grilled, this chapter should be of the very greatest use, and every word should be read and digested carefully. Apart from the somewhat exotic fashion *au bleu*, the cooking of fishes by braising, *au gratin*, and *à la meunière* will to a great many be a revelation of deliciousness and simplicity. The *gratins* in particular afford an admirable way of imparting often to quite a dull fish an interest which transforms it into a first-class dish, and in those fishes of which we have tired because of their insipidness we shall see a remarkable change if we turn to the *court-bouillon* for their 'poaching'.

This, by the way, is a word which should never be forgotten. Fish should never be *boiled* – unless it is to make a soup of some kind, in which case the flavour must be boiled out into the liquid in which it is cooked. To *poach* a fish, however, is a very different matter, and produces a very different result.

The frying of fish *à la meunière* is another fashion to which I should like to draw special attention. It is simple, it is quick, and it is delicious; and yet how many times have we encountered fish cooked in this way on the tables of our friends?

The instructions in this chapter demand serious attention, and once their simple procedure is mastered, the cooking of fish in all its possible ways need have no terrors, even for the mistress when the cook is out!

BUYING FISH AND SHELLFISH

Absolute freshness and good quality are essential. Freshness in fish can be recognized by the lively brilliance of the eyes, by the rosy colour of the gills, and by the stiffness of the flesh. If the eyes are dull and the fish limp, it is not fresh, as the limpness comes from the fibres relaxing. This lack of freshness can also be recognized by the smell.

Lobsters, crawfish (*langouste*), crayfish, and so on ought to be taken alive. The flesh of these shellfish when dead is soft, and has lost the best of its qualities. Molluscs and shellfish such as oysters, clams, cockles, mussels, etc. ought to feel heavy in the hand and have their shells tightly shut. If the shells are open, the shellfish should be rejected.

As far as is possible, freshwater fish ought to be alive, and only killed when the time comes for cooking them. All the same, these fish will keep better than sea-fish, and they can be kept for a day or two by wrapping them in a good covering of fresh grass.

According to their kind, fish weighing from five to seven ounces will do for one person: and those of half a pound to three-quarters for two persons. Two pounds gross of salmon and salmon trout should be allowed for five people; but if a cut piece is bought, two pounds will be enough for six.

Taken by the whole fish, about half a pound of turbot or large brill should be allowed per head.

A lobster weighing a pound or just over is enough for two.

A crawfish (*langouste*) of two pounds is enough for four.

According to their size, two or three crayfish (*écrevisses*) are allowed per head.

GRILLING FISH

All fish that is to be grilled should first be cleaned, scaled or well scraped, dried or well wiped with a clean cloth (especially if the fish has been washed first), and, if the fish is thick-fleshed, scored here and there. By scoring I mean making little slits in the flesh on each side, the reason for this being that these help to hasten the cooking of the fish.

Flat fish, such as sole, have their heads cut off diagonally. The end of the tail is trimmed with scissors, and the black skin is removed. The white skin is left on, but it should be well scraped, and the fins cut off. For other fish of this kind, it is usual to make an incision on the black side and in the middle of the fish, penetrating to the backbone, and from head to tail.

When the fish are prepared in this way, brush them over with oil and put them on a *very hot* grill. If it is not hot enough, they may catch, stick to the bars, and break when they are turned over. During the cooking, continue to brush them over with oil from time to time.

The heat of the grill must naturally be governed by the thickness of the fish you are grilling. The smaller the fish, the fiercer the heat should be: if it is a large and thick one, the cooking should be conducted more gently so that the heat will gradually penetrate the flesh.

Very large fish, which would be cumbersome to grill whole, can be cut across into slices of about an inch to an inch and a half thick. These can then be treated in the same manner as small whole fish.

FRYING FISH
Deep Fat Frying

The best fish for frying, in general, are the flat fish: sole, turbot, plaice, lemon sole, and so on; and after them the other white-fleshed fish such as whiting, saithe, and cod, the last two being cut into fillets or cutlets (steaks).

The best frying medium to use is oil for this can be heated up to 280° F. without burning, whereas the best beef kidney fat cannot exceed 175° F.

Fat used for frying fish should never be used for any other purpose, for the repeated frying of fish will leave its flavour in the fat.

It should be remembered that any fat before being used should be strained, for it is sure to contain some of the burnt flour or breadcrumbs of food which has been fried in it, and these will burn and speck whatever is fried in it next.

It must be carefully noted in frying fish in deep fat that:

(1) The proportion of fat to fish is correct. There should always be plenty of it, for the more there is, the quicker it will heat up and the longer hold its heat, and you will be sure (which is most important) that the fish are completely submerged in the fat.

(2) If you are frying a certain number of fish, or pieces of fish, at the same time, you must remember that they will considerably reduce the heat of the fat when they are plunged into it, and you

must counteract this by putting the pan at once on to a strong heat, so that it will recapture its original temperature as quickly as possible.

(3) The frying fat must be very hot (slightly smoking) when the fish is plunged into it, so that it 'seizes' at once. That is to say, it must be hot enough to form a fried envelope, as it were, round the fish, which will prevent the fat from penetrating into the fish, and so making it indigestible.

All thick-fleshed fish should be scored, as has been explained already.

Whatever sort the fish is, whether whole or in fillets or in cutlets, it should first be rolled in slightly salted milk, or in beer, then rolled in flour and shaken to remove the flour which does not stick to it. Having been plunged into the fat, the fish will be found to be cooked when it rises to the surface. It should then be drained on a clean cloth, dried and slightly salted, and served on a dish with a grid or on a napkin or doyley.

A heap of very green fried parsley should be put at each end of the dish, and the fish may be surrounded with quarters of lemon.

At the same time there should be handed separately some such sauce as *béarnaise*, *tartare*, *rémoulade*, etc.

À LA MEUNIÈRE
Shallow Frying

The cooking of fish in this particularly attractive manner seems to be little known in the majority of English kitchens. It is extremely simple, but needs some care. It is suited only to small fish or the slices of larger ones.

The method is this. The fish (whole, in fillets, or in slices) are simply seasoned with salt and pepper and fried in a frying-pan in very hot butter. When they are golden on each side, they are taken out and dished, a little lemon juice is squeezed over them, and a few pinches of roughly chopped fresh parsley are added. A piece of butter is then put into the pan in which they were cooked, and when this has become *noisette*, that is, slightly browned and giving out a nutty flavour, it is quickly poured over the fish, which is served immediately while the butter is still foaming.

It should be observed that cooking fish *à la meunière*, simple as it sounds, needs some care. Too great a heat will brown the skin, and the appearance and flavour of the fish will be spoiled. If the cooking is too slow, the fish get soft. Fish properly cooked in this way should be a beautiful golden brown.

There are a number of variations on this method, by which the fish, after being cooked, is garnished with certain things, e.g. slices of orange, or of mushrooms, or shrimps: in which case the dish, while still *à la meunière*, takes its name from the added ingredient. For example, *Sole meunière à l'orange*, *aux champignons*, *aux crevettes*, and so on. But the plain *meunière* is the best, and it is pleasant to think that it might have originated in the miller's wife (*la meunière*) taking the little trout from her husband's hands, her own large and floury from baking, throwing the fish into fresh butter, and then, when they were cooked, sprinkling a little parsley over them: the lemon, I am sure, came later.

By the way, if the fish are simply fried golden in this way, and the parsley, lemon, and nut-brown butter are dispensed with, they are simply called *dorées*, and not *à la meunière* at all.

COOKING FISH *AU BLEU*

The important point in this method of cooking is that the fish should be alive. It should be taken from the water, stunned, cleaned through the gills, and trimmed. Be careful to handle it as little as possible, and do not scale or scrape it or even wash it, so as to leave on it the natural slime which plays an important part in making it look blue.

Put the fish on the grid of a fish kettle, sprinkle them with boiling vinegar, and cover them with a *court-bouillon* prepared beforehand. If the fish are fairly large, the *court-bouillon* should only be warm; but if they are small, like river trout, tench, and so on, they should be plunged into the *court-bouillon* while it is boiling.

Cook them in the usual manner, keeping the liquid just trembling, and serve them on a napkin, surrounded by parsley, removing the scales at the time of serving.

Fish cooked in this way can be served either hot or cold. If hot, they should be accompanied by a slightly salted melted butter and steamed or boiled potatoes. If cold, a *sauce ravigote* or a *sauce gribiche* may be offered.

BRAISING FISH

Only large fish such as salmon, turbot, trout, brill, etc. are suitable for braising, either whole or in large pieces; and for the cooking of these, special utensils of special shapes are necessary. These are the long fish kettle for salmon, trout, bass, grey mullet, and so on; and the turbot kettle for fish of the same shape as the turbot. Both these utensils are furnished with a grid, on which the fish is placed, and this makes it easier to lift it out when it is being dished, and to slip it off on to the serving dish. If these large fish are cooked in an unsuitable utensil, grave risk is run of breaking them when they are being dished.

To braise the fish, butter the bottom of the pan well, scatter on it some carrot and onion cut in rounds, and add a *bouquet garni* (page 31). Season the fish with salt and pepper, and let it stew very gently in the oven with the lid on for a quarter of an hour. Then moisten with fish *fumet* (page 32) and red or white wine according to the recipe being followed. If red wine is used in the moistening liquor, increase the proportion of thyme in the *bouquet garni* a little. The liquor ought to come nearly half-way up the fish. Bring to the boil, and continue to cook in the oven, gently and evenly as is necessary in all braises, basting frequently. When the fish is cooked, the liquor is strained, then properly reduced and added to the sauce accompanying the fish.

POACHING FISH

The fish is placed in the fish kettle or turbot kettle, according to its shape, and covered with the *court-bouillon* (page 31), which has been prepared beforehand. In the case of salmon, trout, bass, grey mullet, etc., this *court-bouillon* should be cold. The *court-bouillon* for turbot and brill (page 31) should be prepared only just as it is wanted. In either case, the fish should be completely immersed. For a fish weighing four pounds, salmon, trout, etc., about six quarts of *court-bouillon* will be needed. For a slice weighing about half a pound or so, a pint and three quarters.

As soon as the *court-bouillon* comes to the boil, draw the utensil to the side of the fire, and keep the liquid just gently trembling so that cooking proceeds by a gradual penetration of heat into the fish; that is to say, simply *poach* it. Uncontrolled boiling will not help matters in the least, and will risk the fish being broken. The times for the fish mentioned above are: ten minutes for two pounds, fifteen minutes for four pounds, twenty minutes for six pounds, and thirty minutes for fish weighing from eight to ten pounds.

White fish like turbot, brill, sole, etc. take seven to ten minutes for every two pounds. For fish weighing from eight to ten pounds, the poaching time as calculated above must be lessened by four or five minutes for every two pounds. For a fish weighing a pound and a half to two pounds, three quarts of *court-bouillon* will be needed, and the time of poaching should be from eight to ten minutes.

NOTE: The time of poaching is calculated from the moment the liquid comes to the boil.

It is better to use vinegar in court-bouillons intended for oily fish (herring, mackerel, gurnard, whole salmon, and so on), as well as in court-bouillons intended for lobster, langouste, and crab: in short, in those cases where the court-bouillon is not afterwards used to make a sauce. The proportion of vinegar is half a teacupful to a quart of water.

GLAZING

In the case of certain fish cooked whole or in pieces, and of cold fish cooked again in a border or in scallop shells, the procedure known as glazing (*glaçage*) is demanded.

This is usually done in the case of fish masked with a very buttery sauce, and it consists in obtaining very rapidly a thin golden coating on the surface of the sauce. This can be obtained by fierce heat, either in the oven or with a salamander. Glazing must be done very quickly because if it is done too slowly the sauce may curdle.

A type of sauce for glazing is *sauce vin blanc* (page 50).

LIGHT GRATINS

These are of two sorts. The first is obtained on a fish nearing the completion of its cooking, by sprinkling it with fine browned breadcrumbs and dotting it with pieces of butter or pouring some melted butter over.

The second is by the use of *sauce mornay* (page 48), or in some cases white wine sauce (page 50). This form of *gratin* can be used:

(1) for whole fish poached and masked with *sauce mornay* for cooked fish heated up in scallop shells or in a border of Duchesse potatoes or rice. The reduced cooking liquor of the fish is generally added to the sauce;

(2) for various white meats;

(3) for certain vegetables. *Sauce mornay* which is to be used with vegetables is sometimes combined with a certain amount of *Duxelles* (page 31).

The operation of the *gratin* consists in sprinkling the objects with grated cheese, which is then sprinkled with melted butter. The melted cheese then forms a light crust over the sauce. As in glazing, the objects should be exposed to a fierce heat, a very hot oven or a salamander. In certain cases, a few fine browned breadcrumbs may be mixed with the cheese.

RAPID GRATINS

Fish treated in this way is always ready-cooked fish, and as far as possible should be cut in small regular slices. It is usually prepared in a border or in scallop shells. The agent of the rapid *gratin* is the same as in the case of the complete *gratin* (see below), that is, a *sauce gratin* or a fairly thick *Duxelles*. The operation consists in warming up the fish and covering it with just the necessary amount of sauce. This is then sprinkled with brown breadcrumbs and melted butter. Here the only object is to obtain the formation of a browned surface, and since the fish is already cooked, all there is to be done is to brown the top under fierce heat.

COMPLETE GRATINS

In the case of this *gratin*, the fish and its garnish are raw. The agent is a fairly thick *Duxelles* (page 31). In the cooking of a complete *gratin*, three points must be borne in mind: (1) the size of the fish; (2) the amount of sauce to be used; and (3) the degree of heat to be applied. Whatever the fish, the aim of this form of cooking is to cook the fish, reduce the sauce to its proper thickness, and to produce a browned top, all at the same time.

The larger the fish, the larger the quantity of sauce and the gentler the heat should be.

If there is not enough sauce in proportion to the size of the fish, the sauce will reduce and the *gratin* form before the fish is cooked: if, on the other hand, too much sauce has been used, the fish will be cooked and the *gratin* will have formed before the sauce has thickened properly.

The smaller the fish, the less sauce it will need, and the greater the heat applied to it should be: the fish should cook, the sauce reduce, and the *gratin* form all at the same time.

To make a complete *gratin* requires a good deal of attention. It is really a matter of experience, but that experience is easily acquired.

CHAPTER TWO

*

Auxiliary Preparations for Fish Dishes

THERE are always a number of basic and auxiliary preparations which must inevitably enter into the composition of other dishes. The simplest way of dealing with these would, of course, be to repeat the recipe with every dish for which it was needed. This would be convenient to those to whom these auxiliary recipes are unfamiliar; but it would take up much too much space.

These recipes have been collected together in this chapter so as to be easily found, more especially for the sake of the housewife who has discovered, for one reason or another, that the business of the kitchen devolves more and more upon herself, and who will not be so used to these recipes as is the professional chef or cook.

At the end of the chapter has also been added a short selection of the better-known garnishes for various fish dishes, which will be found useful in the kitchens of large houses where entertaining is often on a grander and more lavish scale than in the ordinary household. But these garnishes will in most cases be found quite simple and by no means beyond the scope of the ordinary kitchen.

AUXILIARY PREPARATIONS FOR FISH DISHES

Aspic. Aspic is very clear fish jelly flavoured with some wine or other. The preparation of a *maigre* aspic is the same as that of all others, namely: Line a border mould with jelly, and decorate the bottom and sides with truffle, hard-boiled egg white, gherkins, capers, tarragon leaves, etc. Set this decoration with a little more jelly, and also set a layer of jelly in the bottom of the mould. On this arrange the ingredients of which the aspic is to be composed, either fillets of sole, roes, slices of lobster or crawfish (*langouste*), and so on. Fill up the mould with jelly, and let it set. Turn it out when you are ready to serve it, and not before. It can be served on a dish or on a base of some kind.

Bouquet garni. This is made of folded parsley stalks containing bay-leaf, thyme, and celery in quantities proportionate to the size of the bouquet. It is then tied up with cotton or thread. In certain cases, where specially described, chervil, tarragon, or fennel may also be included.

Court-bouillon for salmon, trout, etc. Proportions: seven quarts of water, four ounces of coarse salt, not quite half a pint of vinegar, five ounces of carrot and the same of onion cut in round slices, half an ounce of parsley stalks, half a bayleaf, a sprig of thyme, and not quite half an ounce of coarsely ground peppercorns. Bring to the boil, and boil gently for three quarters of an hour. Strain and leave to get cold.

NOTE: Bass, grey mullet, and other fish of that kind can be cooked in water salted in the proportion of half an ounce of salt to every quart of water.

White court-bouillon for turbot and brill. Proportions: six quarts of water, a quart of milk, five ounces of salt, and five slices of lemon without rind or pips. This *court-bouillon* is prepared in the turbot kettle in which the fish is to be cooked.

Duxelles. Chop up finely half a pound of mushroom stalks and trimmings, and squeeze them in a cloth by twisting it, so that as much of their moisture as possible is extracted. Lightly brown half a chopped onion in an ounce of butter and three dessertspoonfuls of olive oil, add two chopped shallots, the mushrooms, salt, pepper, and grated nutmeg. Stir on a hot fire until all the moisture in the mushrooms has evaporated, then pour the *Duxelles* into a basin, press it lightly down, and keep it covered with a buttered paper.

NOTE: This Duxelles is in frequent use in the kitchen. In the preparation of fish it is the basis of the *gratin* sauce, whether for complete or rapid *gratins*. (See pages 28 and 29).

Farce de poisson (Fish forcemeat). Proportions: one pound net of the flesh of pike, whiting, or other fish; nine ounces of cold panada (see page 34), half a pound of butter, two whole eggs and two egg yolks, half an ounce of salt, a very good pinch of white pepper, and a tiny pinch of grated nutmeg.

METHOD. Pound the fish finely with the seasoning in a mortar, and keep it aside. Then pound the panada, mix the two together, and add the butter. When these are well mixed, add the eggs and the egg yolks, one after the other, pass through a very fine sieve or tammy-cloth, and put the forcemeat in a basin. Work it there for a few moments with a spatula to make it smooth, then put it aside in a cool place, covered with a buttered paper.

Farce pour poisson à braiser (Forcemeat for braised fish). Mix together half a pound of raw soft roes and the chopped flesh of four whitings; a quarter of a pound of breadcrumbs first soaked in milk and then pressed as dry as possible; a quarter of a pound of raw mushrooms chopped up and pressed dry; two ounces of chopped onion and one ounce of chopped shallot, both lightly fried in butter and left to get cold; two whole eggs; a dessertspoonful of chopped parsley, a small piece of crushed garlic, salt, pepper, and grated nutmeg. Mix to a paste with a spatula.

Farce mousseline (Mousseline forcemeat). Pound finely a pound of fish or shellfish meat with nearly half an ounce of salt, a pinch of white pepper, and the whites of three small eggs added by degrees. Pass through a fine tammy-cloth, put the forcemeat into a basin, and keep it on ice for an hour. Then, still on the ice, work into it by small degrees a pint of good cream.

NOTE: This forcemeat is principally used for mousses and very fine quenelles.

Fines herbes. Finely chopped equal parts of chervil, chives, parsley, and tarragon.

Fumet de poisson (Fish fumet). For two quarts of *fumet*, put two pounds of chopped-up raw fish bones and trimmings in a buttered pan with two ounces of minced onion, several parsley stalks, and a dozen peppercorns. Let this stew for a while with the lid on, then add a quart of white wine and a little over two and a half pints of water. Add a pinch of salt and boil gently for twenty-five minutes. Then strain through a fine conical sieve, and keep for use.

Gelée de poisson blanche (White fish jelly). Make a fish *fumet* as above. Then, for a pint and three-quarters of *fumet* add nine ounces of chopped or pounded whiting flesh; the white part of a leek and a few parsley stalks cut in small pieces; the white of an egg, and about three-quarters of an ounce of gelatine softened in cold water. Clarify in the usual way, and strain through a napkin.

Gelée de poisson au vin rouge (Red fish jelly). This jelly is usually prepared with a red wine *court-bouillon* in which the fish itself has been cooked.

Or: Prepare a fish *fumet*, substituting red wine for white, and follow the directions given above for white fish jelly.

Glace de poisson (Fish glaze). Fish glaze is obtained by the reduction of fish *fumet*. If desired, a special *fumet* can be prepared, as follows: stew in butter two pounds of fish bones and trimmings with half a minced onion, a small bouquet of parsley stalks, and two ounces of mushroom peelings. Add a glass of white wine, reduce it almost completely, then moisten with a quart of well-strained ordinary *fumet*. Boil gently for twenty-five minutes, strain through a very fine sieve, decant after it has been left to settle, and then reduce to the consistency of syrup.

Herbes à tortue (Herbs for turtle soup). These herbs comprise basil, sage, marjoram, savory, rosemary (this in lesser quantity than the others), thyme, bayleaf, coriander, peppercorns, and a little mint.

Marinade au vin blanc (White wine marinade). Fry lightly, in three dessertspoonfuls of olive oil, half a carrot, an onion, the white part of a leek and two shallots, all minced up, with two whole cloves of garlic, a sprig of thyme and a third of a bayleaf, parsley stalks, several peppercorns, and a clove. Moisten with just over three pints of white wine and not quite half a pint of vinegar. Boil gently for thirty to thirty-five minutes.

Marinade au vin rouge (Red wine marinade). The same ingredients as for the white wine marinade, but moisten only with three and a half pints of red wine instead of white, and add no vinegar.

NOTE: These marinades are generally used cold, but they may sometimes be used hot, if the fish under treatment only need a short time in the marinade.

Mirepoix ordinaire. Stew in butter equal amounts of onion and carrot, and celery in lesser quantity, all cut in little dice. Add a fragment of thyme and a small bit of bayleaf.

NOTE: The mirepoix used for fish does not contain ham or bacon, as does that for use with meat.

Mirepoix bordelaise (Bordeaux mirepoix). Cut in small dice two ounces of the red part of a carrot, the same of onion, two small shallots, and two parsley stalks. Add a pinch of powdered thyme and bay-leaf. Stew in butter until the vegetables are quite cooked, then turn out into a basin, and keep for use.

Nage, ou court-bouillon pour crustacés (*Court-bouillon* for shellfish). Stew in butter a large carrot and two onions minced up. Moisten with a pint and three quarters of white wine, and the same of water. Add a *bouquet garni* and a few peppercorns tied up in butter muslin. Bring to the boil and cook gently for half an hour. Serve hot.

Panade au pain (Bread panada). Soak as many breadcrumbs as you want in boiling milk, seasoning with a little salt. When the milk has been completely absorbed, stir the mixture over a hot fire until it ceases to stick to the spatula or wooden spoon. Then spread it out on a plate or dish in a thin layer, and let it get cold before using.

Panade à la farine (Flour panada). Put in a saucepan eight table-spoonfuls of water, an ounce of butter, and a pinch of salt. Bring to the boil, and then add, off the fire, three ounces of sieved flour. Stir this over the fire until the mixture no longer sticks to the spatula, spread it on a dish in a thin layer, and let it get cold.

Panade à la frangipane (Frangipane panada). Mix in a saucepan three ounces of flour, three egg yolks, two dessertspoonfuls of melted butter, and a pinch of salt. Moisten with a pint and three quarters of boiling milk, bring to the boil, and stir over the fire until the right thickness is reached. Let it get quite cold before using.

Pâte pour coulibiac (Coulibiac pastry). This is ordinary brioche pastry without sugar, made as follows: a pound of sieved flour, half an ounce of salt, six ounces of butter, four eggs, half an ounce of yeast, and four scant tablespoonfuls of warm water. (1) With a quarter of the flour, the water, and the yeast, make your leaven. Roll it into a ball, cut the top in the form of a cross, and keep it in a warm place until it has doubled its size. (2) Mix the rest of the flour with the butter, the eggs, and the salt dissolved in a few drops of water. Work the dough with the hands, pulling it about and kneading it so as to make it elastic. Finally, mix in the yeast, put it in a basin, cover it, and leave it to ferment for five to six hours.

Pâte à choux commune (Choux pastry). Put in a saucepan three quarters of a pint of water, a pinch of salt, and three ounces of butter. Bring to the boil, and add, off the fire, nine ounces of flour. Stir this dough on a hot fire until it no longer sticks to the spatula, and finish it, off the fire, with six large eggs added one after the other.

Pâte feuilletée, or *Feuilletage* (Puff pastry). Sieve a pound of fine wheat flour; make a hollow in it and put in the middle a third of an ounce of salt and half a pint of cold water. Mix together, and be careful that, in winter or summer, its consistency is exactly that of the butter you are to use with it, in order to make certain of the perfect blending of the two ingredients when the dough is rolled out. When mixed, leave it for a quarter of an hour. Spread out the dough on your board in a square, and spread on it a pound of butter, which in winter should be well worked and softened. Fold in the corners of the dough in such a way as to enclose the butter completely and to form a perfect square. Leave this for ten to fifteen minutes before beginning to roll it out, then roll it out twice. This means rolling out the dough in a band about eighteen inches long, and then folding it in three. Put the dough in a cool place for ten or fifteen minutes, then roll it out four more times, twice at a time, leaving it for ten minutes in between.

NOTE: It is important to let the dough rest as described, because if it is rolled too quickly it may become elastic, and so tend to shrink in cooking. The trimmings of puff pastry can be used in the kitchen for making *barquettes, croustades,* tartlets, and so on.

Pâte à foncer (Cold-water pastry). Make a hollow in the middle of a pound of sieved flour, and in it put nine ounces of well-kneaded butter, a third of an ounce of salt, and eight tablespoonfuls of water. Add the flour by degrees, mix twice, and wrap the pastry up in a cloth, leaving it for an hour at least before you want to use it.

NOTE: If you have no puff pastry trimmings, this pastry can be used for *barquettes* and *croustades* (*vol-au-vent* cases) served as hot hors-d'œuvre

Pâte à frire (Frying batter). Mix in a bowl a quarter of a pound of flour sieved with a pinch of salt, two dessertspoonfuls of olive oil or melted butter, and eight tablespoonfuls of lukewarm water or beer. When needed for cooking, add two small egg whites stiffly whisked.

NOTE: As far as possible, frying batter ought to be made a little in advance. The batter made with beer is used principally for fruit fritters.

Pâte à pannequets (Pancake batter, for *hors-d'œuvre*). Mix a pound of flour with half an ounce of salt, four eggs, a pint and three quarters of milk, and three ounces of melted butter.

Pommes de terre duchesse (Duchesse potatoes). This composition is used for various croquettes, and for bordering dishes, as described in the recipe sections that follow. Cook your potatoes, cut in quarters, quickly in salted water, keeping them fairly firm. Drain them throughly, pass them through a fine sieve, put the purée into a pan, and dry it over a quick fire. Season it with salt, pepper, and grated nutmeg, and for every two pounds of the purée add three ounces of butter and six egg yolks, or four yolks and one whole egg. Spread it out on a dish, and let it get cold before using.

Pommes de terre dauphine (Dauphine potatoes). Make a purée of potatoes as described above. Dry it, and for every two pounds add two ounces of butter, three or four egg yolks, and half a pound of ordinary choux pastry dough made without sugar (see page 35). Let it get cold before using.

Purée de champignons (Mushroom purée). To two-thirds of a pint of Béchamel sauce (page 44) add four tablespoonfuls of cream, and reduce it to eight tablespoonfuls. Pass a pound of cooked fresh mushrooms through a coarse tammy-cloth. Put this purée into a sauté pan, add an ounce of butter, and stir over a hot fire until all evaporation has ceased. Mix this purée with the Béchamel sauce, season with salt, pepper, and grated nutmeg, simmer for five minutes, and finish, off the fire, with just over an ounce of butter.

Cuisson de champignons (Mushroom stock). When mushrooms are stewed in butter for a garnish, the stock which comes from them should be carefully kept, as it provides a fine flavouring agent, which is referred to in the course of the following recipes.

Roux brun (Dark roux). This is the binding element in the brown sauce called *espagnole*. Mix four ounces of flour with just under four ounces of clarified butter. Cook gently on a low fire until the mixture is a deep brown.

Roux blond (Light roux). The binding element in *velouté*. Mix flour and butter in the above proportions, and cook gently until the mixture is a golden brown.

RICE

Riz à l'indienne. Cook half a pound of Patna rice in a quart of boiling salted water, stirring it from time to time. It will take a quarter of an hour to cook, and you must then drain it and wash it under the cold tap. The best way to do this is to drain it in a sieve and let the cold water run over it. Let it drain again, then spread it out on a napkin stretched on a board or tin. Let it dry in a very cool oven.

This rice is generally used as an accompaniment to *Lobster à l'américaine* and to poached fish.

Riz pilaff maigre (Pilaff, without meat stock). Lightly brown half a chopped onion in butter, and add half a pound of Carolina rice. Stir it over the fire until the rice gets very white, then moisten it a little more than twice its height in the pan (just under a pint) with clear fish *fumet* (page 32). Season it with a small bouquet of thyme, parsley, and bayleaf, put on the lid, and cook in the oven for eighteen to twenty minutes. When it is cooked, each grain should be separate. When you take it from the oven, stir it lightly and mix in an ounce and a half of butter.

Rizotto maigre (Risotto, without meat stock). Proceed exactly as for the pilaff above, but when it comes to adding the fish *fumet*, do not do so all at once, but by degrees, adding it three or four times as it is absorbed by the rice. After it is cooked, mix in two ounces of grated Parmesan and an ounce of fresh butter. Truffle, tomato pulp, or tomato purée can be added if desired.

GARNISHES

Américaine. Slices of lobster tails prepared like *sauce américaine*; button mushrooms. *Sauce américaine.*

Batelière. Glazed button onions; button mushrooms; crayfish cooked in *court-bouillon*; fried eggs. *Sauce marinière.*

Cancalaise. Poached oysters; shelled prawns. White wine sauce.

Cardinal. Slices of lobster tails; slices of truffles. *Sauce cardinal.*

Chambord. *Quenelles* of fish forcemeat, decorated; button mushrooms; truffles cut in olive shape; gudgeons egg-and-breadcrumbed and fried; crayfish cooked in *court-bouillon*; slices of soft roe fried *à la meunière*. A sauce made with the fish stock.

Chauchat. Thick rounds of hot boiled potato, arranged overlapping one another round the fish. *Sauce mornay.*

Commodore. Large *quenelles* of fish forcemeat decorated with truffles and crayfish tails. *Sauce normande* finished with crayfish butter.

Daumont. Large mushrooms stewed in butter, garnished with a *salpicon* of crayfish bound with *sauce Nantua*; little *quenelles* of creamy fish forcemeat; slices of soft roes egg-and-breadcrumbed and friend. *Sauce Nantua.*

Dieppoise. Poached and bearded mussels; peeled shrimps' tails. White wine sauce.

Doria. Cucumbers cut olive-shaped and stewed in butter, arranged round the fish cooked *à la meunière.*

Florentine. The fish is set on a bed of blanched leaf spinach stewed in butter. It is then covered with a *sauce mornay.*

Grand Duc. Asparagus tips bound with butter; slices of truffle. *Sauce mornay.*

Indienne. Rice prepared *à l'indienne* (page 37). Curry sauce.

Joinville. *Julienne* shreds of mushrooms and truffles; crayfish tails. *Sauce Joinville.* (On the fish itself, slices of truffles, and large prawns with their tails peeled.)

Marinière. Poached mussels and shrimps. *Sauce marinière.*

Matelote. Glazed button onions; button mushrooms; crayfish cooked in *court-bouillon*; heart-shaped *croûtons* fried in butter. *Sauce matelote.*

Montreuil. Olive-shaped boiled or steamed potatoes arranged round the fish. White wine sauce on the fish and shrimp sauce on the potatoes.

Nantua. Crayfish tails and slices of truffle. *Sauce Nantua.*

Niçoise. Peeled, pressed, and roughly chopped tomatoes stewed in olive oil, with a touch of garlic, fillets of anchovy, little olives, and capers. Finish with chopped tarragon.

Normande. Poached oysters and mussels; prawns' or shrimps' tails; mushrooms, gudgeons, egg-and-breadcrumbed and fried; crayfish cooked in *court-bouillon*; small *croûtons* fried in butter. *Sauce normande.*

Trouvillaise. Small poached mussels; shrimps' tails; minced mushrooms. Shrimp sauce.

Walewska. Tails of Dublin Bay prawns, or thin slices of lobster tails; slices of truffle. *Sauce mornay.*

CHAPTER THREE

*

Savoury Butters and Sauces

THIS, of course, is one of the most important chapters in the book. A sauce cannot always make a dish, but it can do wonders with it. I often think that we neglect sauces in this country, where you will find many people who think that because a dish is sauced it means that the fish is of inferior quality and the flavour of the sauce is there to disguise it. White sauce (with or without bits of hard-boiled egg), anchovy sauce, and cheese sauce, these are about all we enjoy (?) with fish, and then generally to use up cold fish that has been left over.

The French are a nation of sauce-makers, while we prefer our roasting and grilling. There is a French saying that, while one can achieve success in roasting, one has to be born a sauce-maker. That no doubt is true of such Masters as Carême, whose sauces were so marvellous that someone said: 'We should wish Carême to prepare the sauce, were we under the necessity of eating an elephant, or our grandfather!'

Nowadays I believe that sauces might even come into their own in this country, and a study of this chapter will tell you all there is to know about them. You may not be able in your own kitchen to make such a finely flavoured sauce as you get at Prunier's, but that will only be because you cannot possibly expect to have at your command the flavoured stock of a large restaurant, where so many trimmings of fish and shellfish are always available. But at any rate the simpler sauces are at your command, if you will take the trouble to make them, and here are all the recipes assembled.

For making sauces, lemon juice can be used instead of white wine for moistening the fish when it is cooking. This is better when the lemon juice is combined with mushroom. This applies to sauces used to mask such fish as sole, turbot, John Dory, cod, halibut, rock salmon, as well as scallops.

Vinegar may also be used in sauces, but only in very small quantities.

A dessertspoonful per person is quite enough, and it must be used only on condition that it is entirely reduced, as in the following sauces: béarnaise, white butter, and in the reduction for making sauce hollandaise for fish. Actually vinegar can be used for all 'condiment' sauces, replacing mustard, piccalilli, etc.

SAVOURY BUTTERS

NOTE: These butters should be used within twenty-four hours of being made.

Beurre d'ail (Garlic butter). Blanched garlic, well pounded and mixed with an equal quantity of butter. Pass through a fine sieve.

Beurre d'amandes (Almond butter). Four ounces of almonds freshly skinned and pounded into a fine paste with a few drops of water. Mix with six ounces of butter, and pass through a fine sieve.

Beurre d'anchois (Anchovy butter). Two ounces of fillets of salted anchovies, washed, pounded with three ounces of butter. Pass through a fine sieve.

Beurre blanc (White butter). (1) Reduce a good glass of white wine vinegar to which you have added a chopped shallot. Before the reduction is complete, draw the pan from the fire, and add by degrees half a pound of softened butter, stirring continuously. Finish with a little freshly ground pepper from the mill. Certain experts are in favour of adding roughly chopped parsley to this butter. (2) Proceed as above, substituting very dry white wine for the vinegar. (3) As above, using Muscadet instead of vinegar. This is called *Beurre blanc nantais*.

Beurre de caviar (Caviar butter). Two ounces of caviar pounded very well indeed; add six ounces of butter, and pass through a fine sieve.

Beurre Colbert. This is a *maître-d'hôtel* butter (page 42) to which is added a dessertspoonful of melted meat glaze for every four ounces of butter. If a *maigre* butter is wanted, the meat glaze can be replaced by fish glaze or fish *fumet* reduced until it is a syrup.

Beurre de crevettes (Prawn butter). Prawns pounded with an equal weight of butter. Add a few drops of carmine. Pass through a sieve.

Beurre d'échalote (Shallot butter). Blanch some chopped shallot quickly, squeeze it in the corner of a cloth, pound it in a mortar, and add an equal weight of butter. Pass through a sieve.

Beurre d'écrevisses (Crayfish butter). The heads and shells of crayfish cooked in an ordinary *mirepoix* (page 33), pounded finely with an equal weight of butter, and passed through a sieve.

Beurre d'estragon (Tarragon butter). Blanched leaves of tarragon, plunged into cold water, pressed dry, and pounded with an equal quantity of butter. Pass through a sieve.

Beurre fondu. Put two tablespoonfuls of milk into a saucepan on a quick fire. Add about half a pound of salted butter by dropping it in in small pieces. Bring to the boil, and strain as soon as the mixture has boiled. The melted butter will now have thickened.

Beurre de hareng (Herring butter). Skinned fillets of herring pounded and mixed with twice as much butter as herring. Pass through a sieve.

Beurre de homard (Lobster butter). (1) The hard and soft roe and the creamy inside parts of the lobsters are pounded with an equal quantity of butter. Pass through a sieve.

(2) Lobster shells dried and pounded very fine. Add an equal quantity of butter, melt in a *bain-marie*, stirring now and again, and pass through a sieve.

Beurre de laitance (Soft-roe butter). Poach some soft roes with butter and lemon juice, let them get cold, squash them to a paste, and add twice their weight of butter and a teaspoonful of mustard for every four ounces of roe.

Beurre à la maître-d'hôtel (*Maître-d'hôtel* butter). Soften five ounces of butter, and add a dessertspoonful of chopped parsley, salt, pepper, and a few drops of lemon juice.

Beurre manié (Blended butter). This butter is used for binding sauces, etc., at the last moment. It is made with five parts of butter and three of flour, mixed and pounded together by means of a fork.

Beurre meunière. Butter cooked to the *noisette* stage – that is to say, until light brown and smelling of nuts – and completed with lemon juice and chopped parsley.

Beurre de Montpellier. Blanch some watercress, tarragon, parsley, and chervil in equal quantities, as well as a rather larger quantity of young spinach leaves. Drain, plunge into cold water, and press dry. Pound them, adding (in proportion to their amount) chopped and blanched shallots, gherkins, capers, fillets of anchovy, and a touch of garlic. To each two ounces of this purée add three hard-boiled egg yolks, salt, pepper, three quarters of a pound of butter, and four dessertspoonfuls of olive oil. Pass through a sieve. The colour of this butter should be a tender green.

Beurre de moutarde (Mustard butter). Softened butter to which mustard is added in proportion, according to taste or to the purpose for which the butter is to be used. When this butter is prepared as an accompaniment to a fish, the mustard is mixed with melted clarified butter.

Beurre noir (Black butter). Cook the butter in a frying pan until it just begins to turn brown. Finish it with a few drops of vinegar swilled in the pan.

Beurre noisette (Nutbrown butter). Butter cooked in a frying pan until it browns lightly and begins to smell of nuts.

Beurre de noisettes (Hazelnut butter). Some sauces need to be completed with this butter, which is made by pounding slightly-dried hazelnuts with a few drops of water and double their weight in butter. Pass through a sieve.

Beurre de paprika (Paprika butter). Fry half a chopped onion in butter with a pinch of paprika pepper. When it is cold, mix with five ounces of softened butter, and pass through a sieve.

Beurre de piment (Pimento butter). Pound up four small cooked sweet peppers. Add five ounces of butter and pass through a sieve. (Tinned red peppers might be used for this butter, if fresh ones are unobtainable.)

Beurre de raifort (Horseradish butter). Add a dessertspoonful of finely grated horseradish to five ounces of softened butter.

Beurre de saumon fumé (Smoked salmon butter). Pound two ounces of smoked salmon and add five ounces of butter. Pass through a sieve.

Beurre de tomate (Tomato butter). This consists of very reduced tomato pulp mixed with double its weight in butter. Pass through a sieve.

Beurre de truffe (Truffle butter). Cooked truffle pounded with a little fish *velouté* (see below). Add twice its weight in butter, and pass through a sieve.

Beurre vert (Green butter). See *Beurre de Montpellier*.

SAUCES
Hot Sauces – The Basic Sauces

Béchamel sauce. Mix together four ounces of butter and five of flour, and cook this for a few seconds only, just to rid it of the flavour of uncooked flour. Moisten it with three and a half pints of boiled milk, and season it with not quite half an ounce of salt, a pinch of coarse-ground pepper, and grated nutmeg, and bring it gently to the boil, stirring all the time. Now add an onion stuck with a clove and a *bouquet* of parsley, thyme, and bayleaf, and let it boil gently for twenty minutes. Then strain it into a bowl, covering the surface with melted butter to prevent a scum from forming.

Velouté de poissons (Fish velvet sauce). Make half a pound of slightly browned *roux* (page 36), and moisten with three and a half pints of fish stock. Bring to the boil, and boil gently for fifteen to eighteen minutes. Pour into a bowl and stir until it is quite cold. The preparation of this *velouté* is the same as that for fish soups, except that it is rather thicker. The secret of the flavour of this sauce lies entirely in the flavour of the stock used.

The Lesser Sauces

Sauce américaine. This is the stock of *Lobster à l'américaine*, lightly bound with blended butter. The sauce is finished with butter, and at the last chopped chervil and tarragon are added.

Sauce anchois (Anchovy sauce). (1) Mix an ounce of flour with two ounces of melted butter, moisten with three quarters of a pint of fresh cream, season with salt and pepper, and bring to the boil. Finish at the last moment with two ounces of anchovy butter or a dessertspoonful of anchovy essence.

(2) To three quarters of a pint of white wine sauce add two and a half ounces of anchovy butter and the fillets of three salted anchovies cut in small dice.

(3) More simply still, add anchovy butter or anchovy essence to melted butter sauce, in whatever proportion you like.

Sauce armoricaine. This is *Sauce américaine* bound with egg yolk and cream, and flavoured with curry.

Sauce aurore. To just over half a pint of fish *velouté* or white wine sauce, add four tablespoonfuls of very red and much reduced tomato purée. Finish with two ounces of butter.

Sauce béarnaise. Put six tablespoonfuls of tarragon vinegar into a saucepan with an ounce of chopped shallot and a pinch of coarsely ground pepper. Reduce this to about four dessertspoonfuls. Let it get nearly cold, stir in four egg yolks, and thicken the sauce by adding half a pound of melted butter by small degrees over a low heat. Pass the sauce through a muslin, correct the seasoning, and finish with a dessertspoonful of chopped chervil and tarragon.

Sauce Bercy. Put four tablespoonfuls of white wine and the same of fish *fumet* in a saucepan with a dessertspoonful of chopped shallot, and reduce it by a third. Add not quite half a pint of fish *velouté*, bring to the boil, and finish with two ounces of butter and a teaspoonful of chopped parsley.

Sauce blanche, dite Sauce bâtarde (White sauce). This is particularly a household sauce. Mix an ounce of flour with an ounce of melted butter, and pour *all at once* into the saucepan a little over half a pint of slightly salted *boiling* water. Mix quickly by stirring with a whisk. Add a binding of three egg yolks mixed with a little cream or milk. Keep the sauce just moving, but not boiling, on the side of the fire, then pass through a sieve, and finish with five ounces of butter and a little lemon juice.

Sauce bourguignonne. In an ounce of butter and two dessertspoonfuls of oil (nut oil, if you want to preserve the local touch), fry but do not brown four ounces of *mirepoix* composed of carrot, onion, and celery. Drain off the fat, moisten with a pint of good red wine (Burgundy), add salt, pepper, a tiny bit of crushed garlic, a bouquet of parsley, thyme, and bayleaf, and some mushroom trimmings, and boil gently for twenty minutes. Pass it through a conical sieve and bind it with blended butter. Finish with a couple of ounces of butter. (If liked, you can add a little burnt brandy.)

Sauce canotière. Bind three quarters of a pint of stock, made from freshwater fish cooked in a white wine *court-bouillon*, with two ounces of blended butter. Boil for a few seconds, and bind with three egg yolks. Finish with two ounces of butter and a few drops of lemon juice.

Sauce cardinal. To just over half a pint of fish *velouté* add four dessert-spoonfuls of very good fumet of sole, a dessertspoonful of essence of truffles, and two ounces of lobster butter. This sauce should be bright red in colour.

Sauce crème (Cream sauce). To a little over half a pint of Béchamel sauce add four tablespoonfuls of double cream.

Sauce crevettes (Shrimp sauce). This sauce can be made, as desired, with either white wine sauce or a *hollandaise*. In either case, finish the chosen sauce with two ounces of shrimp butter (for each three quarters of a pint of the sauce) and an ounce of small peeled shrimps. The colour of the sauce should be a fresh pale pink.

Sauce currie (Curry sauce). Chop up an onion finely and cook it in butter without browning it, with a sprig of thyme, a piece of a bay-leaf, and a blade of mace. Add a pinch of curry powder, four table-spoonfuls of good fish *fumet*, and just over half a pint of fish *velouté*. Boil gently for ten minutes, then pass through a sieve, and finish with several spoonfuls of cream or coconut milk.

Sauce diplomate. This is a fine white wine sauce, to which has been added a lobster broth, in the proportion of one-third broth and two-thirds sauce. Add a dessertspoonful of tiny dice of truffle for each three quarters of a pint of the mixture.

Sauce au fenouil (Fennel sauce). Boil two ounces of fennel in salted water for three minutes. Drain it, plunge it in cold water, and press it dry. Then add it to three quarters of a pint of melted butter sauce (*sauce blanche*). This sauce is used principally with salmon and mackerel.

Sauce genevoise. To a *mirepoix* with a salmon's head or bones, and a bouquet of parsley, thyme, and bayleaf, add white wine from the Geneva district. Reduce to about half, bind with a creamed butter, and add a little *sauce hollandaise* or egg yolk.

Sauce génoise. This is the same as *sauce bourguignonne*, except that a red wine from Genoa is used instead of Burgundy.

Sauce gratin. Put four tablespoonfuls of white wine and the same of fish *fumet* into a saucepan with a dessertspoonful of chopped shallot, and reduce by a half. Add four dessertspoonfuls of *Duxelles* (page 31) and eight tablespoonfuls of fish *velouté*. Finish with butter and chopped parsley.

Sauce hollandaise (enough for twelve people). Put into a saucepan two large dessertspoonfuls of water and a pinch of coarse-ground pepper, and let it reduce. Then add six egg yolks, and on a very low heat or in a *bain-marie* stir in by small degrees half a pound of clarified butter. Correct the seasoning, finish with a few drops of lemon juice, and pass through a sieve.

Or: Mix six egg yolks with a few spoonfuls of water. Heat up slowly, whipping all the time until the eggs are foamy; then as above add half a pound of butter, season, and sieve.

If the sauce seems to be getting too thick as the butter is added, you can dilute it by adding a few drops of water.

Sauce homard (Lobster sauce). To three quarters of a pint of cream sauce add two ounces of lobster butter made with the soft roe or the pounded hard roe. Season with a few drops of anchovy essence, and garnish with small dice of lobster meat.

Sauce aux huîtres (Oyster sauce). To three quarters of a pint of white wine sauce add a dozen poached and bearded oysters, as well as their stock reduced and passed through a fine cloth.

Sauce Joinville. A white wine sauce finished with shrimp or prawn broth, and garnished with small shrimps.

Sauce laguipierre. This is made in the same way as *sauce canotière* (page 46).

Sauce livonienne. With three quarters of a pint of white wine sauce mix two good dessertspoonfuls of fine *julienne* shreds of the red part of carrot stewed in butter, a dessertspoonful of truffle cut in the same fashion, and a little chopped parsley.

Sauce marinière. This is a *sauce Bercy* to which has been added the reduced stock of mussels. It is garnished with small poached and bearded mussels.

Sauce matelote. This is made with a chopped-up salmon head and a *maigre mirepoix* (page 33) fried in butter without browning. This is *flambé* with brandy and moistened with red wine, and the following ingredients are added: a piece of celery, crushed garlic, mushroom trimmings, salt, coarsely ground pepper, thyme, and bayleaf. This is all boiled until reduced to half, then strained, bound with blended butter, and finished with fresh butter. The fish which this sauce accompanies is always garnished with button mushrooms, glazed button onions, and heart-shaped *croûtons* of bread fried in butter.

Sauce mornay. To three quarters of a pint of Béchamel sauce add, while it is still boiling, a binding of two egg yolks and two ounces of grated Parmesan and Gruyère mixed. Finish with the much reduced stock of the fish for which the sauce is intended, several spoonfuls of cream, and two ounces of butter.

Sauce Nantua. This is a very creamy Béchamel sauce finished with two ounces of very red *Beurre d'écrevisses* (page 42) for every three quarters of a pint of the sauce. It is garnished with the peeled tails of very small crayfish.

Sauce Newburg. Fry lightly in butter a lobster cut across in pieces. Swill the pan with sherry, then add enough cream to cover the pieces of lobster, and cook for twenty minutes. Strain the sauce and add a few spoonfuls of Béchamel sauce to which you have added the lobster soft roe kept back for the purpose. Add some more cream, and finish with a little *sauce hollandaise*.

Sauce normande. This is a *sauce vin blanc* to which have been added some oyster stock and the reduced stock in which the fish in question has been cooked.

Sauce aux œufs (Egg sauce). Mix a dessertspoonful of flour with two ounces of melted butter, and moisten with enough milk to make a slightly thick sauce. Season with salt and a little grated nutmeg. Bring to the boil, and boil for several minutes; then, while hot, add three small hard-boiled eggs cut in large dice. This sauce is served in particular with boiled salt cod (*morue pochée*).

Sauce persil (Parsley sauce). This is either a Béchamel or more simply a white sauce (*sauce blanche*), well buttered, to which have been added the juice of a lemon and plenty of parsley, chopped, blanched, and pressed dry. It is served frequently with salmon, mackerel, trout, and so on.

Sauce poulette. To three quarters of a pint of fish *velouté* add several dessertspoonfuls of reduced mushroom stock (page 36) and a binding of three egg yolks beaten with a little cream. Finish with two ounces of butter and a few drops of lemon juice.

Sauce régence. This is a *sauce normande* to which have been added the reduced stock of mushrooms and a little essence of truffle.

Sauce riche. This is made in the same way as *sauce diplomate*.

Sauce soubise (Onion sauce). Finely chop four large onions and stew them in butter. Add three quarters of a pint of Béchamel sauce, finish cooking slowly, and pass through a sieve. Season, and finish with butter and cream according to the use for which the sauce is intended.

Sauce suchet. Cut up equal portions of the red part of carrot and the white of leeks and celery into fine *julienne* shreds so that there are four ounces in all. Stew these in butter, and finish their cooking with a little light fish *fumet*. When they are cooked, reduce the liquid completely, and mix the *julienne* with three quarters of a pint of white wine sauce.

Sauce tomate (Tomato sauce). Make a *mirepoix* without bacon (page 33) and fry it without browning in four ounces of butter. Stir in three dessertspoonfuls of flour, let this brown a little, and then add eight pounds of tomatoes with the seeds and juice pressed out, three and a half pints of tomato purée, salt, pepper, sugar, a bouquet of parsley, thyme, and bayleaf, not quite half an ounce of crushed garlic, and a pint and three quarters of stock. Cook very gently, pass through a sieve, and keep for use when wanted.

Sauce vénitienne. Put into a saucepan eight tablespoonfuls of tarragon vinegar and a good dessertspoonful of finely chopped shallot. Reduce by a good half, and add this reduction to three quarters of a pint of white wine sauce. Pass through a sieve, and finish with two ounces of green butter (page 44) and chopped chervil and tarragon.

Sauce Victoria. This is a white wine sauce made with fish *velouté*, and finished with a shrimp or lobster butter. In the dish *Sole Victoria* (page 164) a lobster butter should be used.

Sauce Villeroy. To three quarters of a pint of fish *velouté* or ordinary *velouté* add several dessertspoonfuls of mushroom stock and three egg yolks. Stir over the heat until the sauce reaches the consistency of a thick mash. (It should always be prepared at the time when it is wanted, and is used only for coating various objects which are to be served *à la Villeroy*.)

Sauce vin blanc (White wine sauce). To three quarters of a pint of fish *velouté* add four tablespoonfuls of fish *fumet*, and bind with two egg yolks. Butter the sauce, and finish it with a little fresh cream. The reduced poaching stock of the fish which it is to accompany should always be added to this sauce.

Cold Sauces

Aïoli. For four people you want eight small cloves of garlic, a pinch of salt, an egg yolk, and half a pint of olive oil. Pound the garlic to a fine paste in a mortar, add the egg and the salt, and mix them together. Then continue pounding while you add the oil drop by drop, as in making a mayonnaise, afterwards pouring it in more freely. When the Aïoli gets too thick, thin it with a few drops of lemon juice and warm water. If it curdles, thicken it again in the same way as mayonnaise (page 51). Some like to add to the Aïoli a small proportion of mashed baked potato.

Sauce andalouse. To just over half a pint of mayonnaise sauce add four tablespoonfuls of thick and very red tomato purée, and two small sweet red peppers cut in *julienne* shreds.

Sauce bohémienne. Take two good dessertspoonfuls of cold thick Béchamel sauce, and mix with them two egg yolks, salt, pepper, and a few drops of vinegar. Then add about three quarters of a pint of olive oil in the same manner as in making mayonnaise sauce, and finish it with a little finely chopped tarragon.

Sauce chaudfroid blanche (White chaudfroid sauce). In certain cases, for coating slices of lobster, fillets of fish, etc., *chaudfroid* sauce is used instead of mayonnaise thickened with jelly. This sauce is made as follows: put into a sauté pan three quarters of a pint of fish *velouté*, and while stirring it over the heat, add by degrees just over half a pint of good white fish jelly and six tablespoonfuls of cream. Let the sauce reduce by a third, and proceed in the same way as for an ordinary *chaudfroid* sauce.

Sauce chaudfroid à l'aurore. With three quarters of a pint of *sauce aurore* proceed as with fish *velouté* above.

Sauce Escoffier. This is a mayonnaise to which have been added grated horseradish and chopped chervil and parsley.

Sauce gribiche. Boil six eggs hard, and pound the yolks into a fine paste; add half a dessertspoonful of French mustard, salt, and pepper, and finish with oil and vinegar in the same way as in making a mayonnaise. Finish the sauce with gherkins, capers, chervil, tarragon, and parsley, all chopped, and several hard-boiled egg whites cut in thin *julienne* shreds.

Sauce mayonnaise. There is no professional secret for making mayonnaise. It is, indeed, one of the easiest sauces to make, and in a few minutes a mayonnaise for fifteen people can be made. No mechanical whisk or spatula is needed, simply one of those small wire whisks generally used for making sauces. Mayonnaise is more easily made in summer than in winter, and the oil used for it should never be too cold, but rather at the temperature of the kitchen. It may even be slightly warmed. The coldness of the oil is likely to make it curdle, as is also the too rapid addition of the oil when the mixing is beginning.

This is the way to make it. The proportions are: for eight egg yolks, one tablespoonful of Dijon mustard, salt and pepper to taste, two dessertspoonfuls of vinegar, and two pints of olive oil. Put the eggs, mustard, salt, pepper, and a dash of vinegar in a salad bowl. Mix them with a small whisk, and add the oil drop by drop to begin with, until the mixture of egg and oil starts to thicken. Then pour the oil in a thin uninterrupted stream, stirring quickly from right to left or left to right, whichever you like. As the oil is added the sauce will become thick, and then a few drops of vinegar can be added to dilute it.

Sauce mayonnaise liée à la gelée. To three quarters of a pint of mayonnaise add little by little eight tablespoonfuls of cold melted thick jelly.

NOTE: If, in spite of all, your mayonnaise curdles, all you have to do is to start again with a little mustard, adding the curdled mayonnaise by degrees, if there is a small quantity of the sauce; but if a larger quantity, start with another egg yolk.

Mayonnaise sauce will keep quite well for several days, but in winter see that it is kept in a warmish place. When you want to use mayonnaise sauce made the day before or some days earlier, simply add a few drops of vinegar and stir vigorously.

Sauce niçoise. This is a mayonnaise to which is added a quarter of its volume of much reduced tomato purée, pounded sweet red pepper, and chopped tarragon.

Sauce ravigote. This is a *vinaigrette* made with five parts of olive oil and two of vinegar, a little French mustard, very finely chopped onion washed and pressed dry, chopped parsley, chervil, and tarragon, and pepper and salt.

Sauce rémoulade. To three quarters of a pint of mayonnaise sauce add a good dessertspoonful of French mustard and two dessertspoonfuls of chopped gherkins, capers, parsley, chervil, and tarragon mixed together. Finish with a few drops of anchovy essence.

Sauce russe. Add to a mayonnaise some of the creamy parts of a lobster and some caviar, both passed through a fine sieve. Season lightly with French mustard.

Sauce tartare. Mayonnaise sauce to which are added finely chopped gherkins, capers, olives, parsley, and chives. Season with pepper.

Sauce verte (Green sauce). Blanch in boiling salted water, for ten minutes, watercress leaves, young spinach leaves, chervil, tarragon, parsley, and chives, about two or three ounces in all. Drain these herbs, plunge them in cold water, and squeeze them in a cloth so as to extract as much moisture as possible from them. Now pound them in a mortar, pass them through a very fine sieve or tammy-cloth, and add this purée to three quarters of a pint of mayonnaise.

Sauce Vincent. Take the herbs needed for *sauce verte* above, and add to them twenty leaves of sorrel. Blanch them, plunge them into cold water, dry and pound them as above, but when pounding add three hard-boiled egg yolks. Pass through a fine sieve or cloth, add two raw egg yolks, and use this as a basis for a mayonnaise, adding oil and vinegar as directed above. Season with salt and pepper.

CHAPTER FOUR

*

Hors-d'œuvre

THIS chapter really needs no preface, except to say how much more delightful many luncheon parties would be if the hostesses and their cooks would take a leaf out of Madame Prunier's book. And not only is this collection of *hors-d'œuvre* of use for luncheons, but givers of sherry parties and cocktail parties will find here many hints of supreme value.

The section Hot *Hors-d'œuvre* may really be treated as a section on Savouries. There is no savoury course in France, and you will find in this selection of dishes that many fall into the category of savouries in this country, and others, such as the *beignets, bouchées, coquilles, cromesquis, croquettes,* and the delicious *sausselis,* are what we generally know as 'entrées', and are particularly suitable either as a main dish at luncheon or a single course at dinner.

By the way, *hors-d'œuvre* is gastronomically correct only at luncheon; never at dinner, except in the case of oysters or caviar.

COLD HORS-D'ŒUVRE
Anchovy and Eel

Anchois en paupiettes. The anchovy fillets are washed and very slightly flattened. The inside is then masked with a purée of cooked fish bound with mayonnaise. They are then rolled up, and served surrounded with a little thread of anchovy butter (page 41).

Anchois aux poivrons. Cut up the anchovy fillets in thin strips, and let them lie for a while in olive oil. Arrange them criss-cross on the dish, alternating the anchovy strips with strips of sweet peppers. Surround them with a border of yolk and white of hard-boiled egg, capers, and parsley, all finely chopped.

Anchois des tamarins. Prepare the anchovies as for *Anchois en paupiettes,* and after dishing them surround the dish with a border of potato cooked in salted water, grated while still warm, and lightly seasoned with vinaigrette.

Anguille fumée. The smoked eel can be bought ready for use. Cut it in very fine strips, and arrange them on a dish surrounded by parsley.

Anguille au paprika, or *à l'hongroise*. Cut the eel in fairly long sections and cook it with white wine and herbs with the addition of a pinch of paprika pepper. When it is cold, remove the backbone, and cut the flesh in fillets lengthwise. Arrange them on a dish, and cover them with the clarified stock to which a very little gelatine has been added. Leave the dish in a cool place to set.

Barquettes

Barquettes are a kind of *croustade*, fashioned in the shape of a small boat, and usually made from scraps of puff pastry or short pastry. They are garnished with fish mousses or cooked shellfish, with a *salpicon* or a purée of some sort. They are always welcome as cold *hors-d'œuvre*. Their garnish can of course be varied according to the materials at hand; and this variety, and the attractiveness of the small boats, depends of course entirely on the imagination and taste of the cook.

Canapés

These 'toasts' are made with crumb of bread cut a little more than a quarter of an inch thick, lightly toasted, and spread with butter while still hot. They are then cut out into whatever shape is preferred, square, rectangular, round, oval, lozenge-shape, and so on. As in the case of the *barquettes*, their garnishes may be widely varied according to taste. A few examples are given here.

Canapés aux anchois. Spread the toast with anchovy butter, and garnish with criss-crossed fillets of anchovy. Surround each piece with a little border of finely chopped hard-boiled egg and parsley.

Canapés au caviar. Spread the toast with caviar butter. Garnish with fresh or pressed caviar and surround with a border of fresh butter.

Canapés aux crevettes. Spread the toast with prawn butter. Garnish either with chopped prawns or with halves of prawns, arranged according to taste.

Canapés danois. Made with plain untoasted brown bread, cut in squares, spread with horseradish butter and a surround of fresh caviar. In the middle is set a thin slice of smoked salmon in the form of a cornet, sprinkled with very finely grated horseradish.

Canapés de homard. Spread the toast with lobster butter. Put in the middle a slice from a lobster tail, and surround it with chopped hard-boiled egg bound with mayonnaise.

Canapés au poisson. Spread the toast with soft roe butter. Garnish with a *salpicon* of cold white fish, bound either with a thick mayonnaise flavoured with tomato or with a *sauce chaudfroid à l'aurore* (page 51).

Canapés rochelaise. Spread the toast with soft roe butter. In the middle put a fine poached oyster, and surround it with crayfish butter.

Miscellaneous

Carolines. These are made with ordinary choux pastry. They are half-moon in shape, or may be shaped like small éclairs. They are stuffed with a purée of roes or fish, and covered with a pink or white *chaudfroid* sauce, or glazed with white jelly.

Caviar. The best cold *hors-d'œuvre* of all. Fresh caviar is served in a timbale surrounded by ice, and it is accompanied by finely minced onion, lemon, and brown bread and butter.

Crèmes. These can be made with the remains of white fish, shellfish, tunny-fish, caviar, soft roes, and so on. The selected left-overs are pounded with a little thin Béchamel sauce, then passed through a fine sieve. Enough jelly is then added to make the cream set, and at the last whipped cream is added. The creams are usually prepared in little oiled moulds. Mussels and other shellfish can be used instead, if desired.

Crevettes en aspic. Halves of fine prawns are placed in very small ornamental moulds, decorated or not, between two layers of clear white jelly.

TO COOK PRAWNS: In order to preserve their fine flavour, prawns should be cooked alive in sea water, or at any rate in water strongly salted. One minute's boiling is enough. You must never try to cool them by plunging them into cold water; let them get cold gradually. When they are served plain (*en bouquet*), a decoration of very green parsley is liked by some.

Croûtes d'anchois. Cut some very thin slices of bread, trim off the crusts, and cut into rather long rectangles. Fry these in clarified butter, and let them get cold. Then spread them with fresh butter, and arrange fillets of anchovy symmetrically upon them.

Duchesses. These, like the *carolines*, are made with ordinary choux pastry, but in the shape of a cream bun the size of a small apricot. Take care that they are well dried. Stuff them with a purée of fish or shellfish. Glaze them thickly with white jelly, and sprinkle on them a pinch of chopped pistachio or truffle, or chopped lobster eggs, if the stuffing is of shellfish. Here again variety is the cook's prerogative.

Éperlans marinés (Marinated smelts): see *Escabèche*.

Escabèche. Only very small fish are treated in this fashion, such as smelts, fresh anchovies, and sardines, fillets of sole, small red mullet, and so on, the name of the fish being added in the name of the dish, e.g. *Escabèche* of red mullet. Whatever the fish, the procedure is the same. Flour them and plunge them in smoking oil, leaving them there for an instant or two according to their size. Take them out, drain them, and arrange them in a shallow dish. Heat the oil again, and for each three quarters of a pint of oil add a third of a carrot and an onion, finely minced, and six large whole cloves of garlic. Fry these for a few minutes, and then add half a pint of good vinegar, half a wine-glassful of water, two red peppers, and salt, a sprig of thyme and a bayleaf. Boil gently for a short fifteen minutes, pour it over the fish, and leave them to lie in it for twenty-four hours. Then serve them in the dish, as they are.

Fruits de mer. A *hors-d'œuvre* consisting of any small shellfish (with the exception of oysters). They are served on ice, and brown bread-and-butter is handed with them.

Goujons à la russe. Cook the gudgeon in a *court-bouillon* with white wine (page 31). When cold, drain them, wipe them, and brush them over with mayonnaise bound with jelly. Sprinkle them with finely chopped parsley, and keep them in a cool place until the jelly sets.

Grondins à l'orientale: see *Rougets à l'orientale*.

Harengs marinés. For twenty herrings prepare a marinade as follows: a pint and three quarters of white wine, a pint of vinegar, three quarters of an ounce of salt, two medium-sized carrots cut in thin rings notched at the edges, three medium-sized onions cut in thin rings, three minced shallots, a sprig of thyme and half a bayleaf, a pinch each of sage and basil, parsley stalks, and several peppercorns. Boil this mixture gently until the carrot and onion are cooked. While the marinade is still boiling, pour it over the herrings, which you have cleaned and arranged in a sauté pan or other shallow pan, and let them poach there for twelve minutes, without the liquid coming to the boil. Then put them into a dish, cover them with the *marinade*, and let them get cold. Serve them very cold, with rounds of carrot, rings of onion, thin slices of lemon, and the *marinade*.

Harengs livonienne. Fillet some fine kippers or bloaters; remove the skin and bones, but keep the heads and tails. Cut the fillets in dice, and cut in dice the same amount of cold boiled potato and rather sharp raw apples. Add chopped parsley, chervil, tarragon, and fennel, season with oil and vinegar, mix together, and add a pinch of cayenne. With this salad make imitation herrings, putting back the head and the tail on each.

Harengs Mesnil-Val. (This interesting dish was discovered by M. Jean Barnagaud-Prunier on a fishing expedition to the little village of Mesnil-Val, which is near Dieppe and Le Treport.) Put four fresh herrings into a long dish with twelve cloves, two ounces of juniper berries, half an ounce of dried red pepper (*piment sec*), half an ounce of mace, two ounces of black peppercorns, a wineglassful of vinegar, salt, a little celery, thyme, and a bayleaf. Add a wineglassful of water, cover, and poach gently for eight minutes. Let the fish get cold in the liquid, and serve them in it.

Harengs saurs à la chalutière. Fillet some soft-roed *harengs saurs*, skin them, and cut them in strips. Soak them in milk to remove the saltiness. Pass the roes through a fine sieve, and moisten this purée with enough vinegar to make a broth. To this add onion, chervil, tarragon, chives, and the white of celery, all finely chopped. Season with salt and pepper and a light touch of cayenne. Drain the fillets, arrange them on a dish, and cover them with a broth.

If preferred, the covering may consist of a mixture of two-thirds mayonnaise and one-third of the broth described above.

Harengs saurs are difficult to obtain in England, but kippers or bloaters may also be used for this recipe and are just as good.

Huîtres (Oysters). These can be served either at luncheon or dinner, and should always be very cold. There are served at the same time lemons, thin slices of buttered brown bread, and vinegar with coarse-ground pepper.

(A special section on oysters will be found on page 201.)

Maquereaux marinés. Small mackerel are best for this, and they are treated in the same way as herrings (see *Harengs marinés*).

Moules. The smaller the mussels are, the better. Open them in the usual manner over the fire (page 199), take them from their shells, remove their beards, and blind them either with a mustard sauce with cream or a mayonnaise, *rémoulade*, or *vinaigrette*, etc. They can also, if liked, be flavoured with saffron. If you wish, you can add to the sauce chosen a little of the reduced stock of the mussels.

Œufs farcis. Cut some hard-boiled eggs in half; take out the yolks and keep them for sprinkling on the stuffed halves, or use them to add to the stuffing. Any sort of purée of fish or shellfish can be used, and it should be stiffened with a little jelly. The egg halves can also be garnished with *Salade Russe* bound with thick mayonnaise; and numberless other garnishes can of course be thought of.

Olives farcies. Stone them, and fill them by means of a forcing-bag with fish or shellfish butter.

Pâte de poisson Traktir. Take two pounds of filleted fish, preferably brill or turbot, but fresh cod can be used. One pound of this fish will be used to make a *farce blanche* (white stuffing); i.e. mince the fish in a mincing machine, or pound it in a mortar. To this add half a pound of panada (page 34), to which add either cream or condensed milk. Mix all together to make the stuffing.

Put the other pound of fish in a marinade made of white wine, whisky, thyme, bayleaf, pepper, and salt. Then make a *Duxelles* (page 31) of chopped mushrooms and chopped cooked sorrel, to which add reduction of shallots, white wine, a little minced savory and chervil, pepper and salt, and one third of the white stuffing, so as to have an equal quantity of white and dark stuffing.

Line a mould with pancakes, and use white stuffing to make the bottom layer. Then put a layer of the fillets of fish which have been soaking in the marinade: all the layers of stuffing should then be put into the mould through a piping bag. Put a layer composed of one stripe of white stuffing and one stripe of black stuffing, then a layer of the fish, then a layer composed of one stripe of white stuffing and one stripe of black stuffing, and so on until the mould is full.

Put the mould in a *bain-marie* in a slow oven for half an hour. When you take it out, press the mould to drain off water, leave the mould to cool, and take out the following day.

Poutargue. An eastern preparation made with the dried hard roe of the grey mullet or tunnyfish. It should be cut in thin slices and dressed with olive oil, pepper, and lemon juice. Or it can be grated and used to garnish buttered toast.

Roll mops. Soak some soft-roed salt herrings in milk for at least five hours. Fillet them, and spread the inside of each fillet with mustard mixed with very finely chopped onion. Roll them round in *paupiettes* and tie them. Arrange them in a shallow vessel, put their roes on top of them, and cover them with vinegar which has been boiled with minced onion, a bouquet of parsley, thyme, and bayleaf, peppercorns and cloves, still boiling and strained through a conical sieve. When cold, pass the roes through a sieve, and moisten the purée thus obtained with the vinegar and eight tablespoonfuls of oil for each pint and three quarters of vinegar. Pour this over the *paupiettes*, and let them lie in it for three days before eating.

Rougets à l'orientale. Fry the red mullet in butter or oil. When they are cold, arrange them in a dish, leaving the heads and tails bare, and cover them with *Tomates à l'orientale*, much reduced and very cold. Add rounds of lemon with the pips removed.

Tomates à l'orientale. Warm a little olive oil and put in some finely minced onions and shallots. Add, according to taste, a little finely chopped garlic and some saffron. Make some tomato pulp, removing skin and pips, add this to the onions, etc., mix well together, and then reduce until it gets like a thick jam.

Salades au riz. Rice salads are made in the proportion of two thirds of the cooked rice and one third of the other ingredients. The rice is cooked in salted water, well drained, and dressed with vinaigrette dressing while still warm. Other ingredients used in these salads are: prawns or crayfish (*écrevisses*), thin strips of lobster or crawfish (*langouste*), strips or small pieces of fish left-overs, truffle, sweet peppers, onion, etc.; in a word, whatever mixtures you consider good. The *vinaigrette* used for dressing the rice is usually made with a little mustard.

Sardines à l'huile. Commercial product.

Saumon fumé. English or Dutch smoked salmon. Cut in very thin slices, arrange on a dish, and surround with parsley. Lemon juice, and black pepper freshly ground from a pepper-mill, will be demanded by the wise.

Tartelettes. The same remarks apply as to *barquettes* (page 54).

Tartelettes au thon. Cover the bottom of the tartlets with mayonnaise, and then put in each a fairly thick round of tinned tunnyfish. Surround with a little border of chopped hard-boiled egg and parsley.

Or: garnish the tart with chopped tinned tunnyfish bound with mayonnaise, sprinkling on top chopped hard-boiled egg yolk and parsley mixed together.

Thon à l'huile. A commercial product. Arrange on a dish and surround with chopped hard-boiled egg.

Tomates farcies au poisson. The tomatoes should be the size of apricots. Open at the stalk end and press gently to expel the juice and seeds. Season the inside with salt, pepper, and a few drops of vinegar, and fill them (with a forcing-bag) with a fine mince of cold white fish. Serve surrounded with parsley.

Tomates à la Monaco. Prepare some small tomatoes as above, and fill them with a mince of tunnyfish in oil mixed with onion finely chopped, washed, and pressed, chopped hard-boiled eggs, parsley, chervil, and tarragon, all bound with mayonnaise.

Tomates en quartiers. Medium-sized and very red tomatoes should be used for this. Open them at the stalk end, press out the juice and pips, and lightly crush the divisions inside. Fill the tomatoes up either with a fine *salpicon*, or with a purée or mince of fish bound with jelly, or with a *salade russe* bound with jelly or thick mayonnaise. Keep the stuffed tomatoes on ice for an hour, then cut them in quarters and serve them with parsley round them.

HOT HORS-D'ŒUVRE

Anchoyade provençale. This is how Reboul, the author of the *Cuisinière Provençale*, describes *anchoyade*:

After having washed seven or eight anchovies, soak them for some minutes to remove their saltiness, then wash the fillets, put them on a plate with several spoonfuls of olive oil, a pinch of pepper, and two or three cloves of garlic cut in small dice. You can also add a few drops of vinegar. Cut off the bottom of a loaf to the thickness of about an inch and a half, and divide this in pieces, one for each guest. Put on each several anchovy fillets, and put each piece of bread on a plate. Cut some more pieces of bread in squares; each person takes one of these pieces, dips it in the oil on the plate, and uses it to crush the anchovy on the bread. This dipping is done several times, and when all the oil is used up, the small pieces of bread are eaten, and the crust with the crushed anchovies on it is toasted before the fire.

Attereaux de homard Pahlen. Fill some skewers with alternate slices of lobster tail, large mussels and oysters, both poached, and slices of truffle. Cover these filled skewers with *sauce Villeroy* (page 50) and let them get cold. Then egg-and-breadcrumb them, giving them a cylindrical shape. Fry them at once, pull out the skewers and serve the pieces on a napkin, with fried parsley.

Barquettes, Tartelettes: These, already described on page 54, can be served hot.

Barquettes aux écrevisses. Fry the crayfish in a little butter, *flambez* them with brandy, cook them with fish *fumet* and white wine, and remove the shells from the tails. Garnish the bottom of each *barquette* with mushroom purée, arrange six to eight crayfish tails in each, and at each end put a crayfish's head.

Barquettes aux huîtres. Garnish the *barquettes* with poached oysters and cover them with cream sauce, sprinkling this with chopped truffle.

Barquettes de filets de sole. Garnish the bottom of the *barquettes* with small pieces of fillets of sole and mushrooms bound with a fish *velouté* made with a *fumet* of shellfish (*fruits de mer*). Cover with this sauce, and arrange on top very small poached fillets of sole alternating with slices of truffle.

Barquettes Joinville. Garnish the bottom of the *barquettes* with small pieces of prawns bound with a creamy fish *velouté* finished with prawn butter. Cover with *hollandaise* sauce; in the middle put a thread of *velouté* finished with lobster butter, and at the end of each *barquette* set a prawn with the tail-case removed.

Barquettes de laitance florentine. Garnish the bottom of the *barquettes* with a little leaf spinach stewed in butter, arrange on this the soft roe, poached and cut in slices, cover with *mornay* sauce, sprinkle with grated cheese, and brown quickly under a salamander or a gas or electric grill.

Beignets d'anchois à la niçoise. Take some fine anchovies, soak them to rid them of their salt, then drain them on a plate and wipe them dry. Fillet them with care. Dip these fillets in a light frying batter, and plunge them one by one into very hot deep fat. A very few minutes will cook them. Drain them, and serve on a napkin with fried parsley.

Beignets à la bénédictine. Mix two thirds *brandade* of salt cod (page 107) and a third potato purée. Add two egg yolks per pound of the mixture, and shape in the form of quoits. When the time comes to serve them, dip these quoits in a light frying batter and fry them in deep fat.

Beignets de laitances. Poach soft roes with white wine, drain them, wipe them dry, and dip them in a thick Béchamel sauce mixed with lobster broth. Arrange them on a dish and let them get cold, and when wanted dip them in frying batter and fry them in very hot deep fat.

Beignets mathurine. With a pound of ordinary choux pastry dough mix four ounces of cold salmon flaked up and the same amount of herring fillets cut in dice. Take up the dough in teaspoonfuls, pushing it off with the finger into deep hot fat. These fritters should be treated in the same way as *beignets soufflés.*

Bouchées. *Bouchées* for use as *hors-d'œuvre* should be only two-thirds the size of ordinary *bouchées*: they are named after the principal ingredient of their garnish, or by some other distinctive name, as these that follow.

    Bouchées hollandaise. Garnish the *bouchées* with small pieces of smoked salmon bound with *hollandaise* sauce, and on the top of each place a fine poached oyster.

    Bouchées Joinville. Garnish the *bouchées* with cut-up crayfish tails, mushrooms, and truffles, bound with *sauce Joinville* (page 47). A slice of truffle surmounts each.

Bouchées Montglas. Garnish the *bouchées* with poached and bearded oysters, mussels, mushrooms, crayfish tails, and truffles, all bound with a white wine sauce to which has been added the reduced liquor from the oysters.

Bouchées Victoria. Garnish the *bouchées* with pieces of lobster tail and truffles, bound with a mayonnaise finished with a lobster broth.

Clams à la marinière: see Mussels (page 199).

Clams vapeur. Open the clams in a large pan with very little water and a trifle of pepper. Serve them as they are, handing melted butter separately.

Riʒotto de clams au safran. Open the clams, and keep aside the liquor. Prepare a risotto (page 37), adding a little saffron. With some fish *velouté* and the liquor from the clams make a sauce, and flavour it with saffron. Bind the shelled clams with this sauce, and serve them with the risotto.

Coquillages: clams, palourde, etc. The best manner of appreciating these shellfish is to eat them raw, and they will be found in the cold *hors-d'œuvre* under *Fruits de mer.* They can, however, be eaten hot, as has been shown in the recipes for clams (above), which apply equally well to the other shellfish of this kind.

Coquilles de crevettes. As a *hors-d'œuvre,* these scallops should be half the size of those ordinarily served as a dish.

Coquilles de crevettes au currie. Have ready a curry sauce (page 46). Peel the prawns, warm them in butter without cooking, take them out, swill the pan with white wine, and mix this with the sauce. Put into scallops shells, and brown under a salamander or a gas or electric grill. Serve rice (for curry) separately. (See *Riʒ à l'indienne,* page 37).

Coquilles de crevettes dieppoise. Mix peeled prawns with cooked mushrooms cut in dice, bind with *sauce dieppoise,* and garnish the scallops with this mixture. Cover with the same sauce, and brown lightly.

Coquilles de crevettes crème gratin. Bind the prawns with cream sauce (page 46), and fill the scallop shells with the mixture. Cover with a light *sauce mornay,* sprinkle with grated cheese, and brown.

Côtelettes. These cutlets are made in the same way as the croquettes described below. The only difference lies in their shape. They are egg-and-breadcrumbed, but instead of being fried in deep fat they are fried in clarified butter. Their shape is self-explanatory, and a small piece of macaroni or spaghetti is inserted in the end of each to imitate the cutlet bone. They are dressed in the same way as *croquettes*, and served with the same sauces.

Crêpes aux huîtres, crevettes, etc. Make an ordinary pancake batter without sugar, slightly flavoured with pepper. If a shellfish is used for the filling, it must be poached and drained and its reduced liquor added to the batter. Pour some of the batter into the frying pan, scatter six to eight of the oysters, or prawns, etc. over it, and fry the pancake in the usual way, turning it. Keep them hot as they are made, and serve them as hot as possible.

Cromesquis. These are made of the same preparation as *Croquettes* (see below), but they have a different wrapping.

Cromesquis à la française. Divide the preparation chosen into pieces weighing three to four ounces, put them on a floured board, and give them a rectangular shape. When the time comes, dip them in frying batter and plunge them into very hot deep fat. When the batter is golden and quite dry, drain the *cromesquis*, and serve them on a napkin with fried parsley.

In England it is usual to wrap the *cromesqui* in a very thin slice of bacon or ham before plunging it into the batter, and then frying it.

Cromesquis à la polonaise. Prepare as above, but wrap each in very thin unsweetened pancake. Before frying, dip the side of the pancake where the join is in the frying batter, so as to make sure that it sticks together when cooking.

Croquettes de poissons et crustacés. These can be made of cold cooked fish or shellfish, with various additions, the principal ingredient being half the mixture, and the additions the other half. The various ingredients are cut into small dice, and are technically called a *salpicon*. The sauce which binds them together is generally a fish *velouté*, very much reduced, and bound with egg yolks; but other sauces are also used. The proper proportion is just over half a pint for every pound of the *salpicon*.

METHOD: Mix the *salpicon* with the sauce, spread it out on a plate, and let it get cold. Then divide it in portions weighing from three to four ounces each; shape them as you like (but they are usually cork-shaped), flour them lightly, roll them in egg, and then in fine white breadcrumbs. They must be fried in very hot deep fat, so that the covering of egg and breadcrumbs solidifies at once and so prevents the sauce inside from escaping. Serve them on a napkin with fried parsley, and hand the appropriate sauce separately.

Croquettes à la dieppoise. Mix together equal quantities of small mussels poached and bearded, prawn tails and *cèpes* (see below) previously fried in oil, and bind them with a very much reduced Béchamel sauce flavoured with paprika pepper. Shape, egg-and-breadcrumb, and fry. Hand a white wine sauce separately. (As *cèpes* are generally unprocurable in this country, ordinary mushrooms may be used; but the flavour will not of course be quite the same.)

Croquettes dominicaine. In these the ingredients are two-thirds poached oysters (at least ten oysters for each croquette) and one-third mushrooms cut in dice. Mix them with a Béchamel sauce flavoured with onion and finished with lobster butter. Shape in oval form, egg-and-breadcrumb, and fry. Hand separately a white wine sauce to which has been added the liquor from the oysters, the whole afterwards reduced.

Croquettes de homard. Make a *salpicon* of lobster, truffles, and mushrooms, bound with egg yolks and lobster butter. Shape as you will, egg-and-breadcrumb, and fry, and serve with a *cardinal* sauce (page 46).

Croquettes de merlan à l'indienne. Mix in equal parts rice cooked in fish stock and the flesh of whiting poached with white wine, allowed to get cold, and then cut in dice. Bind with a much-reduced Béchamel sauce flavoured with curry. Make the *croquettes* cork-shaped, egg-and-breadcrumb them, and fry them. Hand a curry sauce.

Croquettes de saumon gastronome. Make a *salpicon* with three quarters salmon flesh and a quarter truffle, and bind them with a much-reduced Newburg sauce (page 48). Shape in rectangles, egg-and-breadcrumb them, fry them in clarified butter, and serve with Newburg sauce handed separately.

Croquettes de sole Nantua. A *salpicon* of poached fillets of sole and crayfish tails mixed with nearly the same weight of Duchesse potato (page 36), and one part reduced Béchamel sauce. Shape in cork-shapes, egg-and-breadcrumb, and fry in clarified butter. Hand *sauce Nantua* (page 48).

Croquettes de turbot à la parisienne. Equal parts of turbot and Duchesse potato (page 36), enlivened by a little chopped truffle. Shape in the form of a pear, egg-and-breadcrumb, fry, and stick a small piece of truffle in the end in imitation of the stalk. Hand a thick fish *velouté* separately.

Croquettes de morue: see under *Croquettes à l'américaine* (page 110).

Croquettes nantaise. Make a *salpicon* of the remains of cold fish and an equal amount of mushrooms. Mix them with a thick reduced fish *velouté*, shape them into rather long rectangles, egg-and-breadcrumb them, and fry them in deep fat. Serve separately a thin well-buttered tomato sauce.

Croustades Joinville. Make some *croustades* (page 35), and fill them with a *salpicon* of fish *quenelles*, mushrooms, prawn tails or crawfish (*langouste*) bound with prawn or shrimp sauce.

Croustilles Saint-Michel. Cut a slice of bread and trim off the crusts. Garnish this with a *salpicon* of white fish bound with white wine sauce flavoured with paprika pepper. Cover with another slice of bread, dip this sandwich in beaten egg, and fry it golden in foaming butter in a frying pan. Serve very hot indeed.

Huîtres: see Hot Oyster Dishes in Chapter 8 (pages 180–212).

Pains de poisson. Make a forcemeat with well-seasoned white fish, and mix with it a third of its weight of a purée of mushrooms stewed in butter. Shape the forcemeat the size of a bridge roll; in the middle of each put a few rounds of hard-boiled egg. Wrap each in a brioche paste made without sugar, giving them the shape of a small long roll. Bake in a hot oven, and serve hot.

Piroguis au poisson. Finely flake some cooked fish, add to it chopped hard-boiled eggs and well-cooked rice, and bind the mixture lightly with fish *velouté*. Roll out some puff-pastry dough a quarter of an inch thick, and cut out scalloped rounds with a circular cutter, four inches in diameter. Put these on a baking sheet, garnish the middle of each with a little of the fish mixture, moisten the edges a little, cover with another round of pastry, pinch the edges well together, brush with egg yolk, and bake in a hot oven.

Rastegaïs (a kind of small *Coulibiac de poisson*, page 127). Roll out some ordinary brioche dough in a piece six inches by eight inches, and garnish it in the same way as a *coulibiac*, with the following ingredients: hard-boiled eggs cut in rounds, then dipped in melted butter and sprinkled with parsley; minced mushrooms cooked in butter; chopped onion first cooked in butter and then bound with fish *velouté*; cooked with chopped *vésiga* (the dried spine marrow of the sturgeon); rice *à la créole*; and whatever fish is chosen cut in slices and stiffened in butter; all well seasoned. For the actual garnishing, proceed as follows: in the middle of the pastry put successive layers of rice, eggs, mushrooms, *vésiga*, fish, then begin again backwards, *vésiga*, mushrooms, eggs, rice. Lightly moisten the edges of the paste, and fold them together in such a way as to enclose the contents tightly, and pinch them well together. The *rastegaïs* will then have the shape of an elongated shoe. Make a little slit in the top, and bake it in a hot oven. Serve separately some melted butter containing chopped parsley.

Rissoles. These are made, usually with trimmings, either of pastry or of ordinary unsweetened brioche dough, in the latter case being called *Rissoles à la dauphine.* Their garnish can be a *salpicon* of prawns, or crayfish tails, or lobster meat as principal ingredient, with mushrooms and truffles as additions. They are always fried in deep fat, and at the last possible moment before serving.

Sausselis. With puff-pastry dough, or trimmings, roll out a rectangular piece as long as you wish, but three or four inches wide. Garnish the middle with a thickish layer of whiting forcemeat (page 31) to which you may have added, if you like, some prawns or shrimps or crayfish tails, lobster meat, or fillets of anchovies cut in dice. Moisten the edges of the dough, cover the garnish with a second piece of dough, pinch the edges together, brush with egg yolk, and mark the top into divisions for helping. Cook in a hot oven, and cut the *sausselis* up immediately before serving.

NOTE: The preparation of the *sausselis* is exactly the same as that of the pastrycook's *Dartois*, the only difference being that the contents of the former are invariably some sort of fish forcemeat.

Petits soufflés de poissons. Small soufflés for *hors-d'œuvre* are made in small buttered porcelain cases, and always from cold fish. And whatever fish is used, it must always be first stewed in butter and then passed through a sieve. To half a pound of this purée add five or six dessertspoonfuls of very much reduced fish *velouté*; warm it up without letting it boil, correct the seasoning, and then add three egg yolks and four whites stiffly beaten. Put the mixture into the cases, and cook them in a slow oven. (In describing these small soufflés, the name of the fish from which they are made is usually indicated: e.g. *soufflés de merlan, d'éperlans,* and so on.)

Various small timbales. These timbales are made in small *dariole* moulds, and in various ways. The method of preparation is as follows: butter the moulds well, and put them on ice for an instant. Put a slice of truffle in the bottom of each, if you like, and line the bottom and sides with a layer of forcemeat about an eighth of an inch thick. Fill up the inside with a *salpicon* of some kind, cover with a layer of the forcemeat, and poach the moulds in a *bain-marie*. They should be accompanied by a sauce appropriate to the garnish inside them.

CHAPTER FIVE

*

Soups

FISH soups are delicious, as everyone knows who has tasted *bisque de homard*, for instance. But how seldom do we ever come across them, except in restaurants. The simpler soups like bouillabaisse are excellent fare: conger soup, mussel soup, how cheap and satisfying they are! But with the exception perhaps of oyster soup, and in poorer homes of broth made with a cod's head, what do we know of them?

In this chapter will be found the soups which are made from fish and shellfish. Turtle soup, that solace of aldermen, is dealt with fully in Chapter Nine.

POTAGES

Potage bisque de clams. There are two sorts of clam: the soft clam and the hard clam. This soup is made with the hard clams. First of all prepare three and a half pints of fish *velouté*, well cooked and skimmed. Then open three dozen hard clams, reserving their liquor. Chop them up and toss them for a few seconds in nutbrown butter (page 43). Add them to the *velouté* with the liquor strained and decanted through a cloth, and add as well half a glass of white wine. Cook gently for fifteen to twenty minutes, pass through a sieve, heat up again without boiling, and finish, off the fire, with three ounces of butter, a touch of cayenne pepper and three dessertspoonfuls of sherry or Madeira.

Potage bisque de crabes. Take two large crabs, crack their claws, remove the meat from them, flake it up with two forks, and keep it aside. Remove all the meat and creamy substance from the bodies of the crabs, pound this in a mortar, and moisten the purée thus obtained with three and a half pints of light fish *fumet*; add four ounces of rice, and cook gently for half an hour. Now pass through a sieve, heat up without boiling, and finish with a cupful of fresh cream lightly boiled beforehand. Season with a touch of paprika pepper. At the last minute add the flesh from the claws which have meanwhile been heated up in a little consommé.

Potage bisque de crevettes. For three and a half pints of this soup, fry in a *mirepoix* (page 33) a pound and a half of live prawns or shrimps. Proceed then as for the *Bisque d'écrevisses* (below), and finish at the last moment with about three ounces of prawn or shrimp butter. Garnish with three dessertspoonfuls of small shelled prawns or shrimps.

Potage bisque d'écrevisses. (1) Fry lightly in butter a finely cut *mirepoix* consisting of half a carrot, half an onion, parsley stalks, and a little thyme and bayleaf. Add the crayfish, washed and cleaned, allowing four or five to each person according to size. Toss these over a flame until their shells are very red, then moisten with a few dessertspoonfuls of burnt brandy, four tablespoonfuls of white wine, and the same of light fish *fumet*. Season with salt and pepper, cover, and cook for ten to twelve minutes, according to the size of the crayfish. At the same time cook four ounces of rice in white consommé. This rice must be well cooked, or, if preferred, it can be replaced by the best quality ground rice.

(2) Shell the crayfish, keeping aside the tails and a dozen heads. Drain and well pound the broken shells, the rest of the crayfish and the *mirepoix*, keeping back the cooking liquor. Add the rice, then the liquor, and pass through a sieve. Moisten this purée with enough consommé to bring it to the right thickness, and heat it just to boiling point. At the moment of serving, finish the soup with a few spoonfuls of cream, a few drops of good brandy, and five ounces of butter. It should be garnished with the crayfish tails cut in small dice, and the heads stuffed with creamy fish forcemeat or with mousseline forcemeat made with lobster.

NOTE: The operation of cleaning the crayfish should never be neglected, in whatever way they are prepared. It consists in drawing out the intestinal tube, the end of which can be found in an opening under the middle phalanx of the tail.

Potage bisque de homard. Cut up in small slices across the body three small live lobsters, season them with salt and pepper, fry them in a *mirepoix* in the same way as the crayfish (above), and finish in exactly the same way as in that recipe. This soup is garnished by dice of the lobster flesh, which has been kept back for the purpose.

Potage bisque d'huîtres à l'américaine. Open three dozen Portuguese oysters, and poach them in their own liquor. Drain, pound in a mortar, moisten with the strained oyster liquor decanted through a cloth, and add three and a half pints of light fish *velouté*. Heat up, pass through a sieve, and finish with butter and a few drops of Madeira. Heighten the seasoning with a touch of cayenne. A garnish of two small poached and bearded oysters for each person can be added.

Potage bisque de langouste. Proceed exactly as for *Potage bisque de homard*, using live crawfish instead.

Potage bisque de langoustines. Make a bisque in the same way as the *bisque d'écrevisses*, using live Dublin Bay prawns instead of crayfish.

Potage fruits de mer. For four people you will want twelve flat oysters, twelve small clams, one quart of mussels, a few shrimps, three egg yolks, half a pint of cream, a pint of milk, four ounces of butter, some cream crackers, two leeks, one medium-sized onion, one stick of celery, twelve ounces of potatoes. Cut the leeks, onions, celery into small dice, and let them stew gently in the butter. Moisten them with the liquor from the shellfish and with the milk, and add the potatoes cut in little pieces. Cook for twenty minutes, and then pass through a fine conical sieve (*chinois*). Bind with the egg and cream at the moment of serving. (This is done by boiling the cream and pouring it gently on the egg yolks, whipping hard all the time so that the egg does not curdle.) Put the bearded shellfish into the soup tureen and pour the soup over them. Hand the cream crackers separately.

Potage Ouka. (1) With two pounds of a fish like salmon or sturgeon and the same amount of fish bones and trimmings, adding a large bouquet of parsley stalks, celery, and fennel, and salt, and moistening with five pints of water and three quarters of a pint of white wine, make some fish stock. Cut in fine *julienne* shreds six ounces of the white of leeks, the same of celery, and two ounces of parsley roots. Stew these in butter, and finish cooking them with a little fish stock.

(2) Clarify the fish stock with chopped whiting flesh (about a pound and a quarter) and five ounces of caviar. Pass through a

cloth. Mix the *julienne* with the stock, and add also dice of the fish used in making the stock. Serve separately some *Rastegaïs* (page 67), or *Kâche de Sarrasin* (below).

NOTE: The following recipe for *Kâche de Sarrasin* is taken from Escoffier's *Guide to Modern Cookery:*

Moisten one lb. of roughly chopped buckwheat with enough tepid water to make a stiff paste; add the necessary salt, and put this paste into a large charlotte mould. Bake in a hot oven for two hours. Then remove the thick crust which has formed upon the preparation, and transfer what remains, by means of a spoon, to a basin. Mix therewith two oz of butter while it is still hot. Kâche prepared in this way may be served in a special timbale. But it is more often spread in a thin layer on a buttered tray and left to cool. It is then cut into roundels one inch in diameter, and these are rolled in flour and coloured on both sides in very hot, clarified butter.

Oyster and okra soup. Blanch a large chopped onion with two ounces of chopped and melted pork fat. Add three tomatoes, peeled, pressed, and chopped, a few okra, and two minced sweet peppers. Moisten with three and a half pints of white stock, season with a pinch of curry powder, and cook gently for a quarter of an hour. Then bind very lightly with arrowroot. A few seconds before serving, add two dozen oysters and the liquor in which they have that minute been poached.

Potage rossolnick au poisson. Make a very light fish *velouté* to which you have added half a wineglassful of cucumber juice. After it has been cooking for twenty minutes, add a dozen bits of parsley root and the same amount of celery root cut in the shape of a clove of garlic and well blanched; twenty pieces of *agoursis* (Russian salted cucumber) shaped and blanched in the same way. Let it cook gently for twenty-five minutes, and then finish with a binding of two egg yolks mixed with a little cucumber juice. The garnish consists of very small *quenelles* of fish forcemeat and dice of cucumber cooked in salted water.

Potage vermicelle à la granvillaise. Open three and a half pints of well-cleaned mussels, adding an onion and a piece of celery both well minced, a few parsley stalks, and about a pint and a quarter of water. When the mussels are opened, strain the water through a cloth, let it settle, and then decant it. Bring this water to the boil again, and in it poach five ounces of vermicelli, and add enough boiling cream (about a pint and a quarter) to make the proper quantity of soup.

VELOUTÉS

TO PREPARE VELOUTÉ FOR FISH SOUPS: Take a pound and a half of fish which do not have too pronounced a flavour, such as whiting, sole, John Dory, etc., and make a fish stock with them. (Avoid using fish like salmon, tunny, sturgeon, mackerel, etc.) Mix four ounces of butter with five ounces of flour, brown it very lightly indeed on a low fire (it should be golden brown), and moisten it with four and three quarter pints of the fish stock. Bring to the boil, add a small handful of fresh mushroom peelings and a bouquet of parsley, and cook for a quarter of an hour, skimming it. This *velouté* has to be made very quickly, because the flavour of the fish would be too strong if the cooking were prolonged. Nor must it have the consistency of ordinary *velouté*: it must be quite light. Pass it through a sieve, and finish it as directed in the various recipes.

NOTE: In any case a fish *velouté*, as a soup, is always finished by a binding of five egg yolks, eight tablespoonfuls of cream, and five or six ounces of butter, for every three and a half pints of the *velouté*. This particular instruction will not be repeated in the recipes that follow.

Velouté bagration. A very light *velouté* of smelt, to which are added three ounces of raw mushroom purée for each pint and three quarters. Cook the *velouté* for six or seven minutes, pass through a sieve, heat up, and add the binding and butter. It is garnished with thin strips of fillets of sole and slices of crayfish tails.

Velouté cardinal. A light fish *velouté* finished with the usual binding and five ounces of very red lobster butter. The garnish is a *royale* made with lobster stamped out with a cutter.

Velouté carmélite. Fish *velouté* flavoured rather strongly with celery. Usual binding and buttering. Garnish: little *quenelles* of whiting forcemeat.

Velouté chanoinesse: see *Velouté cardinal.* It differs in the garnish, which in this case consists of small slices of soft roes poached in butter.

Velouté de crevettes. Prawns or shrimps. Fry in butter, with a *mirepoix*, as in the case of the *Bisque de crevettes* (page 70), a pound and a quarter of live prawns or shrimps. Pound them finely, mix them with a fish *velouté*, and pass them through a sieve. Heat up and add the usual binding and five or six ounces of prawn or shrimp butter. Garnish with small shrimp tails and small 'pearls' of truffle.

Velouté de crevettes cancalaise. The same as above, but add the oyster liquor from the garnish, which consists of three poached and bearded oysters per head.

Velouté dieppoise. Make the *velouté* in the usual way (page 73), keeping it rather thick, and adding to it the white part of three small leeks finely minced and stewed in butter. Pass through a sieve, and finish with the decanted stock of mussels, remembering that this stock is salted. Add the binding and butter as usual. The garnish is small shrimp tails and poached and bearded mussels.

Velouté d'écrevisses (Crayfish). Cook the crayfish in a *mirepoix*, as for the *Bisque d'écrevisses* (page 70), allowing three for each person. Pound the crayfish finely with the *mirepoix*, and mix the purée with about two and a half pints of light *velouté*. Pass through a sieve, bring nearly to the boil but not quite, and finish with the usual binding and butter. The garnish consists of crayfish tails cut in half, these tails having been kept back for the purpose.

NOTE: The garnish of this soup admits of variation according to the ideas or whim of the cook. It may consist of either crayfish tails, little *quenelles* of whiting forcemeat, or of sole *à la crème*, with or without truffles; a *julienne* of truffles, mushrooms, or fillet of sole; asparagus tips; and so on. These garnishes may consist of one or more of these ingredients. But of course any change in the garnish will imply a change in the name of the dish.

Velouté d'éperlans. To three pints of fish *velouté* add three or four ounces of the flesh of smelt, chopped up and stewed in butter. Be careful of the very pronounced flavour of this little fish. Pass through a sieve, adjust to the right consistency with a very clear *fumet* of sole, and add the binding and the butter. Choose whatever garnish you like, so long as it suits this sort of soup.

Velouté de homard. Make a *Lobster à l'américaine* with a small live lobster. Keep back part of the flesh of the tail for the garnish, and finely pound the rest with the stock from the lobster, and mix this purée with two and a half pints of fish *velouté*. Pass through a sieve, adjust to the right thickness with a very light fish stock, heat up, and finish with the usual binding and butter. Garnish with the reserved lobster meat cut in small dice.

Velouté mathurine. A fish *velouté* finished with a *fumet* of sole, bound and buttered in the usual way, and garnished with small creamy *quenelles* of salmon.

SOUPS

Soupe aux clams à l'américaine. Open four dozen clams, remove the hard parts, and keep the 'nuts' in a stewpan. Add to the clam juice enough water to make just over a quart, and add too the trimmings of the clams. Boil gently for ten minutes, then pass this liquid through a conical sieve on to the clam 'nuts', and let them poach in it without coming to the boil. Finish with a little over a pint of boiling cream, three ounces of butter, and about three ounces of water biscuits crushed with a rolling-pin.

Soupe aux clams. Fry in butter five ounces of streaky bacon cut in small dice, two leeks, five ounces of onions, celery, one sweet pepper, two tomatoes skinned and roughly chopped, four ounces of potatoes, all these cut in small pieces. Add a pinch of thyme. Also poach separately three dozen clams, strain their liquor, keep back the 'nuts', and moisten the vegetables with this *fumet*. Cook them for an hour, and add, at the moment of serving, the bearded clams and a few crushed water biscuits. Season lightly.

Soupe au congre. Fry a large onion and the white of two leeks, both minced, in olive oil until they are a golden brown. Add three pressed and chopped tomatoes, four cloves of garlic, several parsley stalks roughly chopped, and two pounds of small conger cut in small cutlets. Stew thus for a quarter of an hour, moisten with five pints of boiling water, and add two cloves, half a bayleaf, a little fennel, and a small pimento. Bring to the boil, and boil gently for three quarters of an hour. At the end of this time, pass the soup through a tammy-cloth, bring it to the boil again, and then poach in it half a pound of rather thick vermicelli.

NOTE: This soup should be very thick.

Soupe aux huîtres à l'américaine. This is made in the same way as the *Soupe aux clams*, using oysters instead of clams.

Soupe aux moules. This soup is made in various ways, the method differing according to the locality.

(1) It can be prepared *à la crème*, in the same way as the *soupe aux clams*.

(2) *À la marseillaise.* Open three and a half pints of small and very clean mussels, together with a large minced onion, several parsley stalks, a small bayleaf, and two and three quarter pints of water, turn them on to a sieve or tammy-cloth, and keep the liquor in a basin. Remove the shells from the mussels, which you must keep warm. With four tablespoonfuls of olive oil, fry to a very light golden the finely minced whites of three small leeks, and moisten them with the carefully decanted liquor from the mussels. Bring to the boil, and add six ounces of rather large vermicelli and a pinch of saffron and of pepper. Cook gently for twenty minutes, and put the mussels back into the soup when you serve it.

NOTE: If you like, you can substitute seven ounces of rice for the vermicelli. Do not forget that the liquor from the mussels is salted, when you come to check the seasoning of the soup.

Soupe aux moules à la ménagère. Open three pints of medium-sized mussels, with an onion, a bit of celery, some parsley stalks, and a glass of white wine. Take them from the shells and keep them back. Pass the liquor through a fine cloth. Stew in butter, but do not brown, an onion, the white part of two leeks, and an ounce of the white part of celery, all minced up; sprinkle with two dessertspoonfuls of flour, cook for a minute, and then moisten with a pint and three quarters of boiled milk. Season with salt, white pepper, and grated nutmeg, add a small bouquet of parsley, and cook gently for twenty-five minutes. Now add the liquor from the mussels well decanted, and pass the whole thing through a fine conical sieve. Bring to the boil again, boil for a few seconds, then throw in the mussels, and finish the soup with a teacupful of cream and two ounces of butter.

Soupe de poisson à la rochelaise. Lightly brown a large onion and the white part of two leeks, both minced, in olive oil. Add four tomatoes pressed and chopped, and two crushed cloves of garlic. Let these 'melt' for a few minutes, then moisten them with two quarts of water, season with salt and pepper, bring to the boil, and add a *bouquet garni* (page 31) and two pounds of small fish, such as weevers, gurnets, whiting, several conger cutlets, a few small crabs, and fifteen mussels or so. Let the soup cook quickly for twenty minutes, then pass it through a tammy-cloth, pressing the pieces of fish lightly, so as to get their flavour. Bring the ensuing stock to the boil, and poach in it gently for twenty-five minutes seven ounces of large vermicelli.

NOTE: These fish soups vary a little according to the locality in which they are found, this being partly due to the various fish found in those parts and also to the seasoning. For instance, in the south of France they are always flavoured with saffron.

TERRINE DIEPPOISE

Terrine dieppoise or Marmite dieppoise. This is prepared with turbot, sole, red mullet, and a few mussels as garnish. For six people get five pounds of fish.

(1) Make a *fumet* by using the fish heads cut into pieces and adding the water coming out from the cooking of the mussels, a few leeks, one and a half pounds of shredded onions, a head of celery, a bottle of dry white wine, and a *bouquet* (thyme, bayleaves, parsley). Cook for thirty minutes. (2) Place the pieces of fish in a saucepan, season with salt and pepper, add the *fumet* as above. Add three ounces of butter and one pint of cream.

Cook very slowly on a low fire for fifteen minutes. Correct seasoning, adding salt and pepper if necessary. Finally place the pieces of fish in a hollow dish and pour the sauce evenly on top; add some fried *croûtons* for garnish and appearance.

BOUILLABAISSES

Bouillabaisse à la marseillaise. The *bouillabaisse* of Marseille is not a fish dish: it is a soup in every accepted meaning of the word. The fish which have been used in its preparation have left all their flavour in the stock. It must be admitted that the gastronomical value of this soup rests in the variety of fish, large and small, which have contributed to its preparation. In any case, if it is not possible to include in it all those enumerated below, there should be five or six kinds, not including the shellfish. For as the characteristic flavour of the *bouillabaisse* is due to each of its ingredients, it is obvious that the more those ingredients are, the more authentic will that flavour be,

Unfortunately, the fish which is the most prominent and most essential in the *bouillabaisse* is the *rascasse*, a Mediterranean fish unknown on these shores. The fish which should be included are: *rascasse*, gurnet, weever (*vive*), John Dory, rock fish, conger, bass, whiting, small crawfish (*langoustes*), and Dublin Bay prawns. For twelve persons allow eight to ten pounds of fish and five pounds of shellfish.

METHOD: Put into a stewpan two medium-sized onions, and the whites of two leeks, both chopped up; four skinned, pressed, and chopped tomatoes; an ounce of crushed garlic, a dessertspoonful of roughly chopped parsley, a pinch of fennel, a bayleaf, a tiny pinch of saffron, the fish cut in pieces across, the *langouste* cut in sections across or the Dublin Bay prawns cut in half lengthwise, and four tablespoonfuls of olive oil. The fish with tender flesh, such as red mullet, bass, whiting, etc., should be put in only later. They should also to be cut in slices across.

A quarter of an hour in advance, cover the whole thing with *boiling* water. Salt and pepper it, and cook *very rapidly* (which will prevent the oil from staying on the surface). After seven minutes, add the tender-fleshed fish, and continue to cook for another eight minutes, still boiling rapidly. Now pour the liquor of the *bouillabaisse* into a soup tureen containing thick slices of the special bread called 'Navette', in sufficient quantity to make the soup very thick after it has been absorbed by the bread. (It should be remembered here that the great cooks of Marseille, of whom Caillat is the accepted master, have declared that it is a mistake to toast or fry the slices of bread.) Turn the pieces of fish into a shallow dish, sprinkle them with a little chopped parsley, and surround them with the slices of *langouste* or the halved Dublin Bay prawns. Serve this fish at the same time as the soup.

Bouillabaisse à la parisienne. For ten or twelve persons: eight pounds of fish, taken from among red mullet, gurnet, weevers, small congers, rock salmon, John Dory, very small turbot; and a medium-sized crawfish (*langouste*) or lobster. Fry lightly in olive oil two medium-sized onions and the white part of three leeks, chopped up. Moisten with just over a quart of light fish *fumet*, and about a pint and a quarter of white wine. Add three large skinned, pressed, and chopped tomatoes, salt, pepper, a pinch of saffron, an ounce of crushed garlic, and a *bouquet garni.* Bring to the boil, and boil for ten minutes. Add the firm-fleshed fish cut in slices across, and the crawfish (*langouste*) cut up in the same way. Six minutes after, add the tender-fleshed fish with a good dessertspoonful of roughly chopped parsley. Then let the whole thing boil as hard as it can for a quarter of an hour. At the end, bind the soup lightly with blended butter (page 42). Serve the pieces of fish and *langouste* in a timbale or shallow dish; surround them with mussels and other opened shellfish. At the same time, serve in a dish some slices of bread fried in olive oil and soaked in the liquor of the *bouillabaisse*.

Bouillabaisse du pays de Cornouailles. For ten to twelve people. Cut up in fairly thick rounds four or five leeks (the white part only), two pounds of medium-sized waxy potatoes, five tomatoes skinned and with their juice and pips removed, three hearts of celery cut in little quarters. Put all these into an earthenware stewpan with three and a half pints of water, salt, pepper, thyme, bayleaf, and roughly chopped parsley. Cook for twenty-five minutes, and then add four pounds of fish, cleaned and cut in small slices across. These fish will have been chosen from among the following: red mullet, gurnet, whiting, mackerel, small turbot, small rock salmon, or fresh tunnyfish. Cook for a quarter of an hour. At the end of the cooking add to the *bouillabaisse* a binding of three egg yolks and four tablespoonfuls of cream. Mix delicately. At the moment of serving, scatter over the soup three dessertspoonfuls of small breadcrumb dice which have been fried in foaming butter.

CHAPTER SIX

*

Freshwater Fish

WHEN I was engaged in editing this book, I wondered whether this chapter would not perhaps be the most popular of all. There are so many fishermen in this country, and so few books, if indeed any, that specialize in the cooking of river fish. It is a sad moment for the devoted disciple of Izaak Walton to find his precious catch destined for a grave under a rose-bush in the garden, because his wife does not know how to cook it – a fate which did indeed befall the catch of a friend of mine. It is true that the fish was a tench (not a very promising subject for culinary skill), and the rose-bush grew and multiplied exceedingly afterwards; but if this book had then been printed, with what pride could they have eaten their tench in the manner of Anjou, which will be found on a later page of this chapter.

A *matelote* of river fish is a charming dish, too, and as far as I am aware almost unknown in this country; but then we live so near the sea, and our rivers are such midgets when compared with those on the Continent, that we rely more on the fishmonger's supply than our own piscatorial skill. But I think there are a great many recipes in the following pages of which old Izaak would have approved.

BARBEL (*BARBEAU*)

The best barbel comes from fast-flowing rivers. Its flesh is somewhat tasteless, and it has the disadvantage of a large number of bones. It should always have a well-seasoned accompaniment.

Two Ways of Preparing a Four-Pound Barbel

(It is unusual for barbel to be larger than this.)

(1) Cook the fish in a strongly flavoured *court-bouillon*, and serve it either *au beurre blanc* (page 41) or with a caper sauce or a Béchamel sauce with egg.

(2) Skin the fish, stick pieces of anchovy fillets into it here and there, bake it with plentiful bastings of melted butter, and serve it either with nutbrown butter or mustard butter – or, if the fish has a roe, with a sauce made from the roe in a purée, thinned down to the consistency of a broth by the addition of melted butter.

Barbeau de la treille verte. This recipe comes from a riverside inn which used to exist on the banks of the Yonne. It is for a barbel weighing about three pounds.

Fry lightly in butter, without browning, two medium-sized onions and two shallots, both chopped up. Spread them in a long earthenware dish deep enough to hold the fish which will be served in it; add three dessertspoonfuls of chopped dried nuts and five ounces of roughly chopped mushrooms. On this bed lay the fish, well seasoned on each side, moisten with two glasses of good red wine, add four ounces of butter divided in little bits, bring to the boil, and continue cooking in a very hot oven for thirty-five minutes, basting often. When the fish is cooked the liquid ought to be reduced practically to nothing. Ten minutes before serving, sprinkle the fish with fine browned breadcrumbs and with plenty of melted butter, and let it brown. At the moment of serving, sprinkle over a little chopped parsley.

Barbeau au beurre rouge: see *Carpe au beurre rouge,* below.

Barbillons (small barbel) weighing from twelve ounces to a pound or so can be (1) used in a mixed *matelote;* (2) grilled, and accompanied by a mustard butter, a shallot butter, or a simple *maître-d'hôtel* butter; (3) treated *à la meunière, à la Bercy, au gratin,* etc.

BREAM (*BRÈME*)

This fish, easily recognized by its flat and oval appearance, is hardly ever eaten save by those who catch it. Its flesh is soft and insipid, and it needs a highly seasoned accompaniment. It is usually cooked plain in butter, *à la Bercy,* or *sur le plat* with red wine.

CARP (*CARPE*)

Carpe au beurre rouge. Whether the carp is cooked whole or in slices, it must be cooked in a *court-bouillon.* The fish for this dish should weigh between two and three pounds. After it is cooked, skin and trim it.

In the long dish, or in the timbale (if it is in pieces), in which it is to be served, heat some butter to the *noisette* stage; put in the carp, sprinkle with a glass of brandy, set it alight and baste the fish with it, then put on the lid and keep it hot.

For the red butter: reduce a glass of good red wine until it has almost disappeared, having at the beginning added a good dessert-spoonful of finely chopped shallot, salt, pepper, and a pinch of sugar to correct the acidity of the wine. Then, by degrees and while shaking the pan on the fire, add five ounces of butter, so that you get a thick and unctuous sauce. Mask the fish with this sauce, sprinkle it with chopped parsley, and serve it.

NOTE: This method can be applied to all dark-fleshed fish, such as eels, tench, barbel, and so on.

Carpe à la bière. Scale and clean a medium-sized soft-roed carp, and keep the roe aside. Raise the two fillets, one from each side, leaving the half head adhering to each fillet. Be careful to remove the little bitter sac in the head. Now melt in butter, without browning, two finely minced onions. Spread this onion on a dish and add a sprig of thyme, a bit of a bayleaf, a piece of celery, several peppercorns, a clove, and three ounces of *pain d'épice* (which can be bought in most Continental grocers' shops in this country). Cut in dice. Season the fillets of carp with salt and pepper, moisten with just enough dark beer to cover them, and cook for twenty-five minutes. Meanwhile poach the roe in salted water with a touch of lemon juice. Drain the fillets and arrange them on a dish. Pass the stock through a sieve. It will be thick enough, owing to the *pain d'épice.* Heat it up, butter it lightly, pour it over the carp fillets and surround them with the roe cut in slices. (A light gingerbread might be used instead of the *pain d'épice.*)

Carpe au bleu: Proceed as outlined on page 25.

Carpe farcie à la bourguignonne. Take a carp of four or five pounds, as heavily roed as possible. Stuff it with a forcemeat composed of breadcrumbs soaked and pressed dry, shallots tossed in butter, the roe passed through a sieve, *fines herbes* (page 32), and butter. Bind with six egg yolks, and mix the forcemeat well together. Sew up the opening in the fish, and put the carp in a deep fish kettle. Moisten it with Beaujolais, season it, and add, if possible, a little fish glaze. Then poach it gently. When it is cooked, drain it and surround it with a *matelote* garnish (page 38). Reduce stock, and bind it. Finish like a *sauce matelote* (page 48), and pour it over the carp.

Carpe à la canotière. This recipe was invented during a holiday of young cooks, and executed by one of them.

Small carp, weighing about twelve ounces, should be used for it. Score them down each side, season them, and lay them on a dish which has first been well buttered and then sprinkled with shallot. Surround them with small fresh mushrooms, peeled; moisten them with white wine, and add about an ounce of butter for each carp. Cook in the oven, basting frequently.

Ten minutes before the cooking is finished, sprinkle them with fine browned breadcrumbs and melted butter, and let this brown. Surround them with trussed crayfish cooked in a *court-bouillon*, and with gudgeon which have been egg-and-breadcrumbed and fried. The carp are, of course, served in the dish in which they were cooked.

Carpe à la Chambord. For this first-class dish take, if possible, a golden carp weighing about four pounds. Remove the skin, and all over each side stick (*piquer*) truffles and raw mushrooms cut in the shape of dice. Season it and put it in a dish with very good red wine, brandy, thyme, and bayleaf. Leave it there to marinate for several hours, or let it marinate overnight. Then drain it, and put it in a thickly buttered dish, add the wine of the marinade, and braise the fish very gently, with frequent bastings. When it is cooked, drain it thoroughly, arrange it on the serving dish, and surround it with decorated *quenelles*, peeled and cooked mushrooms, olive-shaped truffles, small gudgeon egg-and-breadcrumbed and fried, trussed crayfish cooked in a *court-bouillon*, and, if the carp has a roe, the roe cut in slices and cooked *à la meunière*. Pass the stock through a sieve, reduce it quickly by half, then bind it with blended butter, and finish with more butter. Hand this sauce separately.

Carpe à la juive. This Jewish dish is prepared in various ways, but the only difference between them lies in variation of seasonings. This is the usual recipe.

Cut some medium-sized carp in slices about half an inch thick. For

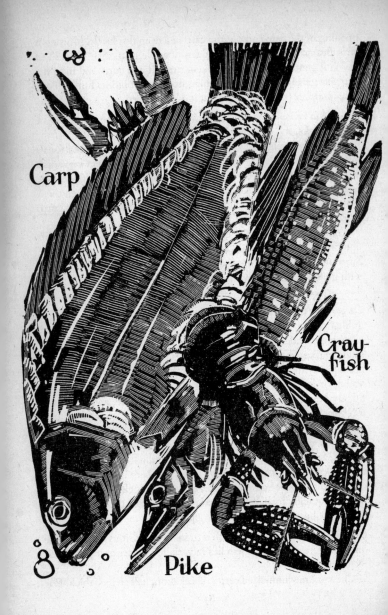

two carp weighing about two and a half pounds each, fry lightly, in eight tablespoonfuls of olive oil in a large sauté pan or turbot kettle, two large onions and five shallots chopped up. Add two ounces of flour, cook for a few seconds, and moisten with a pint and three quarters of white wine and the same of fish stock or water. Season with salt and a good pinch of cayenne, add a large *bouquet garni* and three crushed cloves of garlic, and bring to the boil. In this sauce put the slices of carp, with their heads. Cook gently for twenty-five minutes, then take them out and arrange them on a dish in such a way as to reconstruct the fish's original shape. Remove the bouquet from the sauce, reduce by two thirds, and mix with it, off the fire, half a pint or a little more of olive oil, in exactly the same way as you would in making a mayonnaise. Pour this sauce over the carp after you have corrected the seasoning, sprinkle with parsley, and let them get cold. The sauce will become a jelly.

Laitance de carpe. The soft roe of the carp is very delicate and much sought after. It is usually employed as a garnish, but it can be prepared by itself in the following ways: poached in butter, as a garnish for *bouchées* and omelettes; in little porcelain cases with shrimp or crayfish tails added, and a shrimp sauce or *sauce Nantua*; in fritters and scallops; in a border of Duchesse potato or rice, with a *mornay* sauce; in a soufflé, and in little timbales of the kind called *royale*; cooked *à la meunière*, etc.

Tourte de laitances. If carp's roe cannot be had, the roes of shad or other fish can be used. Whatever they are, they must first be poached with butter and lemon juice, just enough to stiffen them. Make a forcemeat of sufficient quantity for the size of the pie you are making. For this, finely chop the flesh of some perch, carp, or tench with salt, pepper, and grated nutmeg. Mix this with almost the same quantity of *quenelle* forcemeat made with pike (page 31). If this forcemeat is not available, then substitute the same amount of breadcrumbs soaked in milk and pressed dry, a few spoonfuls of cream, and a little egg to bind it. Now take a pie-dish, butter the bottom and sides, and line it with puff-pastry. Put on the bottom a layer of half the forcemeat, then on top the prepared roes and an ounce and a half of butter in small pieces. Cover this with the rest of the forcemeat, and put on a lid of dough about a quarter of an inch thick. Join it well on the edges of the dish, brush with egg yolk, decorate it if you like, make a hole in the top, and put it into a fairly hot oven. In forty minutes it should be done. On taking the pie out of the oven, pour inside a few spoonfuls of melted butter mixed with an equal quantity of fresh cream to which a few drops of lemon juice have been added.

NOTE: There should be plenty of roes in this pie, and only a small quantity of forcemeat; and the latter should be light and spongy enough to absorb the butter and cream added at the end.

Carpe en matelote. Very small carp cut in slices across and treated in a *Matelote batelière* or *Matelote marinière* (page 88). These fish are also used in a mixed *matelote*.

Carpe à la polonaise. The recipe generally used in France for this dish differs slightly from that given by certain authors, in particular from that given by Petit in his *Cuisine russe*, in which he specifies honey where we use caramel.

(1) Chop up a large onion and four shallots, and sprinkle them on the bottom of the fish kettle, also five ounces of *pain d'épice* cut in dice. Clean a medium-sized carp, season it, put it on the grid of the fish kettle, and nearly cover it with two-thirds red wine and one-third fish stock. Braise gently, basting from time to time. (2) Make a light caramel with two dessertspoonfuls of powdered sugar, and dissolve it with a few spoonfuls of wine. When the carp is cooked, arrange it, after draining, on the serving dish. Pass the stock through a sieve, reduce it to make about three quarters of a pint, and add it to the dissolved caramel. Heat up, butter lightly, and add a dozen shredded grilled almonds. This sauce should be handed separately.

Quenelles de carpe. Make these in exactly the same way as *Quenelles de brochet* (page 94), substituting carp flesh for pike.

EEL (*ANGUILLE*)

Anguille grillée à la pêcheuse. Cut the eel up diagonally into pieces three inches long. Score them finely, season them with salt and plenty of pepper, brush them over with olive oil, and grill them very gently. Serve on a *Bercy* butter, rather strong in shallot, to which have also been added a little mustard and some finely chopped nuts.

NOTE: *Bercy* butter is a reduction of white wine with chopped shallots to which are added dice of poached marrow, chopped parsley, salt, black pepper, lemon juice, and softened butter.

Anguille de Bray (Somme) à ma façon (a recipe executed not half a mile from Cléry, during the battle of the Somme in 1916). – Medium-sized eels boned, cut in little pieces, and fried in butter. Fresh *cèpes* gathered not far from there by artillerymen, cut in slices and fried in olive oil with chopped shallot and crushed garlic (but no parsley, for the simple reason that none was to be had). Eels and *cèpes* were finally mixed together, and finished with a drop of vinegar.

NOTE: This dish was much appreciated at the regimental mess of which I had the honour to be the cook. – M. Bouzy.

Coulibiac d'anguille. Make in the same way as *Coulibiac de saumon* (page 130), using slices of fillets of large eels instead of salmon.

Anguille grillée Robinson. Whether the eel is cooked whole (tied in a ring, finely scored, and brushed over with oil) or cut up in pieces, it must first be gently grilled. Put ten tablespoonfuls of good red wine into a saucepan with two dessertspoonfuls of chopped shallot. Reduce to a few dessertspoonfuls, and thicken this with butter, finishing with a dessertspoonful of chopped parsley. Arrange the eel on a dish, surround it with very small new potatoes cooked in butter, or with small *pommes château.* Hand the sauce separately.

Hure d'anguille persillée. Make some fish jelly with a *court-bouillon* of the trimmings of gelatinous fish and some good white braising liquor. Cut up in pieces the requisite number of eels, and let them marinate with finely chopped carrot and onion, garlic, parsley stalks, thyme and bayleaf, lemon juice, white port, and a little brandy, for an hour. Then cook them in the prepared jelly, to which you add the marinade. Cook very gently for an hour. Drain the pieces of eel, remove the bones and any uneatable parts. Pass the stock through a sieve, and reduce it. Now take a rectangular mould, and in it arrange the eel fillets in layers, alternating them with layers of a large amount of chopped parsley, which has been blanched, plunged in cold water, and then pressed dry, so that after each layer of eel there is a strip of green. Finally pour the reduced stock into the mould, and let it get cold in a cool place. (All grease will of course have first been removed from the stock.) To serve, turn the mould out, cut it in slices, and serve them on a napkin with green salad round them.

Matelotes of Eel

Anguille en matelote à la batelière. Cut the eel into small pieces, and fry them lightly in butter with minced onion. Moisten just to cover them with red wine, season them, add a *bouquet garni* and an ounce of mushroom peelings, and cook quickly. Drain the pieces and put them into a sauté pan. Add a dozen glazed button onions, the same number of cooked button mushrooms, and the sauce, bound with blended butter. Simmer for a few seconds, and dish in a timbale or shallow dish. Surround with small heart-shaped *croûtons* of bread fried in butter, and with trussed crayfish cooked in a *court-bouillon*.

Anguille en matelote des canotiers. This *matelote* can be made with eel only, but it is more usually made with other fish as well, such as perch, tench or small carp. The preparation and the garnish are the same as that for *Matelote batelière*, except that the moistening is made with white wine with burnt brandy, and the sauce is more heavily buttered. At the same time, there are served some fried gudgeon, or a mixture of those little fish generically known in France, when cooked, as '*blanchaille*'. They are usually gudgeon, bleak, roach, little perch, and so on. In other words, 'small fry'!

Anguille en matelote à la marinière. Make in the same way as *Batelière* above, but moisten with white instead of red wine, and at the last add a little cream. The garnish is the same as for the *Batelière*.

Anguille en filets à l'Orly. Take the fillets from one or more eels and cut them into strips. Season them, dip them in a light frying batter, and fry them in very hot deep fat. Drain them, arrange them on a plate covered with a napkin, and surround them with fried parsley. Serve tomato sauce separately.

Pâté chaud d'anguille à la flamande. Prepare enough fillets of eel for the size of your pie, cut them in slices, season them, and stiffen them in oil. Line a pie mould with short-crust, and cover the bottom and sides with pike forcemeat flavoured with *fines herbes* (page 32). Garnish this with the slices of eel, arranging them to alternate with layers of the forcemeat, and adding a little sorrel and young *lamier blanc* tops (a sort of white nettle found in France) melted in butter.

When the mould is full, pour in a few spoonfuls of melted butter, close it with a pastry lid well joined on, and cook for an hour and a half in a moderate oven.

Anguille à la provençal. Cut the eel in pieces, roll them in flour, and colour them well in half foaming butter, half oil. Finally add chopped shallot and parsley, crushed garlic, and breadcrumbs; cook a little longer, and serve very hot.

Anguille à la romanaise. Cut the eel in pieces about two inches long, and wrap each up in a very thin slice of raw lemon without peel, and a thin rasher of streaky bacon. Tie them up, and cook them gently in butter, in a stewpan, adding two cloves of garlic. As soon as they are cooked, take out the pieces, untie them, and arrange them on a dish. Remove the garlic, swill the stewpan with a glass of dry white wine, let it reduce, and thicken it with butter. Cover the pieces of eel with it, and sprinkle them with chopped parsley.

Anguille à la tartare. Cook the eel, whether whole and rolled in a ring, or in pieces, in a white wine *court-bouillon*, keeping it rather undercooked than overcooked. Drain it, wipe it thoroughly, egg-and-breadcrumb it, and grill it so as to finish the cooking and at the same time colour the coating of egg and breadcrumbs. Or if you like, fry it in deep fat. Arrange on a dish within a border of gherkins, and hand a *tartare* sauce separately.

Anguille au vert à la flamande. Cut up some small or medium-sized eels in pieces about two and a half to three inches long. Fry them lightly in butter with onion and celery cut in small pieces, moisten with enough white wine to cover the pieces, season, and add, for each two pounds of eel, five ounces of finely cut sorrel, the same of watercress leaves, two ounces of *lamier blanc* tops, a third of an ounce of parsley and the same of chervil, into a little bag containing sage, savory, and mint (a sixth of an ounce of each). Boil very rapidly for twelve to fifteen minutes, and when cooked, bind off the fire with four egg yolks beaten in a little cream. Serve hot or cold.

Bouilliture d'anguilles. Take for preference medium-sized eels; skin them, open them, clean them, and cut them into pieces about two inches long. Season them, and fry them quickly in *nut* oil, with onions and one or two cloves of garlic, all chopped. When all are well coloured, put them into a stewpan, add a little flour, colour this lightly, and moisten with enough red wine and a little water to cover the pieces. Add a *bouquet garni*, stir until it boils, and then cook gently until the eels are cooked. (This recipe is acknowledged to Jourdin.)

Anguille au beurre rouge: see *Carpe au beurre rouge* (page 81).

GRAYLING (*OMBRE*)

This fish is much sought after, but comparatively rare. It can be prepared in all the fashions described later for trout (pages 96–9).

GUDGEON (*GOUJON*)

The best gudgeon come from clear and rapid streams with stony bottoms. They are hardly ever prepared otherwise than fried in deep fat or in butter with *fines herbes* (page 32). They are also used as a garnish for dishes of certain other fish, e.g. *Carpe à la Chambord* (page 84), and they are then egg-and-breadcrumbed and fried in deep fat. They are generally so coated with the egg-and-breadcrumbs that their heads and tails are left uncoated, as if they were wearing a muff; and this method is naturally called *en manchon*.

PERCH (*PERCHE*)

The perch is a beautiful and excellent fish, but it is dangerous to handle because of the pain which the small spikes of its dorsal fin may cause.

Perches à la commère. Allow for each person a perch of six ounces gross. Cook the perch in salted water, slightly acidulated with lemon juice. Drain them, scrape them on each side, and put the fish back into the *court-bouillon* to make sure that they are quite clean. Drain them again, and arrange them on the serving dish. Mask them with butter sauce, keeping it fairly light. Sprinkle over them a mixture of hot hard-boiled egg (white and yolk) and chopped parsley.

Perches à la hollandaise. Prepare and cook in advance for eight minutes a *court-bouillon* composed of water salted with a third of an ounce of salt and acidulated by a dessertspoonful of vinegar for each pint and three quarters, and a bouquet of parsley, thyme, and bay-leaf. Plunge the perch, medium-sized or large, into this, cover the pan, and poach them on the side of the stove, allowing twelve minutes for those weighing from eight to ten ounces. Drain and skin the perch, and put them back into the *court-bouillon*, as directed in the previous recipe. Then arrange them on your dish covered with a napkin, and surround them with quarters of boiled floury potatoes and bunches of parsley. Hand separately some slightly salted melted butter, flavoured with lemon juice and chopped parsley.

NOTE: The proportion of melted butter is generally an ounce for each person.

Perches souchet. Take six perch weighing six ounces each.

(1) Cut two ounces of the red part of carrot into very fine *julienne* shreds, with the same amount of the white part of celery, and half an ounce of parsley root. Stew this *julienne* in butter, moisten it with half a pint and four tablespoonfuls of white wine and as much water, season with a pinch of salt, and finish cooking the vegetables in this. (2) Clean and trim the perch, and arrange them in a shallow dish. Pour over them the boiling *court-bouillon* above, straining it through a conical sieve (but be sure to keep back the *julienne* of vegetables for later use). Put on the lid and poach the fish on the side of the stove for twelve minutes. Then drain them and arrange them on the serving dish, keeping them hot. (3) Reduce the *court-bouillon* by half; then bind it with an ounce and a half of flour blended with butter in the proportion of five parts butter to four parts flour. Let the sauce boil for a minute, then finish it off the fire with two ounces of butter. Mix with it the *julienne* which has been kept back for the purpose, add half a dessertspoonful of very small parsley leaves well blanched, and pour this sauce over the fish.

Other preparations for perch. Perch can be fried (you want little perch weighing about five ounces each for this), grilled, cooked *à la meunière*, *à la Bercy*, *au gratin*, etc. Medium-sized perch can also be used in a *matelote* of perch, or as an ingredient in a mixed *matelote*.

PIKE (*BROCHET*)

The best pike are those weighing from two and a half pounds to four pounds. As the flesh of large fish is inclined to be dry, they are almost always braised.

Brochet à l'angevine, that is to say, pike as cooked in Anjou. Get a pike weighing two pounds, cut it in slices across, and take out the liver. Stiffen the slices in a sauté pan in butter, and then moisten with Anjou wine. Season, add a little chopped shallot, grated nutmeg, and English mustard, and let the fish cook and the sauce reduce at the same time. Finish with two dessertspoonfuls of double cream, and bind with the pounded liver. Add butter, correct the seasoning, and finish with lemon juice. Serve in a timbale with fried *croûtons* round it.

Brochet au beurre blanc. Cook the pike in an ordinary *court-bouillon.* Drain it, remove the skin from the two sides, arrange it on the serving dish, and cover it plentifully with white butter (page 41).

Brochet au bleu. The method of preparing fish *au bleu* is given on page 25.

Brochet aux champignons de rosée. A pike of medium size is best for this dish. Put it in the fish kettle surrounded by very small field mushrooms which have been freshly gathered. Moisten with sherry and thick brown stock, and braise it. When it is cooked, place it on a dish and surround it with the mushrooms. Reduce the stock, finish with butter, a ladleful of cream, and several drops of fine brandy, and pour this (which should look like *café au lait*) over the fish.

Brochet court-bouillonné avec sauces diverses. When pike has been cooked in a *court-bouillon,* it can be served with any of the following sauces, and always then accompanied by boiled or steamed potatoes: caper sauce, *hollandaise, vénitienne,* hot *ravigote.*

Côtelettes de brochet à la mode de Cholet. For fifteen cutlets, prepare a pike forcemeat in the manner described under *Pain de brochet à la normande* (page 94). Divide the forcemeat into portions weighing about three ounces, and shape each with floured hands into the form of a cutlet. Put these into a buttered sauté pan, cover them with slightly salted boiling water, and poach them for about ten minutes. Then take them out, drain them, plunge them into cold water, wipe them dry, and egg-and-breadcrumb them. When the time comes for serving them (so as not to keep them waiting) put them side by side in a sauté pan containing foaming butter, and colour them golden on both sides. Drain them on a cloth, stick in the end of each a piece of uncooked macaroni to imitate the cutlet bone, and put a little frill on it.

Arrange them in a circle on your dish and pour in the middle a very creamy tomato sauce flavoured with *fines herbes* (page 32).

Côtelettes de brochet purée de champignons. With an ordinary pike forcemeat (page 31) make the number of cutlets you want. Poach them with a mushroom purée (page 36) in the middle.

NOTE: If desired, a creamy onion purée can be substituted for the mushroom purée.

Côtelettes de brochet fourrées. Special moulds are made for shaping various sorts of cutlets, and in this case the use of the appropriate moulds is recommended.

Prepare beforehand a *salpicon* (page 234) of mushrooms and truffles bound with *sauce allemande.* Butter the moulds and line them at the bottom and on the sides with an even layer of pike forcemeat. Fill up the centre with the *salpicon*, cover with more forcemeat, and smooth with a knife. Put the moulds into a sauté pan, add boiling salted water, and poach them as above. (On contact with the boiling water, the cutlets will come away from the moulds by themselves.) Then drain them, egg-and-breadcrumb them, fry them golden in butter, and arrange them on the serving dish. They can be accompanied by a light purée of mushrooms, or by an onion (*soubise*) sauce, or some other appropriate sauce.

Filets de brochet. The preparation of these fillets and of the garnish and sauce can be varied according to taste and circumstance. Skin the pike, remove the fillets and cut them up as you like. Arrange them in a buttered fireproof dish, and poach them with very little liquid, basting them from time to time. The liquid will vary according to the dish you are making; e.g. white wine for a white wine sauce. When they are cooked, glaze them at the last moment. Arrange them in a circle on a round dish, and put in the middle the sauce or garnish that you have selected.

Filets de brochet bonne femme. Butter the bottom of a shallow fireproof dish, and sprinkle it with chopped raw mushrooms, roughly chopped parsley, and chopped shallot. Season with salt and pepper. On this arrange the fillets of pike, moisten with white wine and mushroom stock (page 36), and poach them in the oven. Arrange the fillets on the serving dish, reduce the stock, thicken it with butter, and finish it with a little *sauce hollandaise*. Cover the fillets with this, and brown lightly in the oven.

Pain de brochet à la normande. (1) The forcemeat: Pound up one pound of pike flesh and pass it through a very fine tammy-cloth. Work in a mortar eleven ounces of ordinary choux pastry dough without sugar, and add to it by degrees the pike flesh, nine ounces of butter, and several spoonfuls of cold Béchamel sauce. Season with salt, pepper, and nutmeg. Put this forcemeat into a basin, put it on ice, and mix into it four or five egg yolks and four dessertspoonfuls of cream. (2) With this forcemeat fill a well-buttered cylindrical mould, pressing it well down so that there are no air pockets inside. Poach this in the *bain-marie* for forty minutes. (3) Meanwhile, you should prepare a cream sauce (page 46) bound with two egg yolks, to which is added a garnish *à la normande*: that is, crayfish tails, poached oysters, and cooked button mushrooms. Turn out the *pain*, and pour the sauce and garnish over it.

Quenelles de brochet. These *quenelles* are made with ordinary pike forcemeat, but they are better if it is a mousseline forcemeat (page 32). Mould them with a dessertspoon, and place them as they are moulded on a buttered shallow fireproof dish or a sauté pan. Cover them with boiling salted water and poach them. They are done as soon as the forcemeat feels firm to the touch. Drain them on a cloth, arrange them in a circle on the serving dish, and pour the chosen sauce in the middle.

Quenelles de brochet à la graisse, or *Quenelles de brochet lyonnaise*. (1) The forcemeat: Pound up one pound of pike flesh and set it aside. Now pound very finely six and a half ounces of beef kidney fat and just over three ounces of beef marrow. Then add a pound of very cold frangipane panada (page 34) and four egg whites, by small degrees. Put back the pike flesh with a seasoning of salt, pepper, and grated nutmeg, and mix it vigorously with the pestle so as to get a perfect amalgamation. Put the forcemeat into a basin, add a little cream, and, if it is not to be used at once, keep it on ice. (2) Mould the *quenelles* with a dessertspoon in the usual way, and poach them in some good fish *fumet*. Drain, arrange in a circle, and serve with a *sauce Bercy*, *Nantua*, *mornay*, or any other.

Brochet à la Valvins. Take a medium-sized fish. Skin it on both sides, and lard it with anchovy fillets. Season it, and wrap it in oiled or buttered paper. Then bake it in the oven. Serve with a *sauce ravigote*, melted butter flavoured with mustard, or *maître-d'hôtel* butter.

Brochetons (small pike) weighing from nine ounces to a pound can be used in a mixed *matelote*, or fried in deep fat or *à la meunière*, or grilled and served with a butter of some kind, or with *sauce tartare*, *sauce verte*, etc.

ROACH (*GARDON*)

This is described as 'the fisherman's consolation, but of little gastronomical value'. It can be fried like the gudgeon, or take its place in the mixed fry known in French riverside inns as '*blanchaille*'.

TENCH (*TANCHE*)

The removal of the tench's scales presents some difficulty, as they are very small, but this process will be found easier if the fish is first scalded. It is a good fish as an ingredient of a *Matelote à la crème* (*Matelote marinière*, page 88), and it can also be served *au gratin*, *à la Bercy*, *meunière*, fried in deep fat, and so on.

Tanche à la poitevine. Scale and carefully clean a tench weighing about a pound and a half: score its sides, and season it. Thickly butter a shallow dish, and sprinkle over the bottom some finely minced potatoes and a large onion, also minced. Lay the tench on this bed, sprinkle it with a glass of brandy, set it alight, and then moisten with two glasses of dry white wine. Cook in the oven for twenty-five to thirty minutes. At the last moment add a binding of two egg yolks and two dessertspoonfuls of well-whipped fresh cream. Stir lightly, brown very slightly, and serve.

Tanches à la mode de Touraine. Scatter on the bottom of a buttered dish a little chopped shallot, and chopped chives and chervil. Add also a few minced mushrooms or morels, if you can get them. Lay on this some small tench weighing about five to eight ounces each, moisten with cream which has been boiled beforehand, and cook in the oven for twenty minutes, basting now and again. At the moment of serving, correct the seasoning, and sprinkle the fish with chopped parsley, chives, and chervil.

Tanche au beurre rouge: see *Carpe au beurre rouge* (page 81).

TROUT (*TRUITES DE RIVIÈRE*)

Serve one trout, weighing four to five ounces, per head.

Truites au bleu. The essential condition of this picturesque dish is that the fish should be alive. Stun them, clean them as quickly as possible, and plunge them immediately into a boiling *court-bouillon* consisting only of salted water with plenty of vinegar in it.

For quarter-pound trout, poach for ten minutes on the side of the fire. Arrange them on a napkin with parsley round them, and serve separately melted butter and steamed or boiled potatoes.

Truites au Chablis. Make a *court-bouillon* with Chablis, and poach the trout gently in it. With this *court-bouillon*, make a jelly as described on page 32. Decorate the trout with tarragon leaves, little sprigs of chervil, white or yolk of hard-boiled egg, etc., and cover them deeply with the cold jelly.

Truites Doria. The trout are fried *à la meunière* (page 99), and dished with a surround of small heaps of cucumber balls blanched and stewed in butter.

Truites à la bretonne. The trout are fried *à la meunière* (page 99), and served with a surround of shrimp tails and mushrooms fried in butter.

Truites farcies carême. Soft-roed trout should be used for this dish, and should weigh from five to seven ounces each. Pass the roes through a tammy, and add to this purée chopped shallots, mushrooms, parsley and chervil, breadcrumbs, a beaten egg, and a seasoning of salt and pepper. Cut the trout down the back from one end to the other, and remove the backbone. Fill them with the stuffing, wrap each in a heavily buttered paper, and braise them in a very little liquid for fifteen to twenty minutes. Then unroll the paper, and quickly wrap each trout in a thin piece of puff-pastry dough: arrange on a baking tin and cook in a hot oven. They are usually served as they are, but they may be accompanied, if liked, by a cream sauce flavoured with truffle essence.

Truites au fenouil. Butter a dish, and scatter a fine *julienne* of fennel in it. Lightly season your trout with salt and a touch of cayenne, lay them in the dish, moisten with white wine, cover, and poach the fish gently. When they are cooked, skin them and arrange on the serving dish. Reduce the stock, thicken it with butter, heighten the seasoning a little, and pour this sauce over the trout. (This recipe is acknowledged to Jourdin.)

Truites à la grenobloise. These are small trout, seasoned, floured, and cooked in butter: that is, *à la meunière.* Arrange them in the serving dish and keep them hot. In the same pan in which they have cooked, fry in butter some finely chopped mushrooms and a pinch of breadcrumbs, and pour this, when still foaming, over the fish. Finish with lemon juice and a few capers.

Truites à la hussarde. The trout should weigh half a pound each. Fill their stomachs with ordinary fish forcemeat (page 31) mixed with *Duxelles* (page 31), and sew up the opening. Season them with salt and pepper.

For six trout, chop a large onion finely, and scatter it on the bottom of a buttered dish. Lay the trout on this, moisten with half a pint of Chablis, and add two ounces of butter in little dabs and a small *bouquet garni.* Bake in the oven for half an hour, basting frequently. Drain the fish, remove the thread which sewed them up, and arrange them in the serving dish. Rub the stock through a fine conical sieve with a wooden spoon, reduce it for a few seconds, bind it very lightly with blended butter (page 42), and finish with three ounces of butter and a few drops of anchovy essence. Cover the trout with this sauce, and glaze quickly.

Truites à la mode de Héas. (Héas is a small Pyrenean summer resort near Troumouse.) The trout should weigh about five ounces. For six trout prepare four ounces of *Duxelles* (page 31) with fresh mushrooms. Season and flour the trout, and cook them in a frying pan in clarified butter. Spread the *Duxelles* on the serving dish, arrange the trout on it, and sprinkle them generously with the chopped yolk of hot hard-boiled egg mixed with chopped parsley. Sprinkle with nut-brown butter (page 43), using about an ounce of butter for each fish. The dish should be served as quickly as possible so that the butter is still foaming when it comes to the table.

Eel

Tench

Rainbow Trout

Truites à la meunière. Wipe the trout, season them, roll them in flour, and cook them in a frying pan in clarified butter. Arrange them on the serving dish, scatter chopped parsley over them, sprinkle them lightly with lemon juice, and pour over some nutbrown butter cooked *à la noisette* (page 43).

NOTE: It should be observed that cooking fish *à la meunière*, simple as it sounds, needs some care. Too great a heat will brown the skin, and the appearance and flavour of the fish will be spoiled. If the cooking is too slow, the fish get soft. Fish properly cooked in this way should be a beautiful golden brown.

Truites à la normande (*aux ciboulettes*). Butter a dish thickly, lay the trout on it, add a dessertspoonful of water, the juice of a lemon, salt, pepper, plenty of chopped chives, and some chopped parsley. Cook them in the oven for ten minutes. Meanwhile, boil as much double cream as you will want for a sauce. After the ten minutes' cooking, pour this over the fish, sprinkle with breadcrumbs, and brown in the oven.

Truites au rubis. Proceed as if for *Truites au Chablis* (page 96), using a good red Burgundy or Bordeaux in place of the white wine.

THREE DISHES OF RIVER FISH

La meurette (from Bourgogne). For this dish you will want a variety of fish such as eel, perch, small pike, tench, trout, and so on. Scale them, clean them and trim them, and cut off their heads. Now cut them across into pieces of the same size, and put them in a copper pan or earthenware basin. Sprinkle them with a good glass of brandy, and leave them to marinate for an hour or two. Now toss in butter some minced onions and leeks, a few potatoes (which will supply the binding element), a large *bouquet garni* with celery, several crushed cloves of garlic, salt, and pepper. Moisten with good Burgundy and cook for half an hour. Pass this *fumet* through a fine sieve or tammy on to the pieces of fish, and let them cook in it for eight to sixteen minutes. Put some pieces of toasted bread rubbed with garlic in the bottom of a shallow dish, and put the pieces of fish on them. If the sauce is too thin, let it reduce by half, then bind it lightly with blended butter. Finish it with more butter, correct the seasoning, and pour it over the fish.

La pouchouse (from Franche-Comté). For ten people you will want five pounds of fish: small carp, tench, perch, eels, small barbel, small pike, etc. Prepare the fish and cut them in slices across, all the same thickness but not too large. In an earthenware pan put an ounce of minced onion, four finely crushed cloves of garlic, a *bouquet garni*, the pieces of fish, salt, pepper, and three or four ounces of butter. Stiffen the pieces of fish in the butter, *flambez* them with a glass of brandy, moisten with just enough red wine to cover them, and boil for fifteen to twenty minutes. In another eathenware pan fry in butter some rather lean streaky bacon cut in dice and blanched, some button onions and button mushrooms. Take out the pieces of fish and put them into the pan with the garnish above. Reduce the stock in the other pan by half, strain it into the second pan, bind with blended butter (page 42), and simmer for a minute or two. Serve as it is, adding some small *croûtons* of bread fried golden in butter.

Waterzoï. The following fish are suitable for making *Waterzoï*: small pike, eel, chub, small carp, tench, perch, small barbel. If you cannot include all these fish, you should have at least three or four different kinds. You will need, for ten people, six pounds of the fish, and they should be alive.

Having cleaned them, cut them in slices across, and put them into a stewpan with salt, pepper, a bouquet of parsley stalks, and a piece of celery. Moisten with water just to cover the pieces. Cook rapidly for twenty minutes so that the liquid reduces as the fish are cooking. At the last, add a little finely crushed biscuit or oven-dried bread, and boil on for another two minutes. Hand separately slices of brown bread and butter.

CHAPTER SEVEN

*

Saltwater Fish

WHEN we come to the fish from the sea, Madame Prunier has endless advice to give us. She has always been a little puzzled why it is we cannot as a rule get such fish as bass, gurnard, sea bream and so on in the fishmonger's shop, and I am inclined to think that the reason is that even if we were to see them there we should neither recognize them nor know what to do with them if we bought them. This chapter should remove that reproach.

Many writers, and not least among them E. V. Lucas, have complained that they cannot get in the hotels and restaurants of this country any other fish than sole (of varying quality) or turbot. If Madame Prunier has her way, English people will soon become much more 'fish-conscious', and by asking for the cheaper and more unfamiliar fish will soon find that a demand is created. And they are delicious, bass and grey mullet especially, the former being a favourite of George Moore, who was always complaining that it could never be found in London.

A glance through the recipes in this chapter will soon convince the reader that here is imagination at last applied to fish in a way which we had never dreamed it could be. The usual boiled or fried or grilled pale before this magnificent array of dishes. Attention is particularly drawn to the many ways of preparing herring and mackerel. The skate recipes (page 139) should also be noticed, and the remarkable collection of salt cod dishes – remarkable to a country where this fish is eaten only on Good Friday, and then with egg sauce and parsnips. Fresh cod, too, is treated as it deserves, a fish which Escoffier claimed to be so excellent that if it were less common it would be held in as high esteem as salmon.

All of the fish treated in this chapter can be obtained in England, some of them, like shad and sturgeon, being less familiar than others.

BASS (*BAR*)

An excellent fish which might be seen more in the shops were the demand for it greater. It resembles the salmon in its shape, though not in the colour of its flesh, which is very white. Its only disadvantage is that it has rather many bones. Large bass are principally poached, and served with melted butter, *maître-d'hôtel* butter, *sauce hollandaise*, etc. The smaller fish can also be poached, but they are more usually grilled, fried in deep fat or *à la meunière*, and even filleted. Nearly all the ways of serving salmon are applicable to bass.

Bar au bleu. For this you will want a fish weighing about three pounds. Put it in the fish kettle with half a bottle of red wine, the same of white wine and a pint and three quarters of fish *fumet* or stock. Add fluted rounds of carrot (which will serve afterwards as a garnish), two finely chopped onions, two cloves, two cloves of garlic, a *bouquet garni*, a few mushroom stalks, salt, and coarsely ground pepper. Bring to the boil, and let the fish poach on the side for ten to fifteen minutes. Strain half of the stock through a fine cloth, remove any grease, bind it lightly with blended butter (page 42), and add a little tomato purée and a few drops of anchovy essence. Arrange the base on a dish bordered with the carrot rings, and hand the sauces separately.

Bar bouilli sauce crevettes. For six persons you will need a bass weighing about three pounds. Cook it in a *court-bouillon* (page 31), arrange it on a napkin in a dish, and surround it with parsley. Serve separately a shrimp sauce (page 46).

Bar braisé cardinal. For ten people take a five-pound bass. Braise it with very dry white wine, basting it often. Lay it on a dish and round it place crayfish or fine prawns with their tails peeled. Hand a *sauce cardinal* (page 46) seasoned with paprika pepper.

Bar braisé Polotzoff. A medium-sized bass, of about three pounds, is wanted here. Stuff it with mousseline forcemeat (page 32) of sole, with chopped chives added. Braise it with a fine *mirepoix* (page 33) and fresh chopped tomatoes. Reduce the stock with half-glaze (*demi-glace*) sauce, and thicken with butter. Arrange the bass on the dish, cover it with the sauce, and garnish it with stuffed olives, *croustades* of mushrooms *à la crème*, and small tomatoes stewed in butter.

Délices de bar Grand Vatel. Fillet a bass, cut the fillets in small slices and stiffen them in butter. Let them get cold. Now wrap each of them in brioche dough, shape into a rectangle, and bake in the oven. Serve separately a *Bercy* sauce (page 45).

NOTE: If you like you can wrap up with the fish slices a little 'melted' sorrel mixed with chopped hard-boiled egg yolks. In this case, *maître-d'hôtel* butter should be handed instead of the sauce. (This recipe is acknowledged to J.-B. Féès.)

Bar à la dinardaise en médaillons. Cut the bass into small slices, of the same size and the shape of a medal. The fish should weigh two pounds and of course be filleted. Keep the head and tail for cooking separately. Egg-and-breadcrumb the slices and cook them in the oven on a buttered dish. Meanwhile, have prepared a *chiffonnade* (see below) of spinach and sorrel *à la crème*, put this on the serving dish, and arrange on it the slices of bass. At each end place the cooked head and tail of the fish, and cover the whole with a light *sauce mornay* (page 48). Brown quickly in the oven just before serving.

To prepare a *chiffonnade*, first carefully shred the sorrel and spinach, and remove the mid ribs. Carefully wash the leaves, and squeeze them between the fingers of the left hand and the table top, as you cut them into fine strips with a sharp knife. Melt them in a little butter, and finish them with cream in the usual manner.

Bar froid. This is bass poached in *court-bouillon* and left to get cold. Wipe it, arrange it on your dish, and decorate as you wish. Mask it well with jelly, and surround it with a *salade parisienne*, a vegetable salad with which are mixed dice of lobster or *langouste* and a binding of mayonnaise.

Bar rôti Jean-Bart. For six people take a bass of three pounds or thereabouts. Incise it on each side, season, and roast in the oven, basting with butter. Meanwhile cut in rings six large onions, season, flour and fry in oil, keeping them crisp. Arrange the bass on a dish, surround it with the fried onions, and hand a *sauce Bercy* flavoured with mustard.

Bar rôti sauce genevoise. For this you will want a bass of three and a half to four pounds. Lay it in a thickly buttered baking pan, season, surround with rounds of carrot, onion, celery, *bouquet garni*. Sprinkle it with butter, and roast slowly for forty or fifty minutes. When it is cooked, put it in the serving-dish and skin it on both sides. Moisten the stock with three quarters of a pint of very dry white wine (for in the neighbourhood of Geneva some very good white wines are made). Reduce this by three quarters, and strain it into a saucepan. Put it back on the fire, and add four tablespoonfuls of cream. Reduce again, this time by half. Remove the pan from the fire, and add a binding of four dessertspoonfuls of *hollandaise* sauce. Season as you like. Cover the bass with this sauce, and surround it with steamed potatoes cut in the shape of a hazelnut.

Bars pochés carême. Take some small bass weighing about half a pound each and cook them for ten minutes in a *court-bouillon* with white wine (page 31). Drain, skin on both sides, and keep hot. With half of the *court-bouillon*, some stock of oysters, mussels, and mushrooms well reduced, make a white wine sauce and bind it with two egg yolks. Make a garnish of oysters, mussels, and mushrooms, bound with some of the sauce, and fill some little *croustades* with this garnish. Cover the bass with the rest of the sauce, arrange the *croustades* round them, and serve very hot.

Bars poêlés gourmande. These are small bass of a pound to a pound and a half, for two or three persons. Cut them down the back from head to tail, and remove the backbone. Season them, egg-and-breadcrumb them, and cook them in clarified butter. Hand with them a *sauce béarnaise.* (This recipe is acknowledged to Charles Alamagnie.)

Bar à l'angevine. Remove the backbone from a three-pound bass Keep the head and trimmings to make the sauce. Stuff the bass with a mixture of purée of mushrooms, one dessertspoonful of sorrel purée, and half a pound of purée of spinach, all bound with a beaten egg, a little cream, and some breadcrumbs, and seasoned with powdered thyme and savory. Bake the bass gently in the oven, basting it well. Arrange the fish on your dish, reduce the stock, adding two dessertspoonfuls each of vinegar and white wine, and some chopped shallot, then moisten with a pint of cream, thicken with butter and then with two egg yolks at the last moment, and brown lightly. (This recipe is acknowledged to M. Bouzy.)

BRILL (*BARBUE*)

This fish resembles the turbot, but its shape is more elongated. Whether large or small, all the recipes for small turbot and sole can be applied to it. It should be remembered, when cooking brill, that its flesh is more fragile than that of the turbot.

Barbue à l'ambassadrice. For ten people take a six-pound brill. Cut it down the back, lift up the fillets, and remove the backbone. Stuff the inside with a *chasseur* garnish (minced mushrooms tossed in butter with chopped shallots and parsley) much reduced and strongly flavoured with tomato. Put the fillets back in place and join them with a line of mousseline forcemeat of whiting (page 31) squeezed through a forcing-bag with a grooved pipe. Then braise the fish. When it is cooked, arrange it on your dish, surround with small heaps of asparagus tips bound with butter and mushrooms. Reduce the stock, add cream, thicken it with butter, pour it over the fish, and brown it quickly.

Suprême de barbue Saint-Germain. Fillet a small brill, skinned. Trim the fillets, egg-and-breadcrumb them, and cook them in butter. Garnish, on serving, with small grilled tomatoes and croquettes of rice. Hand with them a *sauce béarnaise.*

Barbue Polignac. Cook the fillets in a buttered dish, seasoned and moistened with dry white wine and a little fish *fumet*. Take out the fillets, arrange them on a dish, and decorate them with small strips of cooked mushrooms and truffles. Reduce the stock, add a little cream, and finish with butter. Pour over the fish and brown quickly.

Filet de barbue de Prince. For six persons.

6 fillets of brill of about 4 oz. each	1 lb. 2 oz. fresh tomatoes
1¼ lb. of fresh salmon	¼ pint of fresh cream
5 oz. of mushrooms	6 oz. of butter
4 oz. of peeled shrimps	2 large glasses of dry white wine
2 oz. of shallots	

Make six escalopes of salmon about 2 oz. each and very flat, soak in a marinade of white wine, thyme, salt, pepper, for about an hour. With the rest of the salmon make a mousse (crush the salmon, then pass it through a very fine sieve into a flat saucepan); work the mousse on ice with an egg yolk, one spoonful of fresh cream, salt, and pepper.

Cut the fillets of brill crosswise to make two escalopes. Spread the mousse on each escalope, put on an escalope of salmon and cover with the two fillets of brill. Prepare 2 oz. of shallots finely chopped, 1 lb. 2 oz. of fresh skinned tomatoes, seeded and finely chopped, salt, and pepper, in a well-buttered dish. Place the fillets on the condiments, moisten with a glass of dry white wine and the brine from the salmon escalopes, cook in the oven for about 10 minutes. After cooking, place the fillets on a silver dish and keep hot, pass the liquid in which the fillets have been cooked through a fine sieve into a flat saucepan, reduce to three quarters, add a quarter of a pint of fresh cream, boil, incorporate 4 oz. of butter and pour this sauce on to the fillets garnished with shrimps and mushrooms cut into strips. Glaze in the oven and garnish with puff pastry before serving. (This recipe was created on the occasion of a dinner given at Prunier's in Paris for the eightieth birthday of Curnonsky, '*Prince des Gastronomes*'.)

COD, FRESH (*CABILLAUD*, or *MORUE FRAÎCHE*)

Many despise cod as tasteless and watery; but no less an authority than Escoffier wrote that 'if cod were less common, it would be held in as high esteem as salmon; for, when it is really fresh and of good quality, the delicacy and delicious flavour of its flesh admit of its ranking among the finest of fish'. The following recipes should help to substantiate this dictum.

Cabillaud à la boulangère. Take a piece (cutlet) of the size you need from the middle of the fish. Put it in a shallow fireproof dish, surround it with quartered raw potatoes and well-blanched small onions. Season with salt and pepper, brush over with melted butter, and bake in the oven, basting often with butter. Sprinkle with chopped parsley on serving.

Cabillaud crème gratin. With some cold cod, proceed as for *Turbot crème gratin* (page 169).

Cabillaud à la flamande. Thickly butter a sauté pan, and lay in it the cod cutlets seasoned with salt, pepper, and grated nutmeg. Add a chopped shallot, a small *bouquet garni*, lemon juice, and a little dry white wine, and poach in the oven for ten minutes. Arrange the cutlets in the serving dish, bind the stock with some fine breadcrumbs or finely crushed oven-dried bread. Boil up for a few minutes, and pour over the fish.

Cabillaud en fritot. Cut some thin slices from cod fillets, slit them so as to make a little pocket in each, and stuff them with a little fish force-meat to which chopped mushrooms have been added. Close the slices again and lay them on a buttered dish. Poach them with very little liquid, and let them get cold. When you want to serve them, dip them in a frying batter and fry them in very hot deep fat. Arrange them in a napkin with fried parsley, and hand a tomato sauce.

Cabillaud à la mornay. Cover the bottom of the serving dish with creamy *mornay* sauce (page 48), arrange on this your cod cutlets poached and well drained, cover them with the same sauce, sprinkle them with grated cheese, and brown them quickly.

Cabillaud à la portugaise. Butter a shallow fireproof dish thickly, and lay on it your cod cutlets seasoned with salt and pepper. Add a chopped onion, some crushed garlic, roughly chopped parsley, a sprig of thyme, some peeled, pressed, and roughly chopped toma-toes, and moisten with white wine. Bring to the boil and cook for ten minutes. Arrange the cutlets on the serving dish, reduce the stock, butter it lightly, correct the seasoning, and pour it over the fish.

Cabillaud à la provençale. Proceed as for *Cabillaud à la portugaise* (above), adding a *julienne* of mushrooms.

Cabillaud poché. Cod is usually poached in salted water, but one can also use a well-seasoned and flavoured *court-bouillon*. In either case, and whether it has been poached whole or in cutlets, it should be accompanied by melted butter, or caper sauce, or *hollandaise* sauce, and steamed potatoes.

COD, SALT (*MORUE*)

Salt cod should always have white flesh, and the fillets should be thick. If they are thin and the colour is yellowish, these are signs of age and stringiness. Salt cod should be soaked for at least twenty-four hours to remove the saltiness, and the water should be changed every three or four hours. If it is then still too salt when you want to cook it, it should be placed for a few minutes in warm water. Six or seven ounces of salt cod should be allowed for each person.

Bouillabaisse de morue. Fry in six tablespoonfuls of oil, without browning, four ounces of onion, an ounce of the white part of a leek and the same of garlic, all chopped up. Add two and a half pints of water, a good pinch of salt, a small pinch of pepper, a *bouquet garni* and a touch of saffron. Bring to the boil and boil for five minutes, then add five waxy potatoes cut in thick rounds. Boil for another twelve minutes, and add five pounds of soaked salt cod cut in little pieces about two inches square. Add four more tablespoonfuls of oil. Continue to boil rapidly for a quarter of an hour, and a few seconds before the cooking is finished throw in a dessertspoonful of roughly chopped parsley. Pour the *bouillabaisse* into a timbale or a shallow dish, and serve at the same time, and on another dish, some pieces of toast which have been rubbed with a cut clove of garlic and moistened with some of the liquid of the *bouillabaisse*.

Brandade de morue. Cut three pounds of soaked salt cod in large squares, poach it in water, keeping it rather underdone, drain it, and remove the skin and bones. Now add to it a third of its weight of warm mashed potatoes that have been baked in their jackets in the oven. Pound the salt cod in a mortar, mixing it and pounding it with the potatoes, and working the pestle vigorously so as to get a fine paste. With this paste, incorporate by degrees half a pint of warm olive oil (in which one or two cloves of garlic have been put while it was warming) and the same quantity of warm cream, pounding away all the time, so as to get the *brandade* white and light. Season it at the last minute, and serve it either by itself, or with little *croûtons* of bread fried in butter, or in little *vol-au-vent* cases.

NOTE: This *brandade* is eaten largely in France during Lent, and in the south it is often eaten cold as a *hors-d'œuvre*.

Crêpes de brandade. Make some very thin pancakes with unsweetened batter, garnish them with a very light *brandade*, and fold them over. Serve separately a creamy white wine sauce. (This recipe is acknowledged to M. Cochois.)

Morue cardinal. Make three quarters of a pint of tomato purée, adding chopped parsley and a touch of garlic. When it is cold, mix with it two whole eggs, two egg yolks, and a pound of freshly cooked flaked salt cod. Pour the whole into a buttered mould, and poach it in the *bain-marie*. Turn it out at the moment of serving, and serve with a cream sauce (page 46).

Morue Cantabréca. Take some well-soaked fillets of salt cod and

poach them without letting them come to the boil. Fry lightly in oil
two large chopped onions, add six crushed cloves of garlic, six
roughly chopped tomatoes, six sweet red peppers (tinned ones would
do), two finely cut leeks (the white part only), and a *bouquet garni*.
Simmer for a few minutes, then moisten with a wineglassful of white
wine and the same of the water the cod was cooked in. Cook for ten
minutes. If you then find that the flavour of the tomatoes is not
pronounced enough, add a little concentrated tomato purée. Pass
through a sieve, and correct the seasoning. Flake up the salt cod,
removing skin and bones. In the bottom of a fireproof dish pour
some of the tomato broth. On this lay the salt cod. Cover it with the
rest of the tomato, and let it simmer for a few minutes in the oven.

Coquilles de morue. Make some Béchamel sauce, adding to it some
grated cheese, and mix with it some flaked cooked salt cod and
minced mushrooms, or, if you prefer it, a little truffle. Garnish the
buttered scallop shells with this mixture, smooth it into a dome,
sprinkle it with grated cheese mixed with browned breadcrumbs,
and brown quickly.

Croquettes de morue. Flake or cut in dice some freshly cooked salt cod,
from which all skin and bones have been removed. Mix it with a very
much reduced Béchamel sauce to which grated cheese has been
added. The proportion should be, for a pound of the flaked cod, sixteen tablespoonfuls of the sauce and two ounces of cheese. Spread
the mixture on a plate, and let it get cold. Then divide it into portions
weighing about two ounces each, roll them into balls, and egg-and-
breadcrumb them. Fry them in oil and serve on a napkin with fried
parsley.

Morue à l'espagnole. Flake up some salt cod, and fry it in oil with
finely minced onion. Then add to it some tomatoes, skinned, pressed,
and roughly chopped, some skinned sweet red peppers cut in *julienne*
shreds, a touch of saffron, and a *bouquet garni*. Simmer this mixture
for a quarter of an hour, and serve it either hot or cold.

Filets de morue à l'aixoise. Soak the cod fillets, and stuff them with the
following mixture: onion, tomatoes, garlic, parsley, capers, and
anchovy fillets, all chopped up. Tie the fillets with cotton, put them
into a baking tin, and bake them in the oven, basting them with olive
oil. Then take them out and arrange them on the dish, mix two

dessertspoonfuls of tomato sauce with the stock, and pour it over the fish.

Filets de morue frits. Cut some thin strips from fillets of soaked salt cod, wipe them in a cloth and then dip them in milk. Roll them in flour, dip them in beaten egg, and fry them in very hot oil. Serve with lemon-flavoured tomato sauce, or with a *sauce rémoulade* (page 52).

Croquettes à l'américaine. Pound a half-and-half mixture of flaked cooked salt cod and fresh cod with an equal amount of the pulp from potatoes baked in the oven. Season with a touch of nutmeg. Divide the mixture into portions weighing about two ounces each, roll them into balls, egg-and-breadcrumb them, and fry them in very hot fat. Hand a tomato sauce with them.

Morue au gratin carême. Make a light Béchamel sauce, and add to it plenty of grated cheese. Make a border of Duchesse potato (page 36) round a shallow fireproof dish, and coat the bottom with the sauce. Cover this with flaked salt cod, from which the bones and skin have been removed, mask with the same sauce, sprinkle with grated cheese, and brown in the oven.

Morue au gratin marseillaise. Cut the soaked cod in large cubes, poach them, drain them, and wipe them dry. Now dip them in milk, roll them in flour, and fry them golden in a very hot mixture of oil and butter. Arrange them in a dish, surround them with mussels and mushrooms, cover the whole with a light Béchamel sauce, and brown in the oven.

Morue grand'mère. Stew gently (*faire suer*: see page 209) some white parts of leeks, celery, and a little onion: moisten with milk and cook with some small potatoes. Put a layer of these potatoes in a small shallow dish, alternating the layers with salt cod *à la crème* and chopped chervil. On the top put a little breadcrumbs and grated cheese mixed, and brown in the oven.

Morue grillée Saint-Germain. Take some soaked cod fillets and cut them in two horizontally, so as to make two fillets of each. Dip them in egg yolk beaten with cream, salt, and pepper. Roll them then in breadcrumbs, and flatten them well. Just colour them under the grill, and finish cooking them in a buttered dish in the oven. Serve with them a *sauce béarnaise* (page 45).

Morue à l'italienne. Cut the salt cod in square pieces, roll them in flour, and colour them in oil. Add a few skinned, pressed, and roughly chopped tomatoes, a touch of garlic, *fines herbes* (page 32), and finish cooking them. Arrange in a crown, decorate each piece with criss-crossed anchovy fillets, and garnish the middle with black olives. Hand a pilaff rice (page 37) separately.

Langues de morue à la façon des pêcheurs. Roll the tongues in flour and fry them in oil with finely minced onions and crushed garlic. Moisten with a little fish *fumet* or water, season with pepper, and cook for a quarter of an hour. Add some small potatoes, or large ones cut in quarters, and finish cooking.

Morue à la limousine. Cut the salt cod in quarters and blanch it. Then plunge it into cold water and drain it. Line a sauté pan with large dice (*brunoise*) of onion and white of leek, adding some chopped garlic and a *bouquet garni*. Add the salt cod, moisten with very little water, and cook it. Make separately a white *roux* (page 37), which you will moisten with equal parts of oil and the blanching water of the cod, and cook it for twenty minutes. Also cook in boiling water several small potatoes, keeping them rather firm. Now put the pieces of cod in another sauté pan, add the potatoes, some chopped chervil, cream, and the sauce strained through a conical sieve. Bring to the boil for a minute, then keep on the side of the stove until the moment for serving up.

Morue à la lyonnaise. Fry some sliced onions golden in butter, and add nearly the same amount of *sauté* potatoes which have been kept soft. In another pan, fry the flaked, boned, and skinned salt cod, add the onions and potatoes, fry the three together briskly, shaking the pan to ensure their mixture, and finish with a few drops of lemon or vinegar. Put into a timbale and sprinkle with chopped parsley.

Morue à la marinière. Garnish the bottom of a stewpan with butter, finely chopped onion, crushed garlic, capers, anchovies, parsley, pepper, and a little tomato sauce. Put the pieces of salt cod on this bed, add a little more butter in small pieces, cover tightly and cook for an hour.

Morue à la milanaise. Cut up the salt cod in slices, season them with pepper, dip them in beaten egg, then roll them first in grated cheese and then in breadcrumbs. Fry them in a frying pan in oil and butter, arrange them on the dish, and sprinkle them with lemon juice. Hand a tomato sauce.

Morue à la moscovite (*hors-d'œuvre*). Poach the salt cod, but keep it a little underdone. Remove skin and bones, and finish cooking it in cream with a little chopped fennel. When it is cold, add lemon juice, *fines herbes* (page 32), and a touch of cayenne. Serve separately a cucumber salad.

Morue à la napolitaine. Cooked and flaked salt cod, bound with cream sauce (page 46), between two layers of spaghetti cooked in the usual manner. Sprinkle with browned breadcrumbs and grated cheese, dot over with butter, and brown lightly.

Morue à l'oseille. Put a layer of thinly cut sorrel in a fireproof dish, on it put a layer of thin slices of salt cod fillets, and on them another layer of sorrel. Add some small bits of butter, and cook in a slow oven. Towards the end of the cooking, sprinkle with a few browned breadcrumbs and brown in the oven.

NOTE: If you find the flavour of sorrel a little too acid by itself, you can use a mixture of one-third spinach to two-thirds of sorrel.

Morue à la paysanne. Cook some small floury potatoes in salted water, then skin them and cut them into rounds. Put a layer of them in a shallow dish, add a layer of flaked salt cod, season with pepper and *fines herbes* (page 32), and add a few bits of butter. Fill the dish with alternate layers in this way, heat up well, and serve.

NOTE: If preferred, half butter and half cream may be used.

Morue pochée. Cut the salt cod into square pieces weighing about six ounces, and poach them for ten minutes. Serve with steamed or boiled potatoes and some such sauce as white butter, caper, *hollandaise*, cream, etc.

Morue à la provençale. Proceed as for *Morue à la lyonnaise* (page 111), but substitute oil for butter, and add garlic, capers, and black olives.

CONGER (*CONGRE* or *ANGUILLE DE MER*)

Except in *bouillabaisse*, *haute cuisine* does not use this very firm-fleshed fish. In household cooking it can be used for making fish stock: its flesh can be cut in thin strips, marinated for some time, and then cooked *à l'Orly*: that is to say, egg-and-breadcrumbed, or dipped in batter, and fried in deep fat, being served with a tomato sauce. It is also sometimes cut in slices, cooked in salted water, and served with a white sauce. Here is one very pleasant way with it.

Congre sauté aux câpres. Take the part of the fish from the stomach to the head, and cut it across in pieces about eight inches wide. Bone these as you would a saddle of lamb, then remove the skin on each side. Brush them over with milk, roll them in flour, and cook them gently, after seasoning them with salt and pepper, in foaming butter. When they are served, add a few capers and pour over the butter, which should be nutbrown, not black.

EEL-POUT (*LOTTE*)

This fish, which is also called burbot, blenny, or gunnel, is not very often found for sale in England. It is a firm-fleshed fish, the principal value of which lies in its liver. Filleted, it can be prepared in slices, with a garnish and sauce, according to taste.

Lotte à la bourguignonne. Poach the eel-pout in a stock of red wine, herbs, and spices, prepared beforehand; drain it, and arrange it on the serving dish, surrounding it with mushrooms and button onions stewed in butter. Strain the stock and reduce it, bind it with blended butter, butter it, and pour it over the fish and its garnish. On serving, put some heart-shaped *croûtons* of fried bread round the dish.

Lotte au four. Lard the piece you are going to roast, season it, and wrap it in a well-buttered piece of paper. Put in the bottom of your baking dish some carrot, onion, and a *bouquet garni*, put the eel-pout on this, and add a little white wine and mushroom stock (page 36). Cook in a good moderate oven for fifteen minutes per pound. When the cooking is two-thirds done, remove the paper, and finish cooking the fish without it, basting nearly all the time. Strain the stock, reduce it by half, thicken it with butter, and hand it separately.

Foie de lotte. The eel-pout's liver is cooked like carp's soft roe (page 85) in salted and acidulated water. You can also cook it with butter: but it must be remembered that it will take rather longer than the carp's roe. It can also be used to garnish small china dishes, or served in scallop shells, *au gratin*, and so on.

Quenelles de lotte. With the flesh of the eel-pout, make a forcemeat in the same way and in the same proportions as described for Pike forcemeat (page 31). The forcemeat may be truffled, if liked. To make and poach the *quenelles,* follow the recipe for *Quenelles de brochet* (page 94).

NOTE: See Rockfish, page 124.

GURNARD (*GRONDIN*)

A fish with an enormous bony head, which must not be confused with the red mullet. There are two varieties commonly found, the pink gurnard and the grey. Several of the recipes for red mullet can be applied to the gurnard, but it must be remembered that the gurnard's flesh is very much firmer. The gurnard's best use is the *bouillabaisse,* but the following recipe will be found pleasing.

Grondins beurre blanc. Poach some gurnard fillets in a well-seasoned *court-bouillon.* Reduce a quart of the stock, with the addition of chopped shallot, to half a wine-glassful. Put butter in this, and bring quickly to the boil. As soon as it boils, strain it through a fine conical sieve, and salt and pepper it. Serve the fish with steamed potatoes, and hand the butter separately.

Grondins à l'orientale: see *Rougets à l'orientale* (page 123).

HADDOCK, SMOKED (*ÉGLEFIN FUMÉ*)

Whether whole or in fillets, this fish is poached in plain water to which a little milk is added. The time of cooking, after the liquid comes to the boil, is five to ten minutes for a whole haddock, weighing about a pound, or twice as long for the same weight in fillets. It is served with fresh melted butter and steamed potatoes.

Haddock Monte Carlo. Poach the haddock in cold water, add a little milk. Five minutes is sufficient for one pound of haddock, after it comes to the boil. Reduce the liquid by one quarter, add four spoon-fuls of fresh cream and one spoonful of seasoned *Béchamel* sauce (page 44). Then drain off the haddock, remove the skin and bone, dress it on a dish. While the haddock is cooking, cut some tomatoes and onions in chunks, season and cook them until they are reduced to a purée, then arrange them in small mounds in the centre of the dish, preferably according to the number of people to be served, and on top of each mound put a poached egg.

HALIBUT (*FLÉTAN*)

This fish, which is very little known in France, is very much appreciated in England and Holland for the sake of its delicate and palatable flesh. It is a little like the brill in appearance, but longer, its shape being more like that of a very large lemon sole. As in the case of brill, the various ways of preparing small turbot and the different preparations of sole and fillets of sole can be applied to the halibut.

HERRING (*HARENG*)

For some reason or other there has always been a definite prejudice in the politer kitchens in England against this really delicious fish. It may be because English people know so few different ways of presenting it at table. The numerous recipes that follow should help to disabuse them of the belief that the herring makes a poor and uninteresting dish.

Harengs à la bretonne. Take some soft-roed herrings, egg-and-breadcrumb them, and fry them in clarified butter. Remove the roes, and rub half of them through a sieve. Mix a little Dijon mustard with the purée, and thicken it with melted butter. Egg-and-breadcrumb and fry the rest of the roes. Put the broth of roes in the bottom of the serving dish, arrange the herrings upon it, and surround them with the fried roes.

Harengs à la calaisienne. Cut the herrings down the back and remove the backbones. Stuff them with their roes, hard or soft, mixed with soaked breadcrumbs, chopped shallots and parsley, salt, pepper, a little cream, and a little softened butter. Put the two fillets together again, wrap each herring in buttered paper, and cook them in the oven. Serve a *maître-d'hôtel* butter with this dish.

Harengs à la diable. Score the herrings on each side and spread them with mustard seasoned with a little cayenne pepper. Sprinkle them with breadcrumbs, and grill them, basting them with melted butter.

Harengs farcis. Proceed as for *Harengs à la calaisienne* but substitute an ordinary forcemeat to which chopped hard-boiled eggs have been added, for the *calaisienne* forcemeat. Wrap in paper, and cook in the oven. Serve with them, but separately, some melted butter or a *maître-d'hôtel* butter.

Laitances de harengs: see *Laitance de carpe* (page 85).

Harengs marinés: see under *Hors-d'œuvre* (page 56).

Harengs à la paramé. Stiffen the herrings in butter, and then put them into buttered paper bags with a very dry *Duxelles* (page 31), several drops of lemon juice, and a little butter. Fold over the ends of the paper bags, and finish cooking the herrings in the oven.

Harengs à la portière. Cook the herrings in butter in a frying-pan, spread them with mustard, and add a little chopped parsley. Finally pour over them some nutbrown butter, swill the hot frying pan with a few drops of vinegar, and pour this over as well.

Harengs Mesnil-Val: see page 57.

Filets de harengs mâconnaise. For the *sauce mâconnaise* make a stock with vegetables (onion, carrot, celery) cut in large dice (*brunoise*), seasoning, and red wine (Mâcon), and cook for half an hour. Poach your filleted herrings in this, and serve them garnished with mushrooms, glazed button onions, and *croûtons* of fried bread. Cover with the *sauce mâconnaise*.

Filets de Harengs Trophy. (In 1936 Madame Prunier inaugurated a Trophy for the best herring catch of the season, and this dish was composed to celebrate the event by her late chef, Mr Maurice Cochois.) Fry fillets of herrings in clarified butter, and serve them in this way. Two fillets on each plate, roughly chopped tomatoes tossed in butter on top, then another fillet to make a sandwich. Cover with a light *sauce thermidor* (a mixture of mustard-flavoured *Bercy* sauce and Béchamel) and brown lightly.

JOHN DORY (*SAINT-PIERRE*)

This hideous fish has a rather firm but delicious flesh. It is hardly ever cooked except in fillets, and it can be treated in any of the ways described for fillets of sole. The flesh of the John Dory is excellent for making fish forcemeat. Its name must not be confused with the *daurade*, which is the sea bream.

Filet de St Pierre à l'asturienne. For 6 persons.

3 John Dory of 2 lb. each, to be filleted, making 6 fillets of 7 oz. each	1 spoonful paprika
	4 oz. pimento
	2 oz. parmesan cheese
2 lb. whiting	4 oz. cream
1 oz. chopped onions	2 eggs

Stuff the John Dory fillets with some forcemeat made of whiting to which some very finely chopped onions reduced in butter have been added. Season with paprika. Put the fillets in a buttered dish and moisten with a glass of white wine. Cover with some red sweet peppers and mushrooms cut in large strips. Cook in the oven, basting often. Remove the stock and add two large dessertspoonfuls of cream as well as two of *sauce mornay*. Surround the fillets with small skinned tomatoes cooked in butter. Mask the fish with the sauce, sprinkle grated parmesan on top, and brown under the grill. (Created by Mr M. Muller, Chef de Cuisine, Maison Prunier, London.)

LAMPREY (*LAMPROIE*)

Although this fish is caught in England, notably in the River Severn, it is very seldom to be seen in the fish shops. It is a sort of eel, but finer and fatter than the common eel. It must be scalded before the skin can be removed, and it can be prepared in any of the ways prescribed for the eel. English people will be most familiar with it in its potted form.

LEMON SOLE (*LIMANDE*)

This fish is usually looked on as an economical substitute for the sole, and indeed it is susceptible to a number of sole recipes. The small ones are inclined to be thin, and for that reason are often dipped in batter before they are fried.

MACKEREL (*MAQUEREAU*)

Mackerel are best in the spring, and they should never be used unless they are perfectly fresh.

Filets de maquereau à la batelière. Season the fillets, brush them with oil or with melted butter, and grill them. Hand with them a *sauce verte* (page 52), or a hot *ravigote* sauce (page 52).

Maquereaux antiboise. Fillets fried in butter, and served garnished with roughly chopped tomato and thin strips of the white part of leeks and of celery both stewed in butter. Pour some nutbrown butter over the fish on serving, and finish with a few drops of lemon juice.

Maquereau bouilli au sauce persil. Cut off the head end, cut the mackerel down the back, and bisect the backbone, but do not separate the two fillets. Put it in a shallow dish with enough cold water to cover it; add salt, a little vinegar, and a few sprigs of parsley. Bring to the boil quickly, and let it boil for a few seconds. Then finish cooking it by poaching on the side of the stove for twelve to fifteen minutes, according to size. Drain it on a cloth, scrape off the skin, and serve it in a long dish garnished with parsley. Serve separately a parsley sauce (page 48).

Maquereau bouilli sauce fenouil. Cook the mackerel as above, adding a pinch of fennel. Skin it, arrange it on a dish, and cover it with fennel sauce (page 46).

Maquereau bonnefoy. Cook the fillets *à la meunière* (page 24). Lay them on a hot dish, surround them with steamed or boiled potatoes, and cover them with a *sauce bordelaise* made from chopped shallots, coarse ground pepper, thyme, bayleaves, and white wine reduced and mixed with fish *velouté*, strained, and finished with chopped tarragon.

Maquereau à la boulonnaise. Use soft-roed fish if possible. Cut them in slices across and poach them in a *court-bouillon* with vinegar. Drain the slices, skin them, arrange them in a dish, and surround them with poached mussels. Strain through a cloth the quantity of the *court-bouillon* sufficient for the sauce, and bind it with enough white *roux* (page 37) to make it the right consistency. Finish it with butter, and cover the slices and their garnish with it. Surround the dish with slices of the soft roes, egg-and-breadcrumbed and fried.

Maquereau à la calaisienne : see *Harengs à la calaisienne* (page 115).

La cotriade de maquereaux. Fillet some mackerel weighing about half a pound each, and make a fish *fumet* with the heads and bones. Meanwhile, finely chop some raw potatoes, slice some onions in rings, roughly chop some tomatoes. Butter a shallow fireproof dish thickly, and put the seasoned vegetables on it in layers, adding parsley, thyme, and bayleaf. Lay the mackerel fillets on top, moisten with the *fumet* you have made, sprinkle with butter, put on the lid, and cook in the oven. Sprinkle with roughly chopped parsley on serving.

NOTE: It is usual, in the locality where this dish is eaten, to drink cider with it.

Maquereau à la dieppoise. Fillet the fish, and poach the fillets with white wine and mushroom stock (page 36). Drain them, dish them, surround them with shrimps, mussels and mushrooms, cover with white wine sauce, and brown quickly.

NOTE: When mackerel are poached in *court-bouillon*, whether whole or in fillets, the skin should always be removed before serving.

Maquereau farci à la béarnaise. Open the mackerel by the stomach and remove the backbone. Stuff it with pike or whiting forcemeat (page 31), and reshape the fish to its original form. Put it in a thickly buttered dish, season with salt and pepper, sprinkle with white wine, and cook it in the oven for half an hour. Lay on a dish, and cover with *sauce béarnaise* (page 45).

Maquereau Francillon. Fillet the mackerel, grill the fillets, and serve them on *croûtons* of fried bread which have been spread with a mixture of *maître-d'hôtel* butter and a purée of anchovies. Surround with straw potatoes (*pommes paille*), and hand a tomato sauce.

Maquereau à l'indienne. Cook a mackerel in *court-bouillon*, drain it, skin it, lay it on a bed of rice *à l'indienne* (page 37), and cover it with curry sauce.

Laitance de maquereau (mackerels' roes): see *Laitance de carpe* (page 85).

Maquereau à la meunière. Fillets fried *à la meunière* (page 24).

Filets de maquereaux nantaise. In an earthenware dish sprinkle some chopped raw mushrooms, onion, parsley, chives, and shallots, all chopped up. Arrange on this bed some fillets of mackerel seasoned

Smelt

Mackerel

Monk Fish

with salt and pepper, moisten with white wine (Muscadet), sprinkle with a few breadcrumbs, and cook in the oven. Serve in the same dish.

Maquereau à la normande. Cut the mackerel down the back and withdraw the backbone. Flatten the fish lightly, and poach it in a fish *fumet* (page 32). Dish, surround with a *normande* garnish (page 39), and cover with *sauce normande* (page 48).

Filets de maquereau en papillotes. Grill the fillets, put them in an oiled piece of paper between two layers of dry *Duxelles* (page 31) to which have been added some *fines herbes* (page 32) and some light fish glaze (page 33). Sprinkle with melted butter and lemon juice, fold the paper, and bake in a hot oven until the bag blows out.

MULLET, GREY (*MULET* or *MUGE*)

This fish is distinguished from the bass by its large scales: it is sometimes used instead of it, but it is not of the same quality. Besides those that follow, all the recipes already given for bass may be used for grey mullet.

Mulet aux courgettes. Score the mullet, season it, and put it into a thickly buttered fireproof dish. Surround it with baby vegetable marrows (*courgettes*) cut in rounds, add some *fines herbes* (page 32), sprinkle plentifully with melted butter. and cook it in a slow oven. Serve as it is, in the same dish.

Mulet madrilène. Brush a baking tin with oil, and put in the bottom some thin rings of onion, skinned halves of tomatoes, quarters of sweet red peppers, and a half-root of fennel which has first been blanched. Season the mullet, lay it on the dish, and moisten it with good Muscatel. Bake in a slow oven, fifteen minutes to the pound, basting frequently. Serve as it is, in the same dish.

Mulets en matelote. Use small mullet for this, about ten to twelve ounces each; and cook in the same way as *matelote* of eel (page 88).

Mulet poché au beurre blanc: see *Brochet au beurre blanc* (page 92).

Mulet rôti à l'oseille. For six people you will want a mullet of three to four pounds. Score it down the sides, and cut it down the back from head to tail. Season it, brush it over with oil, and cook it for ten minutes in the oven. Meanwhile have ready a thickly buttered fire-proof dish, put in it a little chopped shallot, some roughly chopped chervil, and half a pound of sorrel cut in thin strips. Let the sorrel 'melt' over the fire. Turn the mullet over on to this bed of sorrel, sprinkle it with melted butter, and cook it in a hot oven for twenty-five to thirty minutes.

Mulet à la niçoise. Fillet some small mullet, and cook them *à la meunière* (page 24), seeing that they are nicely browned. In the dish in which the fillets are to be served, put some butter and oil, a touch of chopped shallot, roughly chopped tomatoes, parsley, and a little thyme, chopped up, half a glass of brandy, and a few breadcrumbs. Sprinkle with butter, lay the fillets on this bed, and put into a hot oven for ten to fifteen minutes. Serve as it is.

MULLET, RED (*ROUGET*)

There are two sorts of mullet generally known in cookery: the red mullet and the surmullet. The latter can be recognized by its redder colour and the golden streaks on its back. The red mullet is the one which has been called the 'woodcock of the sea', and is the commoner of the two. It is an excellent fish, which many prefer to eat with its insides, or at any rate its liver, still intact. The best ways of cooking it are either by grilling or frying in butter, and the recipes that follow are in the main derived from these two processes.

Rougets Danicheff. Poach the fish with chopped shallot, a fine *julienne* of truffles, and very little white wine and mushroom stock (page 36). Dish them; reduce the stock, add a little cream, and cover the red mullet with it. Hand separately boiled or steamed potatoes.

Rougets Francillon. Grill the red mullet, and serve them on pieces of toast cut to the shape of the fish and spread with a mixture of anchovy and *maître-d'hôtel* butters. Surround with straw potatoes (*pommes paille*). Serve separately a thin buttered tomato sauce.

Rougets au gratin: see *Daurade au gratin* (page 135), and proceed in the same way, having regard to the smaller size of the mullet.

Rougets grillés. Score their sides and season them. Smear them with good olive oil, and put them on a very hot grill. They can be accompanied by plain melted butter or by anchovy or *maître-d'hôtel* butter, and steamed potatoes should be served with them.

Rougets grillés Mirabeau. Score a fine red mullet, and grill it. Serve it garnished with a *Mirabeau* garnish and anchovy butter, the last handed separately.

NOTE: The *Mirabeau* garnish consists of criss-cross anchovy fillets and stoned olives.

Rougets à l'italienne. Cook the mullet *à la meunière* (page 24). Dish them, and surround them with fairly coarsely minced mushrooms tossed in butter, and cover with *Duxelles* sauce (page 31). If you like, you can also garnish this dish with very small tomatoes skinned and stewed in butter.

Rougets à la juive. Small mullet should be used for this dish, and they should be floured and fried in oil. Serve separately a *sauce tartare* (page 52).

Rougets à la livournaise. Score and season the mullet; arrange them in a shallow fireproof dish, and cover them with chopped tomatoes which have been lightly stewed (*fondues*) in oil with chopped shallot, a tiny bit of crushed garlic, salt, and pepper. Add a little good white wine, sprinkle with browned breadcrumbs and melted butter or oil, and cook in the oven for fifteen to twenty minutes, according to the size of the fish. When serving, sprinkle over a few drops of lemon juice and scatter over a few capers.

Rougets à la nantaise. Grill the mullet, and arrange them on a dish bordered with scalloped slices of lemon, and cover them with a sauce made in this way. Put some white wine with very finely chopped onion in a saucepan, and reduce almost completely: add a little meat glaze, the insides and liver (and the roe if there is one) of the fish, these last well crushed. Pass through a tammy, thicken with butter, and finish with a little chopped parsley and chervil.

Rougets à la niçoise. Grill the mullet or fry them in oil. Dish them, and cover them with roughly chopped tomatoes lightly stewed in oil, this *fondue* being reduced and seasoned with a touch of garlic. Garnish the tops of the fish with anchovy fillets and stuffed olives. Serve anchovy butter separately.

Rougets à l'orientale. In proportion to the number of mullet, lightly brown in oil some chopped onion; add roughly chopped tomatoes, a *bouquet garni*, white wine, a touch of garlic, chopped sweet red peppers, a little of an infusion of saffron and coriander seeds, salt, and pepper. Cook this for a quarter of an hour, and reduce it. Fry the mullet in very hot oil, arrange them in your dish, cover them with the stewed tomato mixture, and decorate round with slices of unpeeled lemon.

NOTE: This dish can also be served cold, and as such often forms part of the *hors-d'œuvre*.

Rougets en papillotes. Grill the mullet, or fry them in butter. Take a sheet of oiled paper for each mullet, and spread on it a spoonful of very dry *Duxelles* sauce (page 31); lay a mullet on this, cover it with the same sauce, and roll up the paper and fold it. Put the paper bags in the oven, and let them get a light brown, when they will be done.

Rougets au plat: see *Merlans au plat* (page 176).

Rougets à la polonaise. Cook them *à la meunière* (page 24), and dish them. Cover them lightly with reduced fish *fumet* (page 32) bound with egg yolk and cream. Scatter over them some hot hardboiled eggs and parsley, both chopped, mixed with very fine breadcrumbs, and pour over all some nutbrown butter.

Rougets à la vénitienne. Fry the mullet in oil. Dish them, and surround them with button mushrooms and olives stuffed with anchovy purée. Cover with *sauce vénitienne* (page 49).

Rougets Montesquieu. Have the mullet filleted, season them, and dip them first in melted butter and then in chopped onion and parsley. Fry them in butter, and sprinkle with a few drops of lemon juice on serving.

PLAICE (*CARRELET* or *PLIE FRANCHE*)

This fish is easily recognizable by the red spots on its brown side. It is not a prime fish, and is not used at all in high cookery. In the household it is either fried in deep fat, or in butter, grilled (when it can be accompanied by a *maître-d'hôtel* butter or a mustard sauce), or it can be cooked *à la Bercy, au vin blanc, au gratin,* and so on.

ROCKFISH

This is a more or less comprehensive name for a number of fish which are seldom displayed in the fishmonger's in a whole state. It has been known for some years as rock salmon, but the use of this name, owing to its confusion with salmon, is to be discouraged. The fish treated here under this heading are saithe, monk, and flake. These are variously known also as coalfish or green cod (pollack in Scotland), angler or frogfish, and different sorts of dogfish. The corresponding fish in the French edition of this book are *colin* (saithe) and *lotte-de-mer*, or *baudroie* (monk or anglerfish).

All the preparations given for cod can be used for these fish, and when cold they are admirable for making coquilles, mayonnaises, and salads. The *lotte-de-mer* (which should not be confused with the eel-pout – *lotte*) is especially used for *bouillabaisse*, and it is also one of the ingredients of the *Bourride* (page 178). In France it is prepared in smoked fillets, which are grilled or cooked in butter and served accompanied by a highly seasoned sauce. It is also used in the following attractive dish.

Lotte au gratin. A fillet is boned and skinned, and cooked as follows: lay it in a buttered fireproof dish in which you have first put a seasoned layer of very finely chopped shallot and onion and chopped parsley and mushrooms. Moisten with a glass of dry white wine, and cook in the oven. When done, arrange the fish on your serving dish; reduce the cooking liquor, thicken it with butter, and then add a little white wine sauce. Cover the fish, sprinkle with breadcrumbs only, and brown quickly.

NOTE: See Eel-Pout (*Lotte*), page 113.

SALMON (*SAUMON*)

The salmon, king of the migrant fishes, admits of every sort of preparation, whether by boiling, grilling, or braising; an infinite variety even when we exclude the dishes made from salmon already cooked. We give here a few, leaving it to the reader to exercise his skill and ingenuity in improvising others.

The salmon, which is at its best from January to September, can be cooked in the following ways: poached or braised whole; as a piece (*tronçon*) of varying size taken from the middle of the fish; as a cutlet (*darne*): that is, a slice about an inch and a half thick; or in slices (*tranches*) about half an inch thick and weighing about half a pound.

Saumon court-bouillonné: for the method and time of cooking, see note on page 31. – When the salmon is cooked, it is laid upon a napkin on the serving dish, and surrounded by sprigs of curly parsley. At the same time there are handed steamed or boiled potatoes and one or two of the following sauces: *hollandaise,* caper, *mousseline,* anchovy, shrimp, oyster, *Nantua, vénitienne,* hot *ravigote,* or *genevoise;* for which see the chapter on Sauces.

NOTE: With the whole fish or large pieces two sauces are usually served.

Saumon braisé. Put the fish, or the piece, in the grill in the fish kettle, lined in the usual way for braising (page 26), and let it stew gently (*suer*) in the oven for eight to ten minutes. Then moisten it up to halfway with white or red wine, according to the recipe you are following. The cooking is done with the lid on, slowly, with frequent basting, for ten minutes to each pound of fish.

Cadgery de saumon: see page 128.

Côtelettes de saumon. Salmon cutlets can be made in two ways:

(1) Make the necessary amount of salmon forcemeat, following the recipe for pike forcemeat (page 31), substituting salmon for pike, and follow the exact recipe for *Côtelettes de brochet* (page 92).

(2) The cutlets can be made with the same preparation as that for *Croquettes de saumon* (page 127). They are, after all, only croquettes shaped like cutlets, which are accompanied by some broth or sauce according to choice.

Coquilles de saumon. These are made with various sauces in the following manner: cover the bottom of the scallop shells with a spoonful of the sauce chosen, garnish them with flakes of cooked salmon completely freed from all skin and bones, cover this with more of the sauce, and brown quickly in the oven. The coquilles should be silver ones, or failing these, ordinary scallop shells.

Au vin blanc: Garnish the shells with salmon, cover with white wine sauce, and brown quickly.

À la mornay: Garnish the shells, cover with *mornay* sauce (page 48), sprinkle with grated cheese and melted butter, and brown quickly.

Sauce crevettes: Add to the salmon some shrimps, and cover with shrimp sauce.

Au gratin: Garnish the shells, cover with *Duxelles* sauce (page 31), sprinkle with very fine browned breadcrumbs and melted butter, and brown quickly. Take the shells from the oven, and on serving squeeze over them a few drops of lemon juice and add a little chopped parsley.

Froides: Garnish the bottom of the shells with a little seasoned macédoine of vegetables or a fine *julienne* of lettuce leaves. Add the salmon, cover with mayonnaise sauce or green mayonnaise sauce, and surround the shells with a little border of chopped hard-boiled egg (yolk and white) mixed with chopped parsley.

Coulibiac de saumon: see *Pâté chaud de saumon* (page 130).

Croquettes de saumon. (1) Make a *salpicon* with the following ingredients: a pound of salmon, half a pound of cooked mushrooms, four ounces of shelled shrimps, two ounces of truffles. The binding sauce should be a very much reduced Béchamel, with six egg yolks added for every pint and three quarters. The proportion of sauce to *salpicon* is just over half a pint to each pound of the *salpicon*. Mix the *salpicon* with the sauce, pour it out on a dish, and spread it. Brush over the surface with butter, and let it get cold. (2) Divide the mixture into portions weighing about two ounces or a little over and shape them into rectangles, ovals, or cutlets, according to the description on the menu. Egg-and-breadcrumb them, using very fine crumbs. Keep them in a cool place, if they have long to wait. When ready to serve them, plunge them into very hot fat, drain them on a cloth, and serve them in a circle with fried parsley in the middle. Hand the appropriate sauce with them.

Darne de saumon pochée. Make a *court-bouillon* (without vinegar) in sufficient quantity for your needs. Plunge the salmon cutlets in it, bring quickly to the boil, draw the pan to the side of the stove, and let the fish poach for six to ten minutes according to the thickness of the cutlets.

NOTE: The *court-bouillon* usually employed for poaching fish is one containing white wine vinegar. We advise this for large pieces of fish which have to be cooked slowly, but we think the vinegar should be left out in the case of the smaller cutlets, because the acidity tends to spoil the colour of the salmon.

These poached cutlets are always accompanied by steamed or boiled potatoes, and by some such sauce as *hollandaise*, *béarnaise*, or anchovy. Or they can be served with *maître-d'hôtel* butter, plain melted butter, and so on.

Darne de saumon bourguignonne. Poach the cutlet with red wine. Dish it, and surround it with a *bourguignonne* garnish, and finish the sauce as on page 45.

Darne de saumon à la Chambord. Proceed exactly as for *Carpe à la Chambord* (page 84).

Darne de saumon à la Daumont. Poach the cutlet in *court-bouillon* without vinegar. Dish it, and surround it by large cooked mushrooms, little pastry bouchées filled with crayfish tails bound with *sauce Nantua*, and *quenelles* moulded in a small spoon of creamy truffled fish forcemeat. Hand *sauce Nantua* with it.

Darne de saumon à la Riga. Poach the cutlet in *court-bouillon* without vinegar, and let it get cold. Remove the skin, and cover the cutlet thickly with white fish jelly. Dish it, and surround it by little hollowed sections of cucumber, blanched, marinated, and garnished with a macédoine of vegetables bound with mayonnaise sauce, tartlets garnished with the same macédoine, and hard-boiled egg halves filled with caviar. Finally put a border of pieces of jelly round the dish.

Escalopes de saumon. Cut some fillets of salmon, skin them, and cut them in slices weighing about three to four ounces each. Trim them, and poach them on a buttered dish with very little red or white wine, mushroom stock and fish *fumet*. Serve them with a garnish and sauce as desired.

Kadgiori ou Cadgery de saumon. This dish can be made for using up cold cooked salmon, turbot, brill, rockfish, cod, and so on. First make six ounces to half a pound of pilaff rice (page 37), as well as three quarters of a pint of white wine sauce, flavoured, if you like, with curry powder. Flake up a pound of cooked salmon, removing all skin and bone; warm it up in salted water, drain it thoroughly and mix it with the sauce, adding five hard-boiled eggs, cut in large dice while hot. Arrange in a timbale or shallow dish alternating layers of fish and rice. Finish with a layer of rice, and pour over some nutbrown butter (*beurre noisette*) on serving.

Médaillons de saumon. Cut some slices, half an inch thick, from a salmon fillet, trim them into little oval shapes, and poach them gently. Let them get cold. The cover them either with a mayonnaise, *rémoulade*, or green sauce bound with jelly, or with a white or pink *chaudfroid* sauce, and varnish them with jelly. Arrange in a circle on a round dish.

NOTE: The trimmings of the *médaillons* can be poached separately and used for a salmon salad, or some other purpose.

Mousse de saumon (hot). Pound finely a pound of salmon flesh with a third of an ounce of salt, a good pinch of pepper, and two whites of eggs added by degrees. Pass through a tammy, and put the forcemeat into a basin. Work it for a few minutes with a spoon, and put it on ice for an hour. Then, working it with the spatula, mix in about three quarters of a pint of cream, thick and fresh, and lastly two small well-whisked egg whites. With this preparation fill your well-buttered mould, and poach it for forty to forty-five minutes. The mousse is cooked when it feels rather firm and elastic to the touch. It is inadvisable to turn the mousse out immediately on its removal from the *bain-marie*: it is better to leave it for seven or eight minutes so that it shrinks a little inside the mould. This hot mousse can be served with any of the sauces appropriate to salmon.

Mousse de saumon (cold). Pound in a mortar a pound of cold cooked salmon, braised for preference. Pass it through a tammy, put it into a basin and incorporate with it in this order: six tablespoonfuls of very good cold melted jelly, eight tablespoonfuls of fish *velouté*, and eight tablespoonfuls of cream, which must be whipped before being added. Correct the seasoning if necessary. This mousse can be moulded in two ways – in a mould already well lined with very clear jelly and decorated, or in a silver or glass dish. Under the influence of Escoffier, modern kitchen methods have been considerably simplified, and the moulding with the jelly lining, which is a long and painstaking business, has been practically abandoned. This is how you mould it in the silver or glass dish. Take a dish which will just hold the mousse, pour the mousse into it, smooth the top into a slight dome, and decorate it with truffle. Then varnish the top as many times as is necessary to give the mousse a thick coating of jelly. Keep the mousse in the refrigerator or ice-chest until needed to serve.

Mousselines de saumon. Mousselines are really nothing more than large *quenelles* made of the same composition as hot Mousse of salmon (page 129), moulded with dessertspoons and poached in the same way as all other large *quenelles*. They can also be made with a forcing-bag, to the size of an ordinary meringue. Mousselines can also be made in little timbale moulds and poached in the *bain-marie*. They are accompanied, if desired, by a light garnish and by some sauce or other as occasion demands. What sauce and garnish must be decided by the chef when planning his menu.

Mayonnaise de saumon. Garnish the bottom of a salad bowl with *julienne* shreds of lettuce seasoned with salt and a few drops of vinegar. Arrange on this cold flaked salmon, with every vestige of skin and bones removed, in the proportion of between three and four ounces for each person. Cover the whole with a highly seasoned mayonnaise sauce; decorate with anchovy fillets, stoned olives, and capers, and set in the middle of a small lettuce heart. Surround the dish with hard-boiled eggs and quartered lettuce hearts alternately. On serving, a further border can be arranged of thin rings of radish and gherkin, tarragon leaves, and so on.

Pâté chaud de saumon, or *Coulibiac.* This hot salmon pie, which hails from Russia, is a dish which must be eaten once, and then many times after. But you must have a company of ten or twelve people to eat it. For this number you will require: two and a half pounds of pastry for *coulibiac* (page 34); a pound and a half of salmon fillet, cut in small slices, stiffened in butter and allowed to get cold; half a pound of large semolina or rice cooked in white consommé; three hard-boiled eggs, white and yolk chopped together; four ounces of mushrooms and a large onion, chopped, tossed together in butter, and allowed to grow cold, with a tablespoonful of chopped parsley; three ounces of *vésiga* (the dried marrow of the sturgeon), soaked in cold water for five hours to ensure its full swelling, then cooked for four hours in slightly salted water, and then very coarsely chopped. (It has been found that *vésiga* swells to five times its original size during soaking and cooking. In this case, its final weight will be fifteen ounces.)

METHOD: With two-thirds of the pastry, roll out a rectangle sixteen inches long by ten inches wide. Garnish the middle with successive layers of semolina or rice, slices of salmon, *vésiga*, and mushrooms, onions, and egg. Finish with a layer of semolina or rice. Roll out the rest of the pastry, and lay this on top of the garnish. Draw up the edges of the lower rectangle of pastry, moistening them lightly, and join them well to the edges of the top layer, so that the garnish is completely enclosed. Now keep the *coulibiac* in a fairly warm place for a good half hour, so that the pastry rises slightly. Then brush it over with melted butter, sprinkle it with very fine browned breadcrumbs, and make a slit in the top for the steam to escape. Put it in a good moderate oven, in a place where the heat will come especially from the bottom. Bake for fifty minutes, and when removing it from the oven, pour inside it five or six dessertspoonfuls of melted butter.

Saumon au beurre de Montpellier. The fish used for this dish can be either whole or in large or small slices. In any case, it must first be poached, and then let get cold. Skin it, and cover it with Montpellier butter (page 42). Decorate it with truffles in whatever way you like, but the more usual decoration is in the form of scales, with the crescents in truffle. Mask with cold melted white fish jelly. Arrange the piece on a dish, and surround it with halves of hard-boiled egg on end, yolks up. Further decorate the dish outside with pieces of jelly and the Montpellier butter.

OBSERVATION ON COLD DRESSED FISH: Where a whole fish is concerned, one or both sides of the fish are skinned, according to its position on the dish. If it is laid on one side, then only the side on top should be skinned; but if the fish is set on its stomach, then the skin must be removed from both sides. Opinions are divided on this question of dressing the fish, some chefs refusing to allow the position on the stomach, while others, followers of Dubois, admit this position.

Saumon froid à la parisienne. For this dish it is usual to have a small or medium-sized fish, or piece of a fish, that has been poached in *court-bouillon* and allowed to get cold. Remove the skin from the middle in such a way as to leave a rectangle of bare flesh. Cover this skinned part only with mayonnaise sauce mixed with jelly, and when this has set, decorate it with white and yolk of hard-boiled eggs, tiny sprigs of chervil, tarragon leaves, and so on. Mask heavily with white jelly, and decorate with Montpellier butter (page 42) through a forcing-bag. Surround with small artichoke bottoms garnished with *salade russe* bound with thick mayonnaise sauce.

Quiche de saumon fumé. Line a flan case with short-crust pastry. Beat up lightly, as if for an omelette, four whole eggs and two yolks, mix with them three quarters of a pint of fresh cream, season with salt, pepper, and grated nutmeg, and pour this mixture into the flan case. Sprinkle over the top some small dabs of butter, and add enough thin slices of smoked salmon to cover the cream. Bake in a very hot oven for thirty-five minutes. Serve immediately, or the salmon will get tough. The slices should remain on top of the flan and be lightly covered with cream.

NOTE: This mixture can equally well be cooked in little moulds as a hot *hors-d'œuvre.*

Saumon braisé à la régence. Stuff the fish, or the piece of the fish, with forcemeat (page 32). Braise it on a bed of vegetables and herbs (page 31) with a fine white Bordeaux. Do not moisten too deeply. When the fish is cooked, dish it, and surround it with a garnish consisting of little *quenelles* of truffled fish forcemeat moulded with a teaspoon, large decorated *quenelles*, slices of poached soft roes cooked in butter, large trussed crayfish that have been cooked in *court-bouillon*. Serve separately a *sauce normande* (page 48) to which has been added the reduced stock of the fish.

Tourte de saumon à la mode de Valençay. Skin and trim a salmon cutlet about an inch and a quarter thick and weighing about a pound and a half. Season it and let it marinate in champagne for two hours. Chop up some shrimps or prawns, crayfish tails, and oysters, and bind them either with a purée of truffles or of mushrooms, according to your views regarding which flavour should predominate in the final dish. With the carcasses and trimmings of the crayfish, make a red butter in the usual manner (page 42, *Beurre d'écrevisses*). Now line a rather deep flan case with short-crust pastry, lay the cutlet in the middle, and surround it with medium-sized whole truffles. Spread the chopped mixture over the cutlet, cover it with a pastry lid, and join the edges well. Gild with egg, make a slit in the top, and cook in a moderate oven for an hour and a quarter. On taking the tart from the oven, pour into it the crayfish butter which you have just warmed. Serve at once.

Tranches de saumon. It is often found convenient, especially in restaurants (and, I may say, in small families), to cook and serve salmon in slices. These should not be less than seven ounces in weight, and they may be grilled, poached, or fried *à la meunière* (page 24).

Grillées: The slices should be seasoned with salt and pepper, brushed over with oil, and grilled by a fierce heat on both sides to make sure of the outside being 'sealed'. They are then finished by more moderate heat. They can be served on anchovy butter, *maître-d'hôtel*, *Bercy*, and so on.

Pochées: Plunge the slices into boiling *court-bouillon* without vinegar, and then keep the liquid just moving. Ten minutes will be enough. Lay them on a dish covered with a napkin, surround them with steamed or boiled potatoes and parsley, and hand a suitable sauce.

À la meunière: Season the slices with salt and pepper, roll them in flour, and cook them in clarified butter. Continue as for all fish cooked *à la meunière* (page 24).

NOTE: In whatever way the slices are cooked, the bone in the centre must always be removed after they are cooked and before serving.

SALMON TROUT (*TRUITE SAUMONÉE*)

The salmon trout is much in demand for choice dinners, and as it is a smaller fish than the salmon it is never cut up, but always served whole, except in certain cold preparations in which it is served in fillets on a mousse of some kind. Recipes for these fashions will be found in the *Guide Culinaire* by Escoffier, Ph. Gilbert, and Fétu. As all the preparations of salmon, whether hot or cold, can be used for salmon trout, they will not be repeated here. But the two following recipes may be found acceptable.

Truite saumonée braisé, sauce genevoise. Put a salmon trout weighing about two pounds in a baking dish with vegetables cut in rounds (see directions for *Bar rôti*, page 103). Sprinkle with butter, and put the dish in the oven when the vegetables have acquired a light colour.

Moisten with half a bottle of good red wine, and cook for thirty to forty minutes. Drain the fish, and dish it. Strain the stock into a saucepan. Reduce it to half, and then add a light blended butter (page 42), whisking vigorously. Take it off the fire, butter it generously, correct the seasoning, and hand this sauce separately. Also serve steamed or boiled potatoes, if you like.

Truite saumonée fourrée aux crevettes roses. This is a dish for ten people, and you will want a fish weighing about four pounds. Open it at the stomach, and remove the backbone; season with salt and cayenne. Stuff it with a forcemeat made with pike or salmon (page 31), thickened with cream well seasoned and with prawn butter added to it. Wrap the fish up in a thickly buttered piece of paper, and tie it up, but not too tightly. Put the fish on the grid of the fish kettle, moisten with three quarters of a pint of fish *fumet* and half a bottle of Chablis, and add two ounces of butter in small bits. Now braise the salmon trout in the oven, allowing about fifty minutes, and basting it frequently. Then drain it and unwrap it, skin carefully, and dish on its stomach. Now arrange all the way down its back some cooked button mushrooms, and on each mushroom stick a fine prawn with its tail shelled and legs cut off. Cover with white wine sauce, which has been made with the reduced stock enriched with cream, thickened with butter, and bound with *hollandaise* sauce. Season the sauce rather highly. Surround the fish with pastry boats, each garnished with a large *quenelle* of pike forcemeat decorated with truffle, and slices of lobster tails masked with *sauce américaine*.

SEA BREAM (*DAURADE*)

The appearance of this fish is very like that of the freshwater bream, but it is fleshier. Besides the recipes that follow, small and medium-sized sea bream may be grilled, or cooked *à la meunière*. They can also be treated in many of the ways given for fillets of sole. The very large sea bream are always cooked in *court-bouillon*, and served with a well-seasoned sauce.

Daurade Bercy. Score the sea bream, season it and lay it in a buttered shallow fireproof dish, in which you have first sprinkled chopped shallot and roughly chopped parsley. Moisten with white wine, sprinkle with melted butter, and cook in the oven with frequent basting. Arrange the fish on the serving dish, reduce the stock, thicken it with butter, mask the fish with it, and brown quickly in the oven or with a salamander.

Daurade à la bretonne. For six people, take a sea bream of about two and a half pounds. Make a forcemeat as follows: fry lightly in butter, as if for a *Duxelles*, half a pound of chopped mushrooms and a good dessertspoonful of chopped shallot; season with salt and pepper, add parsley, a touch of rosemary, and eight tablespoonfuls of white wine. Let it reduce, then take it off the fire, and finish with three or four ounces of breadcrumbs and a lightly beaten egg. Stuff the fish with this forcemeat, lay it on a thickly buttered dish, surround it with finely minced potatoes, and add a *bouquet garni*. Moisten with a wine-glass of water, and cook in the oven for thirty-five to forty minutes. Serve in the same dish, as it is.

Daurade farcie. Cut a sea bream down the back from head to tail, and take out the backbone without misshaping the fish. Season it inside with salt and pepper, and stuff it with a creamy fish forcemeat (page 31), to which you have added some chopped *fines herbes* (page 32). Put the two fillets together, and cook them in the same way as *Daurade à la Bercy* (page 134).

Daurade au four. Score the sea bream, and season it with salt and pepper. Put it in a generously buttered shallow fireproof dish, and moisten it with fish *fumet* and white wine. Cook in the oven, basting frequently. When the fish is cooked, it should be found to be browned, and the liquid reduced to the proper consistency of the sauce.

Daurade au gratin. Spread a few dessertspoonfuls of *gratin* sauce (page 47) in the bottom of a dish, and add a little chopped shallot and roughly chopped parsley. Put the fish on this bed, surround it with raw mushrooms cut in rather thick slices, cover it with *gratin* sauce, sprinkle with browned breadcrumbs and melted butter, and bake in the oven until browned. This will take about thirty to forty minutes, according to the size of the fish. On removing it from the oven, squeeze over it a little lemon juice, and scatter over it some roughly chopped parsley.

Daurade à la ménagère. Proceed as for *Daurade Bercy* (page 134), but add some minced mushrooms. A few minutes before the cooking is

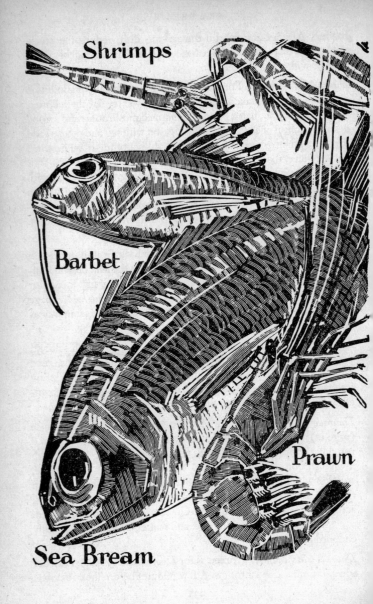

Shrimps

Barbet

Sea Bream

Prawn

finished, sprinkle with browned breadcrumbs, and add a few little dabs of butter to make a thin brown crust.

Daurade rôtie. Lard a sea bream finely with alternate strips of bacon fat and anchovy fillets. Wrap it in oiled paper and bake it in the oven. After cooking, swill the baking dish with a little white wine, reduce it, and thicken it with butter.

SHAD (*ALOSE*)

This is a very popular fish both on the Continent and in America, but it is little known in England.

Alose à l'angevine. Make a forcemeat according to the directions on page 31, with six ounces of raw soft roes, breadcrumbs soaked in milk and squeezed dry, and finely chopped parsley, chives, savory, and a little basil. Clean, scrape, and trim the shad, wash it, wipe it thoroughly, stuff it with the forcemeat, and sew it up. Cut in fine *julienne* shreds half a pound of young cabbage, blanch them, and plunge them at once in cold water. Spread this cabbage in a long fireproof dish, adding the minced white part of three leeks and a small handful of finely cut sorrel. Put the shad on top, season it with salt and pepper, add three quarters of a pint of cream that has been boiled beforehand, and braise the fish in the oven, basting it frequently. Serve it as it is.

Alose à l'avignonnaise. Chop up finely a pound and a half of sorrel, add a large chopped onion, three or four pressed and chopped tomatoes, and a crushed clove of garlic. Fry these lightly in olive oil, season with salt and pepper, and add at the last some chopped parsley and a small handful of fresh breadcrumbs to bind the mixture. Meanwhile fry the shad in olive oil in an earthenware dish with a lid. Spread out on the dish a bed of sorrel, lay the shad on it, cover this in turn with the rest of the sorrel, sprinkle over two dessertspoonfuls of oil and braise the fish in the oven (preferably a baker's oven) for eight to ten hours. After this lengthy cooking, the sorrel will have lost its slightly bitter flavour, the bones will all have melted, and the result will be a delicious dish which was formerly celebrated by the poet Auguste Marin (This recipe was contributed by M. Auternand.)

Alose au beurre blanc. Poach the shad in a *court-bouillon* rather strongly flavoured with white wine, and when it is dished mask it with a few spoonfuls of white butter (page 41), and serve the rest of the butter separately.

Alose farcie et rôtie. Stuff the shad with a forcemeat made with raw soft roes, as described in *Alose à l'angevine* (page 137). In the bottom of a fireproof dish or a baking tin scatter a dessertspoonful of chopped shallot and the same of chopped parsley. Lay the stuffed shad on this, having scored it and seasoned it with salt and pepper. Add a few spoonfuls of white wine, cover with a thickly buttered greaseproof paper, and cook in a fairly hot oven for three quarters of an hour. During cooking, brush the fish over pretty often with melted butter. On serving, sprinkle with a little chopped parsley.

Alose au gratin: see *Sole au gratin* (page 154). The shad may be cooked whole, in fillets, or in cutlets, as preferred.

Alose grillée à l'oseille. Cut the shad down lengthways and remove the backbone. Season with salt and pepper, brush over with plenty of oil, lay it on a very hot grill, and grill it over a hot but not flaming fire. Dish the shad, sprinkle it with melted butter, and hand separately a purée of braised sorrel. If the acidity of the sorrel is not liked, the purée may be made of a third spinach and two thirds sorrel.

NOTE: The directions given above are, of course, for a kind of grill which is unobtainable in private houses. With a gas or electric grill, the cook's judgement must be used to approximate the heat of the grill to that described above.

Alose grillée avec beurres et sauces divers. Whether the shad is cooked whole with its backbone removed, as described in the last recipe, or simply scored on each side, or cut in slices about an inch thick, it is advisable first to marinate it with finely chopped onion, parsley stalks, thyme, bayleaf, lemon juice, and olive oil. Soak a whole shad for one hour; but if cut in pieces, then twenty to twenty-five minutes will be enough.

Serve with the following butters: *maître-d'hôtel*, *Bercy*, anchovy, shallot, *ravigote*, etc. (page 41–2). Or with these sauces: *béarnaise*, mustard, or *sauce matelote* made with either red or white wine.

Œufs d'alose au bacon. Divide the hard roe of a shad in portions, and wrap each in oiled paper. Grill them gently. At the same time grill some thin rashers of bacon. Unwrap the pieces of roe, arrange them on a dish, lay a rasher of bacon on each, and hand a *maître-d'hôtel* butter separately.

Œufs d'alose à l'orange. Season the hard roe of a shad, and cook it in butter. Dish it, squeeze over it a few drops of lemon juice and scatter over it a little chopped parsley. Surround with orange sections, and sprinkle with foaming nutbrown butter (*beurre noisette*).

NOTE: Shad's roe can also be prepared *à la meunière*, in paper bags (*en papillote*) or *sur le plat*.

Tranches d'alose à la meunière: see under Salmon (page 133), and proceed in the same manner.

SKATE (*RAIE*)

The best of the various sorts of skate is that known as the thornback (*bouclée*), for its flesh is more delicate and it is not subject to the alkaline odour of some other kinds. Generally skate is sold in our fishmongers' shops ready prepared for cooking, but in case the whole fish is bought, here are the directions for dealing with it. As far as the cooking is concerned, the directions apply, of course, to the skate ready prepared for cooking.

The cooking of skate. The skate must first of all be scrubbed and washed in plenty of water so as to remove stickiness; the 'wings' are then detached (they are the only eatable parts) and cut into pieces weighing from five ounces to half a pound. They are then cooked in water which has been fairly strongly salted and acidulated with lemon juice or vinegar. The pieces are then drained and skinned (the latter operation being accomplished by scraping each side), and the extremity is cut off, as it consists only of bone. The pieces are then put back into the stock, where they are kept warm for their final preparation.

Raie au beurre noir. It is in this manner that skate is most often served. Have the cooked pieces very hot, drain them, wipe them dry, and arrange them on the dish. Season them with salt and pepper, and sprinkle them with capers and chopped parsley. Pour over plenty of black butter (page 43) and a dash of vinegar which has been swilled in the hot pan. Steamed potatoes should be handed separately.

Raie en fritot. Cut the skate into small pieces, season them with salt and pepper, and let them lie for an hour with minced onion, parsley stalks, thyme, bayleaf, lemon juice, and olive oil. When they are wanted, take the bits out of the marinade, wipe them dry, dip them in frying batter, and fry them in very hot deep oil. Garnish them with fried parsley, and hand a tomato sauce.

Raie au gratin. This dish can be prepared in two ways: with ordinary cooked skate, or with the 'wings' of small raw skates.

In the first place the procedure for rapid gratin must be used, as the skate is already cooked, and all that is needed is the quick browning. But in the second case it is a complete gratin that is needed, as the browning and cooking must be done at the same time. For cooking *au gratin*, see pages 27 and 28.

Raie avec sauces diverses. The skate having been prepared and cooked as already described, it can be served with a cream sauce, a caper sauce, or a Béchamel sauce made with leeks in the Breton fashion. Served cold, it can very happily be accompanied by a *sauce gribiche* (page 51).

Croûtes au foie de raie. This much appreciated and delicate dish is generally served as a hot *hors-d'œuvre*. In England it makes an admirable savoury.

Poach the liver in the *court-bouillon* used for cooking the skate, adding a few vegetables and herbs. Cut out some rounds of breadcrumb about two inches in diameter, fry them in clarified butter, and scoop out a little of the inside. Garnish them with the liver cut in dice or very small slices, sprinkle with nutbrown butter, a little chopped parsley, and lemon juice, and serve very hot.

SMELT (*ÉPERLANS*)

The small smelt are always fried, either *en brochette* – that is, several impaled on a skewer through their eyes – or *en buisson* like gudgeon (page 90). Larger ones may be prepared in certain ways like whiting: that is, *à l'anglaise, Bercy, au gratin, au vin blanc, aux fines herbes*, etc. (pages 174–7). But it must be remembered in adapting these recipes for smelt that the length of cooking time must be shortened in proportion to the size of the fish.

Skate

Sand-Smelt

John
Dory

Gurnet

SOLE AND FILLETS OF SOLE
(*SOLES ET FILETS DE SOLES*)

Among the prime fish the sole is certainly one of the best, and is always in great favour with gourmets. Its very fine and light flesh lends itself to every sort of treatment. Of all soles, the Dover sole is particularly appreciated.

In cookery, sole are prepared either whole or in fillets – whole when the party is a small one, and in fillets when there is a large number of guests and in restaurants. But, with the exception of a few special dishes, the same preparation applies to the whole as to the filleted sole. The following instructions are given as a matter of interest, because in England, in the case of small establishments, this preparation is done by the fishmonger.

To prepare a whole sole for cooking: Cut off the head diagonally at the end of the fillets. Trim the end of the tail, lightly turn back the black skin (the skin of the back) either at this end or the other, take hold of it with the corner of a cloth, and pull it off with a sharp tug. The white skin does not need to be removed, but it should be carefully scraped. Then clean the sole inside, trim the fins round it, and on the skinned side lightly raise the fillets by the backbone, so as to facilitate cooking.

To fillet a sole for poaching: When filleting a sole it is unnecessary to cut off the head. Skin it on both sides, in the manner described above, but pull off the skin from the tail end. Then with a thin-bladed knife raise the fillets from the backbone on both sides, cutting close to the bone. Keep the bones for *fumet* (page 32). Now with a lightly moistened cutlet bat flatten the fillets gently, so as to break the fibres in the flesh. Fillets can be prepared either flat, or folded in half lengthways as they are, or with a stuffing of some sort between. They can also be prepared in paupiettes, as follows: spread the fillets with fish forcemeat, roll them round so that the stuffing is inside, and tie them round with a few turns of thread or cotton so that they will keep their shape, which is that of a large cork.

To poach sole and fillets of sole: In poaching sole the ingredients used are red or white wine, mushroom stock (page 36), or fish *fumet* (page 32). That is to say, one of these only, or two, either wine and mushroom stock, or wine and fish *fumet*. The poaching must be done without the liquid boiling. It must be kept just moving, especially in the case of fillets poached flat, for boiling will make them curl up.

Grilled sole: When whole sole or fillets are grilled, the cooking should be done by a very moderate heat.

In the following pages there are given, in one series, recipes for whole soles and for fillets. Each recipe is headed according to the way the sole should be prepared, e.g. whole, filleted, in *paupiettes*, or in some cases in more than one of these ways.

NOTE ON SAUCES: In almost every case the poaching stock of the sole should be reduced, and added to the sauce accompanying it.

Sole aiglon. Poach the fillets flat in white wine. Arrange them on a purée of mushrooms mixed with a third of its volume of onion purée (*Soubise*). Mask with white wine sauce, and surround with little pastry *fleurons* cooked without being first brushed with egg.

Sole Alexandra. Prepare a whole fish as for *Sole Colbert* (page 149). Arrange it on a bed of roughly chopped tomatoes stewed in butter and substitute *sauce béarnaise* for the *maître-d'hôtel* butter.

Sole Alphonse XIII. Cook fillets of sole flat in butter. Place each on half a fried aubergine, which has been garnished with dice of sweet red peppers and tomatoes stewed to a mash (*fondue*) in butter.

Sole alsacienne. Poach the fillets flat with white wine. Lay them in a bed of braised sauerkraut, cover them with *sauce mornay*, sprinkle with grated cheese, and brown quickly.

Sole à l'ambassadrice. Roll each fillet round the base of a stuffed crayfish head, and poach with white wine. Dish them in a crown, with the crayfish heads outwards. Hand *sauce normande*.

Sole à l'américaine. Poach the sole whole or filleted in an *américaine* stock. Dish surrounded by slices of lobster tail cooked *à l'américaine* and by button mushrooms. Hand *sauce américaine*.

Sole à l'amiral. This should be a whole large sole poached with white wine and fish *fumet*. Arrange on the serving dish, and garnish with crayfish tails and mushrooms round it. Cover with white wine sauce, with the sole stock added and finished with crayfish butter. Surround with a few mussels and oysters cooked *à la Villeroy* (page 203). Decorate with slices of truffle.

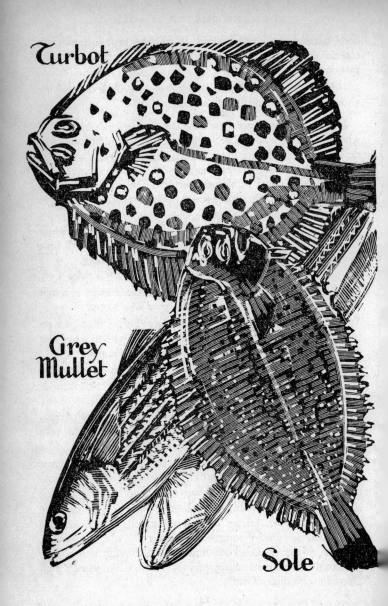

Turbot

Grey
Mullet

Sole

Sole à l'andalouse. Roll the fillets in paupiettes, and poach them with mushroom stock and butter. Arrange each *paupiette* on a small tomato half garnished with rice *à l'indienne* mixed with dice of sweet red peppers. Surround with fried slices of aubergine, and sprinkle with foaming butter. Border the dish with thin slices of lemon.

Sole à l'anglaise. When whole the sole is prepared like *Merlans Colbert* (page 175). Fillets are egg-and-breadcrumbed. In either case they are cooked in clarified butter, and served with a *maître-d'hôtel* butter.

Sole archiduc. These are fillets stuffed with whiting forcemeat flavoured with *fines herbes* (page 32) and paprika pepper, and rolled up in *paupiettes*. Poach them, arrange them in a crown with a *salpicon* of lobster, mushrooms, and truffles, bound with white wine sauce, in the middle. Cover with a creamy *sauce Nantua*, put a slice of truffle on each paupiette, and surround them with little *quenelles* and fried oysters.

Sole Argenteuil. Fillets poached flat, arranged on a bed of green asparagus tips bound with butter, and covered with a white wine sauce.

Sole arlésienne. Poach whole in the same way as *Turbotin Dugléré* (page 171), adding a touch of garlic. Dish; reduce the stock, add some baby vegetable marrows (*courgettes*) cut in the shape of olives, which have been stewed in butter and finished with cream. Pour these and the liquor over the sole, and surround with fried onion rings.

Sole à l'armoricaine. Prepare whole or in fillets in the same way as *à l'américaine* (page 144), but bind the sauce with yolk of egg and cream. The garnish here is slices of lobster and soft roes egg-and-breadcrumbed and fried.

Sole Bagration. Fillets poached flat, covered with *sauce mornay*, sprinkled with grated cheese, and browned. On serving, arrange at each end of the dish a heap of small lozenge-shaped bread *croûtons* fried in butter.

Sole Bannaro. Brush the fillets with melted butter, roll them in fresh breadcrumbs, and cook them flat in the oven with clarified butter. Dish them, surround them with banana rings fried in butter, and sprinkle them with nutbrown butter to which have been added some blanched and splintered fresh almonds, and lemon juice.

Sole batelière. Stuff the fillets, fold them in half, and poach them. Place each on a pastry boat garnished with mussels and mushrooms bound with cream sauce. Cover with white wine sauce flavoured with *fines herbes* (page 32), and on each fillet lay a small fried gudgeon.

Sole Beaufort. The sole is grilled whole. Dish it, cover it with *maître-d'hôtel* butter, and surround it with a garnish consisting of lozenge-shaped bread *croûtons* fried in butter, spread with spinach mixed with mushroom purée, masked with *sauce mornay*, and browned in the oven.

Sole Bénédictine. Folded poached fillets, arranged on a bed of *Brandade* of salt cod (page 108) and masked with cream sauce.

Sole Bercy. Poach the fillets flat with white wine, mushroom stock, chopped shallot, and butter. Reduce the stock, thicken it with butter, pour it over the fillets, and brown quickly. (Or whole.)

Sole bergère. Poach the sole whole or filleted with a little white wine, fish *fumet*, chopped shallot, and raw mushrooms finely minced. Cut some bread (without the crust) into fine *julienne* strips, and fry them in butter. Dish the sole; reduce the stock, butter it lightly, bind it with a little *hollandaise* sauce, and add a pinch of chopped parsley. Pour this over the fish, sprinkle the *julienne* of bread over it, and brown quickly.

Sole Bolivar. Remove the backbone from the sole without spoiling the fish, which you must then stuff with fish forcemeat flavoured with onion and tomato. Moisten with white wine and fish *fumet*, and poach gently. Dish, mask with white wine sauce, and brown quickly.

Sole bonne femme. Using whole or filleted sole, proceed as for *Sole Bercy* (above), but add finely chopped mushrooms. Dish, reduce the stock, bind it with a little fish *velouté*, thicken with butter, pour it over the fish, and brown it quickly.

Sole bordelaise. Poach the sole or the fillets flat with red wine and chopped shallots and seasoning. Dish it; reduce the stock, add a little half-glaze sauce (*demi-glace*) and an appropriate amount of melted meat glaze; thicken with butter. Pour this over the sole, and surround with little pastry *bouchées* garnished with a *salpicon* of mushrooms bound with the same sauce.

Sole bourguignonne. Poach the sole or the fillets flat with red wine and butter. Dish with a *bourguignonne* sauce, and garnish.

Sole à la bretonne. Poach the soles or the fillets flat with white wine and fish *fumet.* Dish; reduce the stock, and add fresh cream. Surround the sole with cooked button mushrooms, pour the sauce over, and brown quickly. Finally, scatter some capers over the sauce, and put pastry *fleurons* round the dish.

Sole Bréval. Proceed as for *Sole bonne femme,* with the addition of roughly chopped tomato.

Sole Byron. Poach the sole with red wine, whole. Dish it, and garnish with button mushrooms. Cover with *sauce génoise* with truffles, to which the stock of the sole has been added. Surround with heart-shaped *croûtons* of fried bread.

Sole cancalaise. Poach the sole or the fillets flat with mushroom stock and oyster water. Dish; garnish with poached and bearded oysters, prawns or shrimps, and button mushrooms. Cover with white wine sauce, and brown quickly.

Sole cardinal. Cover the fillets with fish forcemeat, fold them over, and poach them. Dish them with a surround of slices of lobster tail, cover with *sauce cardinal* (page 46), and put a few slices of truffle on top.

Sole carême. Poach the sole with white wine and fish *fumet,* whole. Dish, and garnish with poached and bearded oysters and poached slices of soft roe. Cover with a white wine sauce flavoured with celery, and surround with little puff-pastry *fleurons.*

Sole Carmen. Grill the sole whole. Dish it, and lay on it strips of sweet red pepper and tarragon leaves. Serve separately a *maître-d'hôtel* butter, slightly flavoured with tomato and mixed with small dice of sweet red pepper.

Sole Castiglione. Prepare fillets as for *Dugléré* (see *Turbotin Dugléré,* (page 171), adding mussels and truffles.

Sole à la catalane. Roll the fillets in *paupiettes* and poach them with white wine and mushroom stock. Put each *paupiette* in a small scooped-out tomato which has been poached in the oven, and garnish with a mash (*fondue*) of onions. Cover with *Bercy* sauce and brown quickly.

Sole Carvalho. Poach the fillets flat with white wine. Dish them, cover them with *sauce béarnaise* to which you have added the reduced stock of the sole, and decorate with blanched tarragon leaves. Put at each end of the serving dish a heap of roughly chopped tomatoes stewed in butter.

Sole Caylus. Poach the sole, whole. Dish it, and surround it with tomato halves which have been stewed in butter and are garnished with a fine *julienne* of carrot, celery and the white part of leeks. Cover with *sauce mornay* and brown quickly.

Sole Cécilia. Cook the fish (whole or filleted) *à la meunière* (page 24). Surround it with asparagus tips bound with butter. Sprinkle with a mixture of breadcrumbs and grated cheese, then with melted butter, and brown in the oven.

Sole au Chambertin. Poach the sole with Chambertin, whole. Dish it; bind the stock with blended butter, cover the sole with it, and surround it with small fried gudgeon.

Sole à la Chambord: see *Carpe à la Chambord* (page 84), and proceed in the same way, being careful to keep to the same proportions.

Sole au champagne. Poach the sole or the fillets flat with champagne. Dish them, cover them with white wine sauce to which has been added the reduced stock from the sole, and surround them with small fried gudgeon.

Sole aux champignons. Poach the sole or the fillets flat with white wine and mushroom stock. Dish them; surround them with cooked button mushrooms, and cover them with white wine sauce to which has been added the reduced stock of the sole.

Sole Chauchat. Poach the sole or the fillets flat with white wine and fish *fumet*. Dish it, and surround with slices of freshly boiled potatoes. Cover with white wine sauce to which the reduced stock of the sole has been added, and brown quickly.

Sole Cherbourg. This consists of stuffed and folded fillets poached with white wine and mussel stock. Dress them in a turban shape, and garnish the middle with a *salpicon* of prawns or shrimps, oysters and mussels bound with white wine sauce. Cover the fillets with shrimp sauce.

Sole Chérubin. Fold the fillets and poach them with white wine. Place each on a boat garnished with mushrooms *à la crème*, cover with white wine sauce, and on each fillet make a criss-cross decoration with thin strips of smoked salmon.

Sole Choisy. Poach the sole or the fillets flat with white wine. Dish them, and surround them with a *chiffonade* of lettuce melted in butter and thin *julienne* shreds of truffle. Mask with white wine sauce and surround with *fleurons*.

Sole cingalaise. Fold and poach the fillets with white wine. Lay them on a bed of pilaff rice (page 37), to which you have added sweet red peppers cut in dice. Cover with a curry sauce.

Sole Clara Ward. Fry the sole or the fillets *à la meunière* (page 24). Dish it; surround it with diced or olive-shaped pieces of celeriac stewed in butter and diced artichoke bottoms tossed in butter. Pour over some foaming butter at the last.

Sole Clarence. Spread on the fillets some whiting forcemeat flavoured with anchovy purée, roll them in *paupiettes* and poach them with fish *fumet*. Arrange them in a crown, garnish the centre with poached soft roes and shelled prawns or shrimps, cover with white wine sauce, and decorate with anchovy fillets.

Sole Claudine. Stuff the fillets with forcemeat, fold them and poach them with white wine, a *mirepoix bordelaise* (page 34), roughly chopped tomato, and lobster broth. Dish in little oval cases garnished with a *salpicon* of lobster bound with *sauce américaine*. Strain the stock, reduce it, thicken it with butter, and cover the fillets with it. Scatter over them at the last a little chopped parsley.

Sole Colbert. Raise the fillets on the skinned side of a sole so as to expose the backbone, and break the bone in two or three places in order to facilitate its removal when the fish is cooked. Egg-and-breadcrumb the fish, press the fillets down again, and fry it in deep fat. When it is cooked, remove the pieces of backbone, and stuff the inside with *maître-d'hôtel* butter.

Sole Coquelin. Cover the fillets with fish forcemeat flavoured with re-duced tomato, add an oyster for each fillet, and fold them over. Poach them with white wine, and dish each on a tomato stewed in butter. Cover with white wine sauce, decorate each fillet with a slice of truffle, and brown quickly.

Coquilles de soles Saint-Jacques. Cut the filleted soles in slices or thin strips, and poach them with white wine and fish *fumet*. Drain them and put them in scallop shells, with slices of lobster tails stiffened in butter, and cooked minced mushrooms. Reduce the stock, finish it as in *Sole bonne femme* (page 146), pour it over the contents of the shells, and brown quickly.

Sole aux courgettes. Cook in butter some minced baby vegetable marrows and roughly chopped parsley, adding chopped rosemary and basil. Lay a sole on a buttered shallow fireproof dish, cover it with this mixture, sprinkle it with brown breadcrumbs and melted butter, and cook in the oven. On serving, add lemon juice and chopped parsley.

Sole Montorgeuil. Poach the fillets flat with white wine and mushroom stock. Dish them; cover them with *mornay* sauce, sprinkle them with grated cheese, and brown quickly. Surround them with a ribbon of tomato sauce, and at each end of the dish arrange a small heap of baby vegetable marrows (*courgettes*) *à la crème*. (This recipe is acknowledged to M. Cochois.)

Sole aux crevettes. Poach the sole with white wine, whole. Dish it, and surround with peeled prawns. Cover with prawn or shrimp sauce. Down the middle of the sole stick a row of prawns with their tails peeled.

Sole Crillon. Poach the fillets with white wine, and arrange them on the serving dish alternately with thin slices of lobster tails. Add to the stock equal parts of *sauce américaine* and thick fresh cream. Reduce it, thicken it with butter, and finish with a liqueur glassful of brandy and a touch of cayenne. Cover the fillets with this sauce, put several slices of truffle on each, and surround them with *fleurons*. (This recipe is acknowled to A. Argentié.)

Croustade de sole marquise. Fold the fillets and poach them in butter. Garnish a very low *vol-au-vent* crust with *Nantua quenelles*: that is, *quenelles* flavoured with crayfish, crayfish tails, and mushrooms bound with *sauce normande*. Cover with *Nantua* sauce, and arrange the fillets with a fine slice of truffle on each.

Sole Cubat. Poach the fish (whole or filleted) with fish *fumet*. Arrange them on a fairly thick mushroom purée, with slices of truffle on them.

Cover with *mornay* sauce, sprinkle with grated cheese, and brown quickly.

Sole à la Daumont. Raise the fillets of the sole on the skinned side, so as to be able to withdraw the backbone without damaging the shape of the fish. Stuff the inside with fish forcemeat made with the addition of a crayfish broth, press back the fillets so as to shut in the forcemeat, turn the fish over on to a buttered dish (that is, stuffed side down), and poach it with white wine and mushroom stock. Arrange the sole on the serving dish, cover it with shrimp sauce, and surround it with the following garnish: large mushrooms stewed in butter and garnished with a *salpicon* of crayfish tails, truffled *quenelles*, and slices of soft roes egg-and-breadcrumbed and fried.

Sole dauphine. Fold the fillets in half, poach them in butter, wipe them, and cover them with *sauce Villeroy* (page 50). When they are cold and the sauce is set, egg-and-breadcrumb them and fry them in clarified butter. Dish them in a crown, and put in the middle a *salpicon* of lobster, *quenelles*, mushrooms, and truffles bound with white wine sauce. Hand a *Nantua* sauce separately.

Sole deauvillaise. Poach the sole (whole) with four ounces of onion stewed in butter but not browned, and with thin cream. Dish it; pass the stock through a sieve, and finish it with butter and fresh cream. Cover the sole with this sauce, and surround it with *fleurons* of puff pastry.

Délice de sole marquise de Polignac. For this you will want a sole weighing about a pound and three quarters. Skin it on both sides, and fillet it. Keep the backbone, leaving the head on. Cut the fillets diagonally in half, beat them a little so as to soften the fibres, and spread them with a fine forcemeat of whiting seasoned with paprika pepper, to which you have added the raw hard or soft roe of a lobster passed through a fine tammy. Put the backbone of the sole on a thickly buttered dish, arrange the fillets on it, season them, moisten them with Pommery, and poach them gently. Now drain the fillets, take the backbone from the dish and put it on the serving dish, and on it lay the eight fillets in two rows with eight peeled and cooked mushrooms in the middle. Reduce the stock by three quarters, add four dessertspoonfuls of fresh cream, take the pan from the fire, and finish with four dessertspoonfuls of *hollandaise* sauce. Pass the sauce through muslin. Cover the fillets (which have been kept hot) with this sauce, and garnish them with eight fine trussed crayfish, which have been cooked in a highly seasoned *nage* (page 34).

NOTE: The fillets should be coated with the sauce only at the very last minute.

Sole dieppoise. Poach the sole or the fillets flat with white wine. Dish them; surround them with prawns or shrimps, mushrooms, and mussels. Cover with white wine sauce and brown quickly.

Sole dorée. Fry the sole (whole) *à la meunière* (page 24) in clarified butter, seeing that it is nice and golden on each side. Serve as it is, drained, with slices of peeled lemon.

Sole Doria. Fry the sole or the fillets *à la meunière* (page 24). Garnish with little heaps of cucumber cut olive-shaped, stewed in butter and bound with cream.

Sole Dugléré. For this dish you use a large sole, either cut in slices across or cooked whole. Follow the recipe for *Turbotin Dugléré* (page 171).

Sole à la Duse. Stuff the fillets, fold them, and poach them with fish *fumet*. Arrange them in a turban shape on a bed of pilaff rice (page 37), and garnish the centre with shelled prawns or shrimps bound with *Nantua* sauce. Cover generously with a thin *mornay* sauce, and brown quickly.

Sole Édouard. Poach the fillets flat with white wine and fish *fumet*. Arrange them on a very fine *salpicon* of lobster and truffles bound with an equal amount of mushroom purée. Cover with *Bercy* sauce made red with lobster shells, and brown quickly.

Épigrammes de filets de sole. Stuff, fold, and poach the fillets. Let them get cold, then egg-and-breadcrumb them and grill them gently. Dress in a turban with a sauce or garnish of some kind in the middle, the name of the garnish being stated in the name of the dish: e.g. *Épigrammes de filets de sole à la dieppoise*.

Sole à la fécampoise. Sole or fillets poached flat with white wine and the stock of mussels. Dish them, garnish them with mussels and shrimps, and cover with *Joinville* sauce. Surround with soft roes egg-and-breadcrumbed and fried.

Sole à la florentine. Poach the sole or the fillets flat with fish *fumet*. Dish on a bed of leaf spinach stewed in butter. Cover with *mornay* sauce to which you have added the reduced stock from the sole, sprinkle with grated cheese, and brown quickly.

Sole à la française. Poach the sole (whole) with white wine and fish *fumet*. Dish it, and cover it lengthways, one half with white wine sauce and the other half with *sauce vénitienne*. Surround with little croustades made of Duchesse potato (page 36) garnished with mussels *à la poulette* (page 201), and with trussed crayfish cooked in *court-bouillon*.

Sole François-Premier. Stuff the fillets with a mousseline of lobster, fold them, and poach them in fish *fumet*. Serve them on half-aubergines garnished with a *chasseur* garnish (minced mushrooms tossed in butter with chopped shallots and parsley), and cover them with tomato-flavoured *béarnaise* sauce. Pour round the reduced stock, to which you have added some fresh cream.

Sole Gallia. Poach the sole or the fillets flat with mushroom stock. Dish them; garnish them with *julienne* shreds of mushrooms and truffles; cover them with a creamy white wine sauce, and surround the dish with little round scalloped *croûtons* fried in butter.

Sole Galliéra. Proceed as for *Sole Choisy* (page 149), replacing the *iulienne* of truffles by a *julienne* of mushrooms.

Sole grand duc. Stuff the fillets, fold them, and poach them with mushroom cooking liquor. Arrange them in turban shape, cover them with *mornay* sauce, and brown them quickly. Garnish the centre with asparagus tips bound with butter, and surround them with stuffed and poached crayfish heads.

Sole grand prix. These should be fine fillets poached flat in a fine white wine and butter. Dish, and cover with *sauce vénitienne*. Arrange on the sole some mushrooms coated with prawn sauce, and surmounted by a piece of truffle cut to represent a jockey's cap. (This recipe is acknowledged to E. Kientz.)

Sole Granville. The sole or the fillets flat are poached in fish *fumet*. They are dished and garnished with prawns or shrimps, mushrooms, and truffles, and covered with white wine sauce. The dish should be bordered with little *canapés* spread with soft roe butter (page 42).

Sole au gratin. Cover the bottom of a shallow fireproof dish with rather thick *Duxelles* sauce (page 31). Lay the sole or the fillets on it, surround them with raw mushrooms cut in rather thick slices and over-lapping each other, put on the sole itself a few cooked mushrooms, cover with *Duxelles* sauce, sprinkle with browned breadcrumbs, dot with butter, and brown in the oven. (See notes on *Complete Gratin*, page 28) On taking from the oven, add lemon juice and chopped parsley.

Sole Grimaldi. Garnish the bottom of a timbale crust with spaghetti bound with butter and cream, and add the flesh from a lobster tail cut in dice. Add six cooked paupiettes of sole, and cover them with prawn or shrimp sauce. Cover with more spaghetti, add another six paupiettes, and finish with a layer of the sauce. Put the lid on the timbale, and serve it on a napkin.

Sole Henriette. Bake some large waxy potatoes in their jackets. Cut a slice from the skin, and withdraw the pulp from the inside without breaking the skin. Now fill the skins two-thirds full with a *salpicon* of poached fillets of sole bound with white wine sauce seasoned with paprika pepper. Cover with *mornay* sauce, sprinkle with chopped nuts, and brown quickly. Serve on a napkin.

Sole aux huîtres. Poach the sole or the fillets flat. Dish them; surround with poached and bearded oysters, and mask with white wine sauce to which the reduced stock of the oysters has been added.

Sole Île de France. Poach the sole (whole), dish it, and surround it with *julienne* shreds of mushroom and truffle. Cover with *Bercy* sauce, brown quickly, and at each end of the dish lay a heap of asparagus tips bound with butter and a heap of roughly chopped tomatoes stewed in butter.

Sole à l'indienne. Fold the fillets, poach them, and lay them on a bed of rice *à l'indienne* to which you have added peeled and splintered fresh almonds. Cover with curry sauce.

Sole Jean-Bart. Arrange in a dome shape on a dish a *salpicon* of prawns or shrimps, mushrooms, and little mussels, bound with thick Béchamel sauce. On this arrange raw and well-flattened fillets of sole, sprinkle with melted butter, and poach them in a cool oven.

Now cover with white wine sauce, sprinkle with chopped truffle, and surround with large mussels put back in their shells, covered with *mornay* sauce, and browned.

Sole Joinville. Mask the fillets with a mousseline of fish (page 32). Fold them, and poach them with mushroom stock. Arrange them in a turban shape on a *salpicon* of prawns or shrimps, mushrooms, and truffles, bound with *Joinville* sauce. Cover with the same sauce, put a slice of truffle on each fillet, and stick a small crayfish on top.

Sole Judic. Fold the fillets and poach them. Arrange them in a crown, putting each on a small braised lettuce half. Garnish the centre with small fish *quenelles*, cover with *mornay* sauce, and brown quickly.

Sole en julienne. Cut the fillets in thin *julienne* shreds. Dip them in milk and then in flour, and fry them in very hot deep fat. Arrange them in a heap on the serving dish on a napkin with fried parsley.

NOTE: Instead of being fried in deep fat, the fish can be fried in clarified butter.

Soles Jules Janin. Remove the backbone of a large raw sole. Garnish the inside with a mousseline of whiting to which plenty of *Duxelles* and *fines herbes* (page 32) have been added. Press the fillets back, and arrange down the join a line of slices of mushrooms and truffles alternately. Braise the sole with Rhine wine, and when it is dished reduce the stock, thicken with butter, enrich with cream, and pour it over the fish, browning it quickly.

Sole Ledoyen. Butter a shallow fireproof dish, and strew in it two chopped shallots, a dessertspoonful of roughly chopped parsley, and two minced mushrooms. Add two dessertspoonfuls of white wine and as much fish *fumet*, and the juice of a quarter of a lemon. Season the sole (whole), lay it on this bed skinned side down, sprinkle it with very finely sieved white breadcrumbs, pour over some melted butter, and put it in the oven. At the end of ten minutes surround the sole with shelled cooked Dublin Bay prawns' tails (*langoustines*), a few dice of truffle, two dessertspoonfuls of thick cream, and a thin ribbon of melted meat glaze. Put in the oven for another five minutes, so that the whole is a nice golden brown. If you like, you can add, on serving, a surround of heart-shaped *croûtons* of bread fried in butter.

Sole louisiane. Cook the sole (whole) *à la meunière* (page 24). On serving, arrange on it rounds of bananas and sweet peppers fried in butter, surround it with a ribbon of tomato sauce, and pour over some foaming butter. Finally, sprinkle it with chopped chervil and tarragon.

Sole mâconnaise. Proceed as for *Sole bourguignonne* (page 147), using a good Mâcon instead of Burgundy.

Sole marchand de vins. Proceed as for *Sole Bercy* (page 146), using red wine instead of white.

Sole maréchal. Poach the sole (whole) with fish *fumet*. Dish it, and surround it with little heaps of mushroom *salpicon* and of roughly chopped tomatoes stewed in butter. Reduce the stock, thicken it with butter and a little fish glaze, cover the fish with it, and brown quickly.

Sole Marguéry. Poach the fillets flat with white wine and fish *fumet*. Dish them, and surround them with mussels and shrimps. Cover with a very creamy white wine sauce, and brown quickly.

Sole marinière. Poach the sole or the fillets flat with white wine and the stock of mussels. Dish, surround with mussels, and cover with *Bercy* sauce to which the reduced stock of the sole has been added.

Sole à la marseillaise. Proceed as for *Sole au vin blanc* (page 164), with the sauce flavoured with saffron.

Sole à la meunière. Flour the sole or fillets, and fry them in clarified butter. Arrange on a dish bordered with decorative slices of lemon, sprinkle lightly with lemon juice, scatter over some roughly chopped parsley, and cover with nutbrown butter.

NOTE: Whole soles and filleted soles *à la meunière* may be garnished as desired. The name of the garnish will follow the word *meunière*, e.g. *Sole meunière à l'orange, aux champignons*, etc.

Sole mexicaine. Roll the fillets in paupiettes, poach them with white wine and fish *fumet*, arrange them on large grilled mushrooms, garnished with roughly chopped tomato which has been stewed in butter with okra and sweet peppers cut in dice. Cover with white wine sauce, and surround with a ribbon of tomato sauce.

Sole Mirabeau. Poach the fillets flat. Arrange them side by side, and cover each alternate one with white wine sauce, the others with *sauce bourguignonne.* Make a little thread of white sauce on the red, and of red sauce on the white, and decorate with anchovy fillets and blanched tarragon leaves arranged in a cross.

Sole Miroton. Poach the fillets flat with white wine and fish *fumet.* Dish them on a rather creamy mushroom purée, and scatter on the fillets some roughly chopped *fines herbes* (page 32). Cover with highly seasoned *Bercy* sauce and brown quickly. (This recipe is acknowledged to Alamagnie.)

Sole Mogador. Spread the fillets with a fine fish forcemeat and with a slice of truffle at the end, fold them, and poach them with white wine and fish *fumet.* Arrange them in turban shape on a border of mousseline forcemeat, and put in the middle a *Nantua* garnish bound with *Nantua* sauce. Cover with the same sauce and surround with trussed crayfish cooked in *court-bouillon.*

Sole Moïna. Fold the fillets, flour them, cook them in butter in a sauté dish, and dish them in turban shape. Swill the pan with port wine mixed with a little meat glaze, thicken this with butter, and pour it over the fillets. Garnish the centre with small quarters of artichokes, and morels *à la crème.*

NOTE: Morels (*morilles*), which are a sponge-like fungus, can be occasionally found in England in the spring; but they can be bought dried, and only need soaking to be cooked in the same way as the fresh ones, though the dried ones are not, of course, so delicious.

Sole monseigneur. Poach the sole (whole) with Chambertin. Dish it, reduce the stock, thicken it with butter, and cover the sole with it. Surround by *quenelles* made of mousseline forcemeat, truffles, and very small poached eggs.

Sole Montreuil. Poach the sole or the fillets flat with white wine and mushroom stock. Dish, and surround with little potato balls steamed or boiled. Cover with white wine sauce.

Sole Montrouge. Fold the fillets and poach them. Arrange them on boats which have been garnished with a *salpicon* of prawns and mushrooms bound with prawn or shrimp sauce. Cover the fillets, half with white wine sauce and half with shrimp sauce, and place a nice white cooked decorative slice of mushroom on each fillet.

Sole Mornay. Poach the sole or fillets flat with fish *fumet.* When dished, cover it with *mornay* sauce, sprinkle with grated cheese, and brown quickly.

Sol aux moules. Poach the sole or fillets flat with white wine and the stock of mussels. Dish surrounded by mussels, cover with white wine sauce and brown quickly.

Sole Murat. Cut the fillets in strips the size of a gudgeon, and fry them in butter. Mix with them the same quantity of potatoes and artichoke bottoms, also fried in butter. Serve in a timbale, sprinkled with roughly chopped parsley and with nutbrown butter poured over at the last.

Sole à la Nantua. Poach the sole or fillets flat. Dish them, and surround with a *Nantua* garnish (page 38). Cover with *Nantua* sauce.

Sole narbonnaise. Fry the sole (whole) *à la meunière* (page 24). Dish it, and surround with minced mushrooms fried in butter, and little potatoes cooked *à la parisienne* (see below). Sprinkle with nutbrown butter, and scatter over some chopped *fines herbes.*

NOTE: *Pommes parisienne* are potatoes cut in pieces a little smaller than a hazelnut. These are seasoned and cooked in butter until golden. When they are cooked, they are rolled in melted meat glaze and sprinkled with chopped parsley.

Sole Nelson. Poach the sole or fillets flat with fish *fumet.* Dish them, cover with white wine sauce, and brown quickly. Put a heap of *pommes noisette* at each end of the dish, and surround the fish with soft roes egg-and-breadcrumbed and fried. *Pommes noisette* are potatoes cut to the size and shape of a hazelnut and cooked golden in butter.

Sole Newburg. Poach the sole or the fillets flat. Dish them and surround them with slices of lobster prepared *à la Newburg* (page 195), cover with Newburg sauce, and put some slices of truffle over the sauce.

Sole niçoise. Poach the sole (whole), dish it, and cover it with white wine sauce finished with anchovy essence. Surround it with heaps of roughly chopped stewed tomatoes, and on the sole lay some olives stuffed with anchovy butter.

Sole normande. Poach the sole or the fillets flat with white wine and the stock of mussels. Arrange on the serving dish with a *normande* garnish (page 39), and cover with *normande* sauce.

Sole opéra. Roll the fillets in *paupiettes*, and poach them with white wine and mushroom stock. Lay each *paupiette* in a tartlet garnished with asparagus tips bound with butter, and put a slice of truffle on top of it. Surround the *paupiettes* with a thread of buttered meat glaze.

Sole Orly. Season the fillets and egg-and-breadcrumb them, or if you wish, dip them in frying batter: there is no strict rule about this. Fry them in deep fat, serve them on a napkin with fried parsley, and hand a tomato sauce with them.

Sole ostendaise. Fold the fillets, and poach them with white wine and the liquor from the oysters which you are to use in the garnish. Arrange them in turban shape, garnish the middle with poached oysters, cover with *normande* sauce, and surround with little quoit-shaped croquettes made with a *salpicon* of fillets of sole, truffles, and mushrooms, bound with a thick Béchamel sauce.

Sole Otéro. Bake some large waxy potatoes in their jackets, cut a slice off their sides, and remove the pulp. Fill the scooped-out shells three parts full with a *salpicon* of lobster, place in each a folded and poached fillet of sole, cover with *mornay* sauce, and brown quickly in the oven. Put a slice of truffle on each fillet, and serve.

Sole parisienne. Poach the fillets flat with white wine. Dish them surrounded by minced mushrooms and slices of truffle, cover with white wine sauce, and border with little potatoes *à la parisienne* (page 158) and trussed cooked crayfish.

Sole sur planche. Cook the sole (whole) *à la meunière.* Put it in a paper bag (*papilotte*), with a thread of *béarnaise* sauce down the middle and slices of truffles. Close the paper bag, set it on an ebony 'plank' which has been heated beforehand, and let the bag brown in the oven.

Sole portugaise. Poach the sole or the fillets flat with white wine and fish *fumet.* Dish them, surround with a stew (*fondue*) of tomatoes with cooked minced mushrooms added, cover with white wine sauce, and brown quickly. Sprinkle some chopped *fines herbes* on top.

Sole Prat. Poach the fillets flat. Dish them and surround them with small cooked mushrooms. Treat as for *Sole au vin blanc* (page 164), but use Noilly-Prat Vermouth instead of the white wine.

Sole Prince Albert. Fold the fillets in boat shape, and poach them with white wine. Dish, cover with prawn or shrimp sauce, and put a small peeled mushroom on each fillet.

Sole Prunier. Poach the fillets with white wine and mushroom stock. Dish them, and surround with poached and bearded oysters. Place over them peeled mushrooms and slices of truffle, and cover with a white wine sauce. (This recipe is acknowledged to A. Lenoble.)

Sole Rachel. Spread some fillets with fish forcemeat with slices of truffle stuck in it, and poach them flat, taking great care in doing so. Cover the serving dish with shrimp sauce, arrange the fillets on the sauce, and surround them with heaps of asparagus tips bound with butter. Stick a prawn with its tail peeled on each fillet.

Sole régence. Poach the sole or the fillets flat with a good white wine. Dish, surround with a *régence* garnish, and cover with a thin white wine sauce.

Sole Rémoi. Cook the fish *à la meunière* (page 24). Dish it on a fine truffled purée of mushrooms, and sprinkle with nutbrown butter. Add a few slices of truffle before serving.

Sole Richelieu. Prepare this in the same manner as *Sole Colbert* (page 149), and cook whole in clarified butter. Garnish the inside of the fish with *maître-d'hôtel* butter, and put a line of truffle slices on the fish.

Sole Riviéra. Cut the fillets in strips the size of a gudgeon, and fry them in butter. Mix with artichoke bottoms and mushrooms (both cut in a thick *julienne*) which have also been fried in butter, and toss the three ingredients together for a minute or two to make sure of their mixing well. Dish them, and add a small heap of roughly chopped fresh tomatoes stewed in butter. At the last pour over some foaming butter, and finish with a squeeze of lemon juice.

Sole rochelaise. Poach the sole or the fillets flat with red wine and chopped onion cooked in butter. Dish, and surround with poached mussels, oysters, and soft roes. Cover with the reduced stock lightly bound with blended butter (page 42) and thickened with butter. Put round a border of small *croûtons* fried in butter.

Sole Rossini. Spread the fillets with fish forcemeat to which has been added a quarter of its volume of *foie gras* purée. Roll them in *paupiettes*, and poach them in some very good white wine. Dish them, cover them with white wine sauce, and scatter chopped truffle over. Surround by very small tartlets stuffed with the same forcemeat as was used for the fillets, this having been cooked on each tartlet in a cool oven. On top of each tartlet put an olive-shaped truffle.

Sole rouennaise. Proceed exactly as for *Sole rochelaise.* When the fish is covered with the sauce, surround it with small smelt egg-and-breadcrumbed and fried, trussed crayfish, and small heart-shaped *croûtons* fried in butter.

Sole royale Montceau. Fold the fillets, and poach them with white wine and fish *fumet.* Garnish the bottom of a low croustade with *quenelles* of pike and slices of lobster tail on each *quenelle.* Cover with *sauce armoricaine,* add the fillets of sole, and put slices of truffle on them.

Sole à la russe. Poach the sole (whole) with white wine with the addition of vegetables designated *à la russe*: that is to say, grooved and very thin rounds of carrot, and fine slices of a small onion. Dish the sole, cover it with white wine sauce to which you have added tiny sprigs of chervil, and brown quickly.

Sole Saint-Germain. Brush the sole or fillets with melted butter, roll in fine white breadcrumbs, and grill them gently. Serve surrounded by *pommes noisette* (page 158), and on the fish lay some blanched tarragon leaves. Hand a *béarnaise* sauce separately.

Soufflé de filets de sole royal. Cut the fillets in strips the size of a gudgeon, poach them with Barsac, and drain them. Add some *fumet* of sole to the stock, reduce it to a glaze, and roll the fillets in it. Prepare a cheese soufflé mixture, using half Cheshire and half Parmesan cheese, and put this and the fillets of sole in alternate layers in a buttered timbale. Finish with a layer of the mixture, and cook like ordinary soufflé. Serve separately a white wine sauce made with Barsac.

Soles soufflées. For six people you will want six small sole each weighing about six or seven ounces. Fillet them, trim the backbones, and put these in a buttered dish with a little fish *fumet*; put them in the oven for a few minutes, and keep them by. Pound six of the fillets, adding a little pike or turbot flesh, with seasoning and a small white of egg. Pass through a tammy, put the forcemeat in a bowl, and work it on ice, adding three dessertspoonfuls of fresh thick cream and then six egg whites stiffly beaten. Correct the seasoning, and add a touch of cayenne. Now arrange the back bones on a dish, spread on each a layer of the forcemeat about a quarter of an inch thick, and on this bed lay the fillets, three on each backbone. Cover these with more forcemeat, smooth it over, sprinkle with clarified butter, and put into a very hot oven. Fifteen minutes, with frequent basting, will be enough. On serving, surround the dish with little *croustades* garnished with a *salpicon* of lobster, truffles, and mushrooms bound with *sauce américaine*. Hand separately a highly seasoned *normande* sauce. (This recipe is acknowledged to P. Escalle.)

Sole Suchet. Poach the fillets with white wine and fish *fumet*, adding a *julienne* of truffles and of celery and the red part of carrot stewed beforehand in butter. Dish the fillets, and cover them with white wine sauce to which has been added the *julienne* of vegetables and truffles, well drained.

Sole suédoise. Poach some macaroni, and bind it with grated cheese and butter. Poach the fillets with half white wine, half fish *fumet*. Arrange on a buttered shallow fireproof dish, sole and macaroni alternately. Cover with white wine sauce, and brown quickly.

Sole Sylvette. Poach the fillets flat with Madeira. Dish them surrounded by artichoke bottoms and minced mushrooms. Reduce the stock, thicken it with cream and butter, and pour it over the fillets.

Sole Sylvia. Roll the fillets in *paupiettes*, poach them, and dish each on an artichoke bottom. Cover with *mornay* sauce, brown quickly, and sprinkle with chopped truffle.

Sole Talleyrand. Spread a layer of spaghetti *à la crème* on the bottom of a buttered shallow fireproof dish; arrange on it the raw fillets of sole, cover with a light white wine sauce, and cook in the oven until the fillets are done. On removing from the oven, add some slices of truffles, and serve in the dish as it is.

Sole Thérèse. Roll the fillets in *paupiettes* after stuffing them with truffled whiting forcemeat. Poach them and dish them. Put a slice of truffle on each *paupiette*, surround them with little hazelnut-shaped potatoes boiled or steamed, and cover with white wine sauce flavoured with essence of truffles.

Sole thermidor. Poach the sole (whole) with white wine. Dish it, surround it with slices of cooked mushrooms, and cover it with a *Bercy* sauce flavoured with mustard.

Timbale de sole à la Bottin. Cut the fillets in strips the size of a gudgeon, and cook them as for *Sole Bercy* (page 146), adding a little meat glaze. Add slices of lobster, shelled prawns, or shrimps, and mussels, and put into the timbale. Reduce the stock, thicken it with butter, and pour it into the timbale. Serve very hot.

Sole Tosca. Mask the fillets with a mousseline forcemeat of sole to which has been added a fine *salpicon* of lobster, truffles, and mushrooms. Fold them, egg-and-breadcrumb them, fry them in oil, and arrange them in a crown. Garnish the centre with a stew (*fondue*) of tomatoes very much reduced, and surround the dish with onion rings dipped in batter and fried.

Sole trouvillaise. Poach the sole (whole). Dish it, and surround it with a *dieppoise* garnish (page 38), cover it with white wine sauce, and brown it quickly. Put a border of *fleurons* round the dish, and down the middle a row of poached oysters.

Sole Urville. Fold the fillets, and poach them: put each in a boat, and cover with *sauce américaine.*

Sole Valois. Poach the sole (whole), and dish it. Cover it with white wine sauce made with a reduction of *béarnaise* sauce, and put a ribbon of meat glaze round the dish.

Sole varsovienne. Prepare this like *Sole à la russe* (page 161), adding: (1) some little triangles (*paysanne*) of celery in the cooking mixture; and (2) a light caviar butter in the sauce.

Sole Vendôme. Poach the fillets flat. Dish them, and cover them with white wine sauce flavoured with tomato. Surround the fish with little *mousselines* of lobster.

Sole vénitienne. Poach the sole (whole) with white wine. Dish it, and serve covered with *sauce vénitienne.*

Sole Victoria. Poach the sole (whole) with fish *fumet.* Dish it, and surround it with small slices of lobster tail, cover it with *sauce Victoria,* and brown quickly. Add some slices of truffle after browning.

Sole Vierville. Poach the sole (whole) with white wine and fish *fumet.* Arrange it on a bed of fresh tomatoes which have been peeled, roughly chopped, and cooked with fish *fumet.* Season well. Reduce the stock, add a little white wine sauce and as much *hollandaise* sauce, cover the sole with it, and brown quickly. (This recipe is acknowledged to Chaumeix.)

Sole au vin blanc. Poach the sole or the fillets flat with white wine. Dish them, cover them with white wine sauce, and brown quickly.

Sole viveur. Prepare a *julienne* of celery and sweet peppers stewed in butter and finish by cooking in fish *fumet.* Poach the sole (whole) with white wine and fish *fumet*; dish it, surround it with the *julienne* of celery and sweet peppers, and a *julienne* of mushrooms and truffles. Cover with fairly highly seasoned *sauce américaine,* and put slices of lobster on the sauce. Serve very hot.

Sole Walewska. Garnish the fillets with slices of lobster and of truffles, fold them, and poach them with fish *fumet.* Arrange them in the dish, cover them with *mornay* sauce, and brown them quickly.

Sole Wilhelmine. Bake some large waxy potatoes in their jackets, remove a slice of the skin, and take out the pulp without breaking the skins. Fold and poach the sole fillets in fish *fumet.* Garnish the scooped-out potatoes with a purée of baby marrows *à la crème,* and poached oysters. Then put a fillet in each, cover with *mornay* sauce, and brown quickly.

Cold Fillets of Sole

Aspic de filets de sole. (1) Poach the fillets, let them get cold, and decorate them according to taste. Line a mould with fine white fish jelly, and arrange the fillets in it, placing them upright along the sides. Garnish the empty space inside with a *salpicon* of fillets of sole, mushrooms, and crayfish tails. Finish by filling up the mould with the jelly, and let it set. Turn it out when wanted on a dish bordered with pieces of jelly.

Sturgeon

Tunny

Aspic de filets de sole. (2) Spread the fillets with truffled fish forcemeat, roll them in *paupiettes*, poach them, and let them get cold. Line a mould with jelly, and arrange the *paupiettes* in it, alternately with *quenelles* truffled and decorated. Finish as above.

Filets de sole moscovite. (1) Make some small *paupiettes* stuffed with creamy fish forcemeat, poach them, let them get cold, and coat them with jelly. Make some small cases from thick slices of blanched cucumber by hollowing them out and grooving them (like cogwheels) outside. Fill these with the *paupiettes*, and surround them when dished with a thin border of fresh caviar. Hand separately a mayonnaise sauce to which have been added some lobster flesh cut in dice and some caviar.

Filets de sole moscovite. (2) Make a border of cold lobster mousse. On it arrange, alternately, small fillets of sole stuffed with the same mousse, folded, and poached; *médaillons* of lobster flesh coated with jellied mayonnaise and decorated as you like. On each fillet place a mushroom stuck with a prawn. Cover the whole thing thickly with jelly. Garnish the middle with tomatoes, peeled, scooped out, and garnished with prawns or shrimps bound with mayonnaise. Hand separately a green sauce.

STURGEON (*ESTURGEON*)

The sturgeon is a migratory fish like the salmon, and is found especially in the great rivers of Russia. It is in season from March to July. Its principal importance lies in the fact that its roe supplies the world-famous caviar. Its flesh, which is firm and dry, needs a good deal of culinary skill to make it palatable.

Esturgeon basquaise. Thin slices of raw sturgeon, seasoned and egg-and-breadcrumbed like an *escalope* of veal, are cooked gently in clarified butter, and served garnished with braised fennel. *Béarnaise* sauce is handed with this dish.

NOTE: The fennel is of course the Florence fennel or *finocchio*.

Esturgeon à la bordelaise. Braise a piece of sturgeon with white wine, let it get cold, and cut it in thin slices. Arrange these slices on a dish, surround them with stoned olives, peeled mushrooms cooked, and button onions stewed in butter. Cover the whole with a white jelly made with the stock. At the time of serving, surround the dish with little tartlets filled with caviar.

NOTE: A salad of celery, beetroot, and horseradish may be served at the same time.

Darne d'esturgeon à la bourgeoise. Take a cutlet from the sturgeon, not too thick. Season it with salt and pepper, and put it in a baking dish which you have already garnished with minced carrot, onion, and celery and with a few parsley stalks. Moisten moderately with white wine and fish *fumet*, and braise gently. When cooked, remove the cutlet and dish it. Stain the stock, reduce it by half, bind it with blended butter (page 42), and add to it several dessertspoonfuls of fresh cream. Skin the piece of sturgeon, cover it with this sauce, and surround it with little potatoes cut in the shape of olives and boiled in salted water.

Fricandeau d'esturgeon. Cut the sturgeon in slices about an inch and a half thick, and lard them like a *fricandeau* of veal. Braise them in just the same way as the meat is braised. This *fricandeau* is accompanied by the stock and any garnish you think suitable – for example, little glazed onions, stuffed olives, and so on.

NOTE: During Lent, the *fricandeau* of sturgeon can be served with a vegetable such as spinach, sorrel, celery, little marrows, *gratinées* potatoes, *cèpes*, morels (*morilles*), and so on.

STERLET

This fish, which also comes from the rivers of Russia, is much appreciated by the gourmets of that country, but it is rarely seen in Paris or London. It belongs to the same family as the sturgeon, and the same recipes can also apply to it. The eggs of the sterlet furnish a very fine caviar, and its marrow, like that of the sturgeon, supplies the *vésiga* which is so essential an ingredient of the *Coulibiac* (page 34).

TUNNYFISH (*THON*)

This fish is regularly caught on the west and Mediterranean coasts of France, and by sportsmen off the coasts of this country. Where it is fished commercially, its most important use is for preserving in oil, and this preserve makes a much appreciated *hors-d'œuvre* in various fashions. In household kitchens it is served hot in the following ways, and always in cutlets (*darnes*) about two inches thick. (It may be noted here that in French cookery the term *rouelle* is applied to the tunny cutlet instead of the more usual *darne*.)

Thon à la bonne femme. Blanch the cutlet for seven or eight minutes, drain it, wipe it, colour it in oil on both sides, and take it out. In the same oil lightly fry an onion, add a tablespoonful of flour, cook it for a few minutes, then moisten with half water and half wine (three quarters of a pint), and half a wineglassful of vinegar. Add salt and pepper, two chopped tomatoes and a *bouquet garni*. When this liquid is boiling, put back the tunny cutlet, and cook slowly for an hour. On the moment of serving, mix with the sauce a few gherkins cut in thin rounds, as well as some chopped parsley.

Thon braisé. Put the tunny in a stewpan which has been lined with large rounds of carrot and onion and a *bouquet garni*, and let it stew gently in the oven for a quarter of an hour. Add a wineglassful of white wine, reduce it almost completely, then moisten with stock to the height of the cutlet. Cook gently for an hour and a quarter. With this braised tunny you can serve a purée of sorrel or spinach, or a highly seasoned sauce. At the same time serve the stock, strained and reduced.

Thon grillé. For grilling, the cutlet ought to be thinner, about an inch thick only. Season it with salt and pepper, and marinate for an hour beforehand with a minced onion, some parsley stalks, thyme and bayleaf, oil, white wine, and lemon juice. Then wipe it dry, brush it over with oil, and grill it gently. When it is almost done, sprinkle both sides with fine browned breadcrumbs. Instead of grilling the cutlet, you can cook it in the oven if you prefer. Whichever way it is cooked, serve at the same time a *rémoulade* or *tartare* sauce.

TURBOT (*TURBOT*)

The flesh of the turbot is firm, white, and extremely palatable. It should be chosen large, with thick fillets and a very white underside. Large turbot are usually served as *relevés* for a large party, but in restaurants (and increasingly in the home as well) turbot is served in slivers and in fillets. The recipes for cooking these fillets are the same as those for chicken turbot (*turbotin*), and a large number of recipes for cooking fillets of sole can also be applied to them. But for the proper treatment of a whole turbot, a turbot kettle of the right size, with its grid, is essential.

Turbot bouilli ou poché. Having prepared the turbot for cooking, make a fairly deep incision down the backbone on the back, which is the brown side. Put the fish in the kettle, on the grid. Cover it with cold water, to which you have added milk (in proportion of one-eighth of the water) and a few slices of peeled lemon with the pips removed. Bring to the boil slowly, draw aside to a corner of the stove, where the liquid will continue just moving. Rapid boiling will do no good, as it will only result in breaking the fish. Poach for seven to ten minutes per pound according to the thickness of the fish. To serve the turbot, slide it gently from the grid on to a napkin in the serving dish, and surround it with parsley. It is advisable to smear the surface of the fish with a piece of butter to give it brilliance. With it should be served steamed or boiled potatoes, and one or two of the following sauces: *hollandaise*, *mousseline*, caper, shrimp, lobster, *vénitienne*, *béarnaise*, white wine, *américaine*, or melted butter, *maître-d'hôtel* butter, etc., etc.

Turbot Prince Albert. Braise the turbot on a bed of vegetables and herbs with a good white wine. After cooking, arrange the turbot on the serving dish and surround it by large peeled mushrooms, tartlets garnished with crayfish tails bound with *Nantua* sauce, large truffled *quenelles*, and oysters and mussels egg-and-breadcrumbed and fried. Cover the fish with white wine sauce, flavoured with oysters and with crayfish butter added. Also arrange two rows of truffles on the fish. Serve some of the same sauce separately.

Cadgery de turbot. With cold turbot, proceed as for *Cadgery de saumon* (page 128).

Turbot crème gratin. Butter a shallow fireproof dish, border it with Duchesse potatoes, making a wall about an inch and a half high, and brushing the top with egg. Put in the middle several spoonfuls of *mornay* sauce, add the flaked turbot, which has been warmed up beforehand, in sufficient quantity to come two-thirds of the way up the border of potato. Fill up with *mornay* sauce, sprinkle with grated cheese, and brown in the oven in such a way that the top of the border does not get too brown.

Coquilles de turbot. These are made in the same way as all other coquilles, with sauces such as *mornay*, or white wine, *au gratin* with *Duxelles* sauce, and so on.

Turbot jurassienne. For four persons take one three-pound turbot and fillet it. Lard the fillets with the fat of bacon and mushrooms. Leave to marinate for 12 hours in Jura wine, one glass of brandy, and one glass of red cooking port; add seasoning, a little spice, and a *bouquet garni*. Then cook it in the liquor for 12 minutes, with two mushrooms per person. Take out the fillets and place on a serving dish. Reduce the stock, bind with 2 oz. cream and 2 oz. butter at last minute; strain and pour over the fillets. Surround with *fleurons*. (This recipe was created in September 1958 by Mr Muller, Chef des Cuisines, Maison Prunier, London.)

Turbot Verilhac. For six persons you will need one four-pound turbot, 12 medium or 18 small Dublin Bay prawns, 1 12-oz. lobster, ½ lb. butter, 2 eggs, 1 pint of cream, ½ bottle of still champagne or dry white wine, a glass of brandy, salt and pepper. Cut the live lobster in pieces across and cut the head in half lengthwise, removing the pouch at the top of the head, which contains grit. Cook the lobster in butter for fifteen minutes, then singe with brandy, add half the still champagne or dry white wine, pepper, very little salt. Reduce to half a glass of liquid. When the turbot has been filleted, season the fillets and put them in a heavily buttered roasting dish, and then in a hot oven for fifteen to twenty minutes, so that they are well roasted, and from time to time moisten with their own juice and butter. Dispose them on a serving dish, preferably earthenware, dress the shelled Dublin Bay prawns on top of each fillet, and keep them hot. To the lobster and the turbot stock, add the other half of dry white wine or still champagne, and reduce this mixture. Then add to this reduction one pint of cream, and reduce again until it thickens. Add two egg yolks, on the side of the fire, so that it does not curdle, salt and pepper, pass the sauce thus obtained through a fine sieve, and pour over turbot and Dublin Bay prawns. Serve very hot. (This recipe was created in spring 1958 by M. Verilhac, Chef des Cuisines, Maison Prunier, Paris.)

CHICKEN TURBOT (*TURBOTINS*)

The following recipes are for small turbot, commonly known in England as chicken turbot, and for fillets of large turbot as spoken of on page 168.

Turbotin à l'américaine. Braise the chicken turbot, and dish it. Surf round it with large mushrooms grooved like cogwheels and slices of lobster flesh, and cover it with *sauce américaine* to which has been added the reduced stock.

Turbotin farci à l'amiral. For six people you will want a chicken turbot weighing from three to four pounds. Make an incision to the backbone on the brown side, from head to tail. Lift the fillets near the backbone so as to form a pocket, and stuff this pocket with lobster forcemeat to which have been added the raw soft roe and some very much reduced tomato purée. Draw the fillets together, so as to enclose the stuffing well. Turn the fish over, and lay it in a suitably sized dish which has been thickly buttered. Moisten with a glass of champagne, and nearly as much fish *fumet*. Cook very gently in the oven, basting frequently, for about forty minutes. Arrange the fish on the serving dish. Reduce the stock by half, and add to it as much *sauce américaine*, rather highly seasoned and finished with chopped tarragon. Cover the fish with some of the sauce, and hand the rest.

Turbotin bonne femme. Proceed exactly as for *Sole bonne femme* (page 146).

Turbotin à la Daumont. Braise it in the manner described under *Turbotin à l'amiral* (above), but do not stuff. Dish it, surround it with croquettes of crayfish tails, mushrooms, large truffled *quenelles*, and soft roes egg-and-breadcrumbed and fried. Cover with *Nantua* sauce with chopped truffles added. Border the dish with puff pastry *fleurons*. Serve the rest of the sauce separately.

Turbotin Dugléré. Braise the chicken turbot with chopped shallot, roughly chopped tomatoes, sprigs of thyme, *fines herbes* (page 32), and white wine, salt, and pepper. When cooked, dish it, reduce the cooking liquor, thicken it with butter, add to it a little white wine sauce, cover the fish, and brown quickly. With breadcrumbs fried in butter write the word '*Dugléré*' on top.

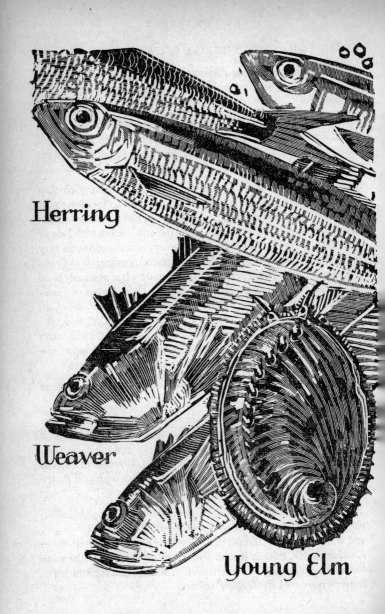

Herring

Weaver

Young Elm

Turbotin au grand vin. Braise the chicken turbot with *a grand vin:* Champagne, Sauterne, Chablis, port, sherry, etc. Dish it, reduce the braising liquor, thicken with butter, enrich with cream, and pour this sauce over the fish. Surround with puff-pastry *fleurons.*

Filets de turbotin. These fillets can be treated in every respect in the same way as fillets of sole. (See the section on Sole, pages 142–66.)

Fricassée de turbotin grand'mère. For six people you will want a chicken turbot weighing two pounds and a sole weighing one pound, each cut in pieces weighing two ounces each. Stew in butter some button onions and mushrooms cut in quarters, add three quarters of a pint of cream, and cook for ten minutes. Put in the pieces of fish, season, and cook gently for a quarter of an hour. Then take out the pieces of fish, and arrange them in the serving dish. Reduce the stock by half, bind it with two egg yolks, add lemon juice, and pour the sauce and the garnish over the pieces of fish. Surround with *croûtons* of bread fried in butter. Hand separately some mussels which have been egg-and-breadcrumbed, fried in oil, and kept very dry.

Turbotin au gratin. Proceed as for *Sole au gratin* (page 154), having regard, as to times, to the size of the fish.

Turbotin à la Mirabeau. Braise the chicken turbot with red wine. With the stock make a *genevoise* sauce. Cover the fish with this sauce, but make outside a border of white wine sauce, on which you will lay some anchovy fillets. Make a decoration in the middle of the fish with blanched tarragon leaves.

Turbotin à la parisienne. Braise the chicken turbot with white wine. Meanwhile, cook a lobster *à la nage* (page 191). Arrange the fish in the serving dish. Remove the flesh from the lobster tail without damaging the shell, and cut it in slices. Put the lobster on the turbot, brushing over the shell with melted butter to make it shine. Surround the base of the lobster shell with a mousse of whiting, on which you will arrange alternately the lobster slices and slices of poached soft roes. Serve separately some steamed potatoes and a sauceboat of *Nantua* sauce.

Turbotin régence. Braise the fish with white wine. Dish it, and surround it with *quenelles* of fish forcemeat flavoured with crayfish broth, mushrooms, slices of poached soft roes, poached oysters and slices of truffles. Cover with white wine sauce flavoured with truffle essence.

Turbotin soufflé. Loosen the fillets as described in *Turbotin à l'amiral* (page 171). Stuff the opening with a mousse or turbot or other fish, to which have been added chopped truffles and stiffly whisked egg whites. Wrap the fish in a buttered paper, and turn it over on to a buttered shallow fireproof dish. Sprinkle it with melted butter, and bake it in the oven. Lay it in the serving dish, surround it with fine whole truffles and small croquettes of truffled fish mousse. Hand separately a *hollandaise* sauce flavoured with essence of truffles.

WEEVER (*VIVE*)

A fish with firm flesh, most suitable for inclusion in a *bouillabaisse*. It is not easily come by in this country, though the Editor has lively childhood recollections of it, as a denizen (no doubt when very young and small) in seashore pools. A number of recipes from those given for whiting are applicable, but the comparative firmness of its flesh must be taken into account in calculating the time of cooking. Care must be taken in handling it, owing to its poisonous and prickly fins.

Filets de vives Bréval. Butter a dish, and put in it some minced mushrooms, chopped shallots, a few chopped onions, and some fresh tomatoes roughly chopped and with their pips removed; season with salt and pepper. Lay on this the skinned weever fillets, add a little dry white wine, cover with buttered paper, and cook in the oven. Reduce the stock, thicken it slightly with butter, add a little white wine sauce and chopped parsley, pour it over the fillets, and brown quickly.

WHITING (*MERLAN*)

The whiting has a delicate but fragile flesh, and the best way to prepare it is whole. But there are a number of recipes for fillets of whiting well worth considering. Below are given a number of recipes for this fish, whole and filleted.

Merlans à la mode anglaise. Open the fish down the back, remove the backbone, egg-and-breadcrumb them, using fresh breadcrumbs, and cook them in clarified butter. Serve *maître-d'hôtel* butter separately.

Merlans bercy. Butter a dish, sprinkle it with chopped shallot and parsley, and lay the fish on this. Season them with salt and pepper, moisten with white wine, and cook in the oven with frequent basting. Dish the whiting, reduce the cooking liquor by half, thicken it with butter, pour it over the fish, and brown quickly.

Merlans Boitelle. Prepare the whiting as for *Merlans bonne femme* (below). Arrange them in a dish bordered with *Duchesse* potato (page 36) lightly coloured in the oven, and arrange round them slices of freshly boiled potatoes.

Merlans bonne femme. Cook the whiting as indicated for *Merlans bercy*, but add minced mushrooms. Finish the sauce with a little *hollandaise* sauce, or with a yolk of egg beaten in a little water.

Merlans à la bretonne. Fry the whiting *à la meunière* (page 24): add capers and peeled shrimps, and edge the dish with slices of lemon.

Merlans à la cancalaise. Poach the fillets with white wine. Arrange them in the serving dish, surround them with peeled shrimps or prawns and poached oysters, cover them with white wine sauce or *normande* sauce, and brown quickly.

Merlans Cécilia. Fry the fillets *à la meunière* (page 24). Dish them surrounded by asparagus tips bound with butter, sprinkle with grated cheese, and brown in the oven. Add a few slices of truffle.

Merlans Colbert. Open the whiting down the back and remove the backbone, breaking it at the beginning of the head and near the tail. Season it, egg-and-breadcrumb it, and fry it in deep fat. Dish, and serve covered with *maître-d'hôtel* butter.

Merlans Crawford. This dish is cooked in the same way as *Merlans Richelieu* (page 177), the difference being that it is cooked without its head, served with a *béarnaise* sauce, and sprinkled with chopped truffles.

Merlans à la dieppoise. Poach the fillets with fish *fumet.* Dish them with a surround of shrimps, mussels, and button mushrooms. Cover with white sauce, and brown quickly.

Merlans à la diplomate. Remove the backbone as for *Merlans Colbert.* Stuff the fish with a mixture of coarsely chopped mushrooms which have been tossed in butter with chopped shallot, parsley, tarragon, and roughly chopped tomatoes, all bound with a little *mornay* sauce. Close the whiting, and poach them with a little fish *fumet.* Drain them, dish them, cover them with *mornay* sauce, sprinkle them with grated cheese, and brown quickly.

Merlans Doria. Fry the fillets *à la meunière* (page 24). Dish them, and surround them with little balls of cucumber stewed in butter and bound with cream.

Merlans au gratin. Score the whiting on the back, and proceed as for *Daurade au gratin* (page 135).

Merlans à l'hôtelière. Egg-and-breadcrumb, and fry the whiting as for *Merlans Colbert.* Dish them on *maître-d'hôtel* butter to which you have added some *Duxelles* (page 31) and a few drops of meat glaze.

Merlans Jackson. Poach the fillets with fish *fumet* and white wine. Cover the bottom of the serving dish with onion purée (*soubise*), to which you have added chopped parsley and tarragon. Drain the fillets well, and lay them on this purée. Reduce the stock, thicken it with butter, cover the fillets with it, and brown quickly.

Merlans en lorgnette (also called *Merlans en colère*). Loosen the fillets by the backbone, and break the bone just by the head. This will leave the whiting whole, but without a stiff backbone. Egg-and-bread-crumb them, roll them into *paupiette* shape, and secure them by means of a small skewer. Fry them in deep fat just before you want them, remove the skewer afterwards, and serve them on a napkin with fried parsley. Hand a light tomato sauce.

Merlans à la meunière: see page 24.

Merlans au plat. Score the whiting on the back, and lay them in a buttered, fireproof dish in which they are to be served. Moisten with fish *fumet* and white wine, add a few dabs of butter, and cook in the oven, basting them frequently until they are done. The fish should be then partly browned, and the cooking liquor reduced to a syrupy consistence.

Quenelles de merlan. These *quenelles* are made with a creamy whiting forcemeat (page 31), and are moulded with two dessertspoons dipped in hot water. Fill one of the spoons with the forcemeat, shaping it smoothly into a dome so that the *quenelle* approaches the shape of an egg. Detach it by slipping the other spoon under it, and put each *quenelle* as soon as made on a buttered baking dish. When all are done, cover them with slightly salted boiling water, and poach them for twelve minutes without letting the water boil, but keeping it just moving. Drain the *quenelles* on a cloth, arrange them in a crown on a round dish, and cover them with the sauce chosen. This may be cream, onion, white wine, *normande*, etc. They can also be covered with *mornay* sauce, sprinkled with cheese, and quickly browned.

NOTE: For this kind of *quenelle*, there are special moulds which much simplify the process.

Mousse de merlan. Pound a pound of whiting flesh with a fifth of its amount of white breadcrumbs soaked in milk and pressed, salt, and pepper, and two egg whites added very gradually. Pass through a tammy. Put the purée into a basin, and work it on ice with a spatula, mixing in about twelve tablespoonfuls of thick fresh cream little by little. Poach this forcemeat in a mould in the *bain-marie*, and serve with it whatever sauce you choose. In certain cases the forcemeat may be enriched by chopped truffle.

Mousse de merlan (cold). See cold *Mousse de saumon* (page 129), and proceed in the same way.

Merlans Richelieu. Prepare exactly as *Merlans Colbert*, but serve with a few slices of truffle on each.

Merlans verdurette. Egg-and-breadcrumb the fillets, and fry them in clarified butter. Dish them on the serving dish. Meanwhile fry some minced fresh *chanterelles* (*girolles*) or *cèpes* (see below) in oil until they are cooked and lightly browned. Drain away the oil, substitute a piece of butter, add chopped shallot and a teaspoonful each of chopped parsley, chervil, and chives, and four leaves of tarragon also chopped. Fry together for a few seconds, and pour the whole, still foaming, over the fillets. The juice of half a lemon can also be added now, if liked. (This recipe is acknowledged to P. Neveu.)

NOTE: It is unlikely that the ordinary housewife will be able to buy fresh *cèpes* or *chanterelles*; but both these fungi grow in our woods, and those who are lucky enough to live near spots where they can be found may like to try this simple recipe for themselves.

MIXED TIMBALES

Timbale argentié. (This timbale is dedicated by M. Bouzy to a former colleague.) Garnish the timbale with little *paupiettes* of sole stuffed with salmon forcemeat, poached and boned frogs' legs, sliced mushrooms, shelled prawns, all bound with a creamy and highly seasoned *sauce américaine*. Stick round the outside some prawns with their tails shelled. Serve separately rice *à la Créole*.

Timbale de Maître Escoffier. For the garnish, cook some large macaroni, keeping them rather firm. Using a paper cornet, fill the macaroni with a fine whiting forcemeat, cut them in short lengths, and poach these for a few minutes in salted water. Mix together in a cream sauce the macaroni, the white part of some scallops stewed in old brandy, and cream, mushrooms, slices of *langouste*, and *quenelles* made with whiting forcemeat.

Timbale Marivaux. Garnish the timbale with slices of lobster and crayfish tails cooked with sherry, truffled *quenelles* of salmon, little stewed morels (*morilles*) or, if they cannot be obtained, small stewed mushrooms. Mix these with a thick broth made from the shells and heads of the lobster and crayfish, thickened with cream and flavoured with a few spoonfuls of *hollandaise* sauce and a touch of paprika pepper.

Timbale Prunier. Garnish *paupiettes* of sole stuffed with fine whiting forcemeat, large mushrooms cut in slices, poached and bearded oysters, and truffles; bind with white wine sauce. (This recipe is acknowledged to A. Lenoble.)

Tourte carême. Blanch some noodles, bind them with cream, and mix them with the fillets of fish, e.g. John Dory, rockfish, turbot, or fillets of sole, cut in small slices. Bind the whole with a sauce made with the stock of mussels and of mushrooms, and finished with egg yolks and cream. Garnish the tart with this mixture; sprinkle with grated Gruyère cheese, and brown quickly just before serving.

Vol-au-vent du vendredi-saint. Garnish the *vol-au-vent* with large *quenelles* made with whatever fish forcemeat you like, shelled prawns or shrimps, mussels, and button mushrooms. Make a sauce with the stock of the mussels and mushrooms, and finish it with egg yolks and cream. Garnish the *vol-au-vent* just before you want to serve it.

MIXED FISH DISHES

La bourride. This is a regional dish from Provence, and this is how you make it for six persons. With six cloves of garlic, a pinch of salt, two egg yolks, and three quarters of a pint of olive oil, make an *aïoli* (page 231). Put a dozen slices of bread a quarter of an inch thick in a dish. Now cut in slices across (*tronçons*) three pounds of fish, such as whiting, bass, sea bream, conger, and so on; in other words, what you can get, but there should not be fewer than three varieties. Line a sauté pan with a large onion cut in rings, a sprig of fennel, and thyme, a bayleaf, and a little piece of dried orange peel. Add the fish, moisten with two and a half pints of hot water, season with salt and pepper, bring to the boil quickly, and boil for twenty minutes. Sprinkle the slices of bread with a few spoonfuls of the fish stock, just enough to soak them. Now mix eight egg yolks and six tablespoonfuls of the *aïoli* in a sauce-pan. Dilute this little by little with the rest of the fish stock strained through a fine conical sieve. Stir it on a low fire until the mixture is thick enough to coat the spoon (like an English custard), but do not let it boil or it will curdle. The result should be a smooth and very light cream. Pour it over the soaked slices of bread so that they are well covered, and serve at once, with the pieces of fish in a separate dish, and the rest of the *aïoli* in a sauce-boat.

La chaudrée charentaise. Make a very rich fish *fumet* with the bones of turbot and soles, the white part of leeks, parsley, chervil, celery, thyme, bayleaf, pepper and salt, bound with a light purée. In this *fumet* cook four-ounce pieces of turbot, John Dory, conger, rockfish, skinned and boned, for a quarter of an hour, as well as gurnard, mackerel, and small sole for eight minutes. The resulting dish should have the appearance of an Irish stew of which the liquor has been strained off. Hand separately some slices of toast, and sprinkle the dish with parsley and chervil before serving.

Grillade au fenouil. This extremely delicious dish from the south of France is simple to do, but requires a double grid with legs on each side to fit over the dish. This recipe can be applied to various fish, but it is particularly good when made with John Dory (*St-Pierre*). The fish is grilled in the usual manner, and then laid in the double grid. On a large dish a heap of dried fennel is laid, the fish on the grid is put over this, and the fennel is lighted. As it burns, the fish is turned over, so that each side receives some of the fragrant flavouring of the burning herbs. Serve with *Beurre au fenouil* (page 197).

CHAPTER EIGHT

*

Shellfish

IN culinary matters the French are far more punctilious than we are, and where we speak glibly of shellfish, they divide that wide term into shellfish (*coquillages*) and molluscs, and crustaceans (*crustacés*) such as crabs, lobsters, crayfish, *langouste*, and so on.

Here again is a great diversity of recipes which will come as a pleasant surprise to us who mostly eat our oysters raw and our lobsters cold. And while I am on the subject of oysters, let me say, without in any way belittling our own Natives (which I personally believe are second to none in the world), that it is the duty of everyone interested in food to try those oysters that come from France and while cheaper are nearly as good. In particular the *Marennes*, a greenish oyster, and the plump little *Belons*. The bright green *Portugaise* is affected by some, and the expert will find pleasure in instructing his friends in the different sorts of this delicious mollusc.

Mussels are another shellfish which ought to be enjoyed more in this country, and those who have tasted and appreciated *moules marinière*, for example, at a restaurant, will be glad to find out how to prepare them themselves.

Of the larger crustaceans, I should like to sing the praises of the *langouste*, or crayfish, which makes many admirable dishes, and is less expensive than the lobster. This creature must not be confused with the freshwater crayfish (*écrevisse*), about which I should like to add a few words. This little creature used to be easily obtainable many years ago in the Thames, and all over the country; and while it has disappeared, at any rate from the lower reaches of the Thames, it is still to be found in streams and small rivers up and down the country. Many people with a stream running through their estates still hold crayfish parties, and the house-party goes down to the stream by night to catch these little creatures. But I suspect that crayfish-catching has gone out of fashion because we have forgotten what to do with them when once they are caught, and here again is Madame Prunier offering instruction and, I hope, setting a pleasant and profitable fashion once more.

CLAMS

See directions for cooking under *hors-d'œuvre*, soups, etc.

CRABS (*CRABES*)

Crabs should be boiled in a special *court-bouillon* or *nage* for shellfish, for which a recipe is given on page 34. The time allowed should be a quarter of an hour for each pound. After cooking, remove the flesh and the creamy parts from the inside of the shell, as well as the flesh from the claws. Great care should be taken in shelling, for nothing would be more unpleasant than to find little bits of shell in the flesh. The body shells should be kept intact.

Crabe en barquettes à l'armoricaine. Mix the crab flesh with *sauce armoricaine* (page 44), and use the mixture for garnishing the barquettes.

Crabe à la bretonne. Put some white wine into a pan with a *bouquet garni* chopped, shallots, and mushrooms, and reduce it. Add a little Béchamel sauce, butter it, mix in the crab flesh, and simmer for seven or eight minutes. Fill some shells (*coquilles*), cover with cream sauce (page 46), sprinkle with grated cheese, and brown quickly.

Crabe en croustade à la Nantua. Mix the crab flesh with *sauce Nantua* flavoured with truffle essence, and garnish the *croustades* with it.

Crabe diablé. Lightly fry in butter some chopped onion and shallot. Remove, and swill the pan with a few drops of brandy, adding then a little Dijon mustard, a little Béchamel sauce, and the flesh of the crab. Season according to taste, and garnish the crab shells with this mixture.

Crabe à l'indienne. Lightly fry some shallots, mushrooms, and tomatoes all chopped up. Add a little Béchamel sauce, four ounces of rice cooked with curry, and the same quantity of crab flesh. Simmer for twenty minutes, and fill the crab shells or some scallop shells with the mixture.

Crabe au paprika. Toss lightly in foaming butter half a pound of crab flesh. Add some cream, a little Béchamel sauce, a pinch of paprika pepper, enough breadcrumbs to bind it, and two egg yolks. Make some round pieces of toast, put a spoonful of the mixture on each, and make them very hot in the oven just before serving.

Pilaff de chair de crabe. Butter a mould or pudding basin, and line the bottom and sides with a fairly thick layer of pilaff rice (page 37). Fill up the middle with crab flesh bound with the sauce required: white wine, curry, shrimp, *américaine*, Newburg, etc. Turn out the pilaff, and surround it with a few spoonfuls of the sauce used.

Rissoles de crabe lorientaise. Bind the crab flesh with *mornay* sauce with plenty of cheese in it. Roll out some puff pastry five inches wide and as long as you like, and place on it, about an inch and a half apart, little heaps of the crab flesh about the size of a pigeon's egg. Moisten the edges of the pastry, fold it in half, pinch the edges together, and cut out the little rissoles with a plain or fluted pastry cutter. Brush them with egg yolk, and cook them in a very hot oven for twelve minutes before serving them.

NOTE: By all accepted rules, rissoles should be fried in deep fat, not baked. But the way it is done in Lorient is given here.

CRAWFISH (SALTWATER) (*LANGOUSTE*)

In view of the confusion which exists between the names of crawfish (*langouste*) and crayfish (*écrevisse*), it has been thought better to refer in these pages to the former as the *langouste*. In appearance it is like a large lobster without the big claws, and although it is fished a good deal off these shores, the bulk of the catches go abroad, where it is more appreciated than here. Its flesh is a good deal firmer than that of the lobster, but it is no less savoury in flavour. Nearly all the hot lobster dishes can be made with *langouste*, for which see pages 188–99 under Lobster. It lends itself more readily than the lobster to the preparation of cold dishes, particularly for banquets. Dressed *à la parisienne*, it always gains the admiration of the diners, especially when two *langoustes* are dressed in this way face to face.

Langouste à la parisienne. Stretch the *langouste* on a board so as to keep its tail out flat, attach it firmly, and cook it in a *court-bouillon*.

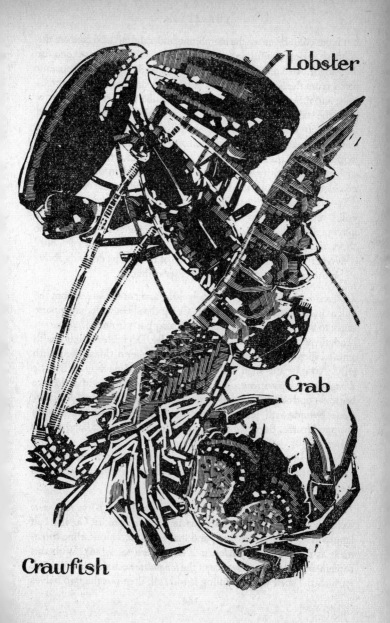

Lobster

Crab

Crawfish

Let it get cold. Remove the membrane under the tail, and take out the tail flesh, being careful not to damage the shell, which is needed for dressing it. Also remove the parts which are edible, flesh and creamy parts, from the head. Cut up the tail flesh in slices of the same thickness, and make on each a decoration in truffle well set in jelly. Now place the shell on a block of crumb of bread shaped like a wedge, and fix it firmly on. (The shell may be filled with a *julienne* of lettuce leaves.) Arrange the slices of the tail on top of the shell, slightly overlapping each other. Surround the *langouste* with artichoke bottoms each garnished with a little heap of vegetable salad, in which has been mixed the flesh from the head cut in dice and bound with jellied mayonnaise, and with hard-boiled egg halves stuffed with their own yolks mixed with chopped truffle and bound with jelly. Hand a mayonnaise sauce separately. Set round the outside of the dishes some slices of jelly.

NOTE: The correctness and beauty of this recipe depends above all on the taste and skill of the cook responsible.

Langouste à la russe. Cook the *langouste*, and cut the slices from the tail, as in *Langouste à la parisienne.* Cover the slices with mayonnaise sauce to which have been added the creamy parts from the *langouste*'s head, the whole sieved and bound with jelly. Decorate each slice with a fluted slice of truffle and two tiny sprigs of chervil. Mask them with jelly. Arrange the shell and the slices in the same way as for the *Langouste à la parisienne*, but surround it alternately with artichoke bottoms and small scooped-out tomatoes, both filled with *Salade russe* bound with jellied mayonnaise, the salad sprinkled with chopped truffle. Border the dish with slices of jelly, and hand a *sauce russe*.

NOTE: In certain cases, and according to taste, you can add as a garnish little barrel shapes of hard-boiled egg in which caviar takes the place of the yolk.

Langouste Wladimir. For two people you will want a live *langouste* weighing about a pound and a quarter, or a little more. Cut it in half lengthwise, remove the flesh, and make with it a mousseline forcemeat as directed under *Mousse d'écrevisses* (page 186). With this forcemeat, to which a few dice of the *langouste* flesh should be added, garnish the shell without filling it too full, then put the two halves together so as to give the *langouste* its original shape. Wrap it up in buttered paper bands, and tie these round with thread. Then poach the *langouste* in a *bain-marie* for twenty-five minutes. When ready to serve, take off the paper, and arrange the two half shells on a napkin. Hand a *sauce américaine* (page 44).

CRAYFISH (*ÉCREVISSES*)

These little river shellfish are not very well known in England at the present time, although many of our streams abound with them. Many years ago they were popular enough, and efforts have recently been made to interest the public here in them. The principal difficulty about them is the fact that when people have once caught them, they do not know what to do with them: a problem which the following pages should help to solve.

In the kitchen there are three kinds of crayfish, or rather, three different sizes. The small ones, which average just over an ounce to an ounce and a half, are used for soups; the medium-sized ones, averaging two ounces, are used for garnishes; while the large ones, weighing about three ounces, are used in the recipes that follow.

It must be noted that before any other preparation the crayfish must be well washed in plenty of cold water, and gutted. The latter operation consists in removing the intestinal tube with the point of a small knife. It will be found in the opening under the middle phalanx of the tail, and care should be exercised in pulling it out so as not to break it. Its presence in the crayfish when cooked would cause an unpleasant bitterness.

Aspic de queues d'écrevisses. Coat a border mould with white jelly, and decorate it as you will. Set the decoration with a little more jelly, and on this, slightly overlapping each other, arrange the peeled tails of crayfish cooked *à la bordelaise* (page 186). Cover with a layer of jelly, and make another layer of crayfish tails, this time arranging them the other way round. Fill up the mould in this way with alternate rows of jelly and crayfish, and when it is full, finish with a layer of jelly. Keep it on ice, and turn it out at the last moment before serving.

Écrevisses à la Bombay. Fry the crayfish in oil with a *mirepoix bordelaise* (page 34). Moisten with white wine and good fish *fumet*, add a *bouquet garni*, some roughly chopped tomatoes, and a pinch of curry powder. Cover and cook for ten minutes. Arrange the crayfish in a timbale, strain and reduce the stock, finish it with cream flavoured with milk of almonds, correct the seasoning, and pour it over the crayfish. Hand separately some rice *à l'indienne* (page 37).

Écrevisses en buisson. Cook the crayfish for ten minutes in a *nage* (page 34) rather heavily flavoured with white wine. Let them get cold in it. Arrange them in the utensil specially made for this dish, mixing them with freshly picked curly parsley.

Écrevisses à la bordelaise. Fry the crayfish in butter with a *mirepoix bordelaise* (page 34). When the shells get very red, pour over a glass of brandy and set it alight. When the flames have died down, moisten with white wine, add peeled, pressed, and roughly chopped tomatoes, a *bouquet garni*, a little meat glaze, salt, and a touch of cayenne. Cover and cook for ten minutes. Arrange the crayfish in a timbale, reduce the stock, thicken it with butter, pour it over the crayfish, and finish by sprinkling them with a little roughly chopped parsley.

Écrevisses à la Magenta. Fry the crayfish as for *à la bordelaise*, and finish cooking them in the same way, using as moistening the stock of lobster *à la américaine*, and seasoning with a little basil.

Écrevisses à la marinière. Fry the crayfish in butter, add onion and celery both finely minced, moisten with white wine, season, and cook them. Arrange them in a timbale, reduce the stock by half, thicken it with butter, and pour it over the crayfish. Sprinkle at the last with a little roughly chopped parsley.

Mousses et mousselines d'écrevisses. Shell some crayfish (tails and claws) cooked *à la bordelaise*. Pound the flesh finely, add the necessary amount of fish *velouté*, and pass through a tammy. To each pound of the purée allow six tablespoonfuls of very strong jelly and half a pint of cream well whisked. Mix the jelly into the purée, and put it on ice. When it begins to set, add the cream.

NOTE: *Mousses* are made in large moulds; *mousselines* in small ones, one for each person. Whether the moulds are large or small, they ought to be lined with jelly before the mixture is put into them.

Écrevisses à la nage. Get ready a *nage* (page 34) well flavoured with white wine, and when this boils, throw the crayfish into it. Cook for seven minutes, and serve them in the *nage* itself, hot or cold. If they are served cold, let them get cold in the liquid itself.

Gratin de queues d'écrevisses à la Nantua. Have at least half a dozen crayfish for each person, two small mushrooms, one fresh truffle for every five, a pint of cream, and a quarter of a pound of butter. Peel and wash the mushrooms, and cook them with water, salt, and lemon juice. Melt a little butter, throw in the crayfish, season them, moisten with a glass of dry white wine and the mushroom stock. Cook for six minutes, then take out the crayfish and drain them. Shell their tails and claws, reduce the sauce, and add the cream and a dessertspoonful of Béchamel sauce. Crush the crayfish shells with the four ounces of butter, add them to the sauce, and pass all through a sieve twice. Now put into a dish the uncooked truffles cut in strips, the crayfish tails and claws, and the mushrooms dipped into the sauce and sprinkled with grated cheese, and browned. Keep the bottom of the dish in a *bain-marie* to prevent the sauce from curdling.

Écrevisses à la Newburg: see *Homard à la Newburg* (page 195) and proceed in the same way.

Écrevisses sans-gêne. Bake some large waxy potatoes in their jackets. Remove a slice from each, remove the pulp, and coat the inside of the skin with a *sauce américaine* (page 44). Fill them two-thirds full with crayfish tails cooked in a *nage*, and little truffled *quenelles* of fish. Finish with a *mornay* sauce, sprinkle with grated cheese, and brown in the oven. As you take them from the oven, put a slice of truffle in the middle of each, a crayfish head at each end, and the claws stuck round the edges.

Soufflé d'écrevisses. Allow three dozen crayfish for six persons. Get ready a cheese soufflé mixture: that is to say, a very much reduced Béchamel sauce flavoured with grated Parmesan, salt, and a little nutmeg. Add three raw egg yolks and the well-whisked whites in the proportions usually advised in making soufflés. Pour the mixture into a buttered soufflé dish with alternate layers of crayfish tails and truffles in slices or dice. Cook like an ordinary soufflé.

Timbale de queues d'écrevisses. In a mould about three inches high (that is, of the shape of a timbale) bake a pastry case 'blind', with a lid of pastry. When the rice or dried peas have been removed from the case brush the inside with egg, and let it dry in a cool oven. Cook some medium-sized crayfish *à la bordelaise* (page 186), and shell them. Mix them with whatever sauce you have chosen, adding little *quenelles* of truffled fish forcemeat, button mushrooms, and slices of truffles. At least half of the contents should be crayfish tails. Pour this mixture into the pastry timbale, crown the top with empty crayfish heads, put on the pastry lid, and serve on a napkin.

Suprêmes d'écrevisses au grand vin. First prepare the crayfish in the *bordelaise* fashion (page 186), substituting a fine vintage wine for the usual white wine. Shell the crayfish tails, and keep them aside. With the shells and the heads, etc., make a *mousse.* Arrange the *mousse* in a shallow timbale or a glass dish, and put it on ice. When it has set, make a decoration with the crayfish tails and slices of truffles and set it with jelly.

Écrevisses à la viennoise. Cook the crayfish in a good *court-bouillon* with white wine, and arrange them in a dish. Reduce the stock, thicken it with butter, and season it with paprika pepper. Pour it over the crayfish and sprinkle them with a little roughly chopped parsley.

DUBLIN BAY PRAWNS (*LANGOUSTINES*)

These are quite well known in England, and are very often seen in the shops. They can be prepared in the same way as crayfish, and the very large ones in the various fashions given for lobster (pages 188–99). They can be a very good substitute for the *scampi* of Venice.

Pilaff de langoustines: see *Pilaff de crevettes* (page 207), and proceed in the same way, but using Dublin Bay prawns.

ESCALLOP (*COQUILLE SAINT-JACQUES*):
See SCALLOP

LOBSTER (*HOMARD*)*

Homard à l'américaine. For six people you will want three live lobsters weighing about a pound and a quarter each. First, fry lightly

* For the killing of lobsters a humane method advocated by the R.S.P.C.A. is described in their pamphlet *The Killing of Crabs and Lobsters for Table*, by Joseph Sinel. It will be understood that the author and the editor of the present work are bound to have regard to the possibility of suffering inflicted on any living creature. Notwithstanding this, they are of opinion that the cutting up of a live lobster is the better method from the point of view of preparation of the dishes in question.

in oil a *mirepoix bordelaise* (page 34). Cut the tail of the lobster in pieces across, remove the claws, and cut the head in half lengthwise. Remove the little pouch at the top of the head, which contains a little grit: keep aside the creamy parts of the head, as well as the greenish part known as the coral. Crush the shells of the claws, add both the claws and the slices of the tail to the *mirepoix*, and fry until the shell is a bright red and the flesh stiffened. Pour over a glass of good brandy and set it alight, then moisten with dry white wine and fish *fumet*, or better still, consommé. Add a few roughly chopped tomatoes, a *bouquet garni*, and a tiny bit of crushed garlic, and cook for twenty minutes. Arrange the slices, the claws and the halves of the head in a timbale. Reduce the stock and bind it with the creamy parts, and the coral from the head crushed on a plate, with a little butter. Thicken with blended butter (page 42), correct the seasoning, and finish with chopped parsley, chervil, and tarragon. Pour this sauce over the pieces of lobster.

NOTE: With *Lobster à l'américaine*, a dish of rice *à l'indienne* (page 37) is usually handed.

Homard à l'américaine Prunier. This is Prunier's version of the famous dish. Proceed as above, and when the sauce is strained add to it some good *velouté*, a tablespoonful for each pint and three quarters of the sauce. In this case the lobster is extracted from the shell before being served.

Homard à l'armoricaine. Proceed as for *Homard à l'américaine*. Arrange the pieces in a timbale. Strain the sauce, bring it to the boil, and then on the side of the stove bind it with egg yolks and cream being pouring it over the lobster.

NOTE: If you like, add as a garnish some mushrooms *à la crème*.

Homard à la bordelaise. Remove the legs and claws from the lobster, and crack the claws. Fry the whole lobster lightly in oil and butter until it is red, then add the claws and the legs. Pour over a glass of brandy and set it alight, moisten with white wine and fish *fumet*, add a few roughly chopped tomatoes, a *bouquet garni*, a small piece of garlic, and a little meat glaze, and cook for a quarter of an hour. Then take out the lobster, with the legs and claws, cut the flesh from the tail in slices, and remove the flesh from the claws and legs. You will have prepared beforehand a *mirepoix bordelaise* (page 34); now moisten it with the lobster stock, add the slices and the flesh from the claws, and bring just to the boil. Keep it just at boiling point for five minutes, then put the lobster flesh into a timbale. Reduce the stock, strain it, thicken it with butter, correct the seasoning, pour it over the lobster, and finally sprinkle with a little roughly chopped parsley.

Homard cardinal. Cook the lobster in a *court-bouillon*. Cut it in half lengthwise, remove the flesh from each half of the tail and cut it in slices. Put the two halves of the head on a dish, and in the bottom of each spread a little *cardinal* sauce (page 46). Add the flesh from the claws cut in dice, some minced cooked mushrooms, and slices of truffle. Arrange on top the slices of tail flesh, overlapping one another. Cover with *cardinal* sauce, sprinkle with grated cheese, and brown in the oven. On serving, put a few slices of truffle on each half lobster.

Homard au champagne. Fry the lobster in butter, and after the shell has coloured lightly, moisten with very dry Champagne and cook for twenty-five minutes. Then drain the lobster, cut it in slices across, shell the slices, and put the flesh into a timbale. Reduce the stock, add some cream, bind it with egg yolks, season it with cayenne, and pass it through a sieve. Then pour it over the pieces of lobster.

NOTE: A few slices of truffle may be added.

Homard chez lui. Take a small live lobster weighing between three quarters of a pound and a pound, and cook it *whole* according to the method *à l'américaine* (page 188). When it is cooked, remove the tail shell without breaking it, wash it, and put back into it the tail flesh and the flesh from the claws and legs. Keep warm, sprinkled with a little brandy. Now arrange the lobster, head and shell, on its back on a base of rice *à la créole*, and cover the flesh with a rich *sauce américaine*. Add slices of truffles and chopped chervil and tarragon. Serve very hot, with a *sauce américaine* handed separately.

NOTE: The base of rice, while useful for holding the lobster in place, also acts as a garnish to be eaten with it.

Homard Clarence. Cook the lobster in a *court-bouillon*. When it is done, halve it lengthways and remove the flesh from the tail, claws and legs. Cut the tail flesh in slices, and that from the claws and legs in half. Remove the flesh and creamy parts from the head, pound it with a little cream, and pass it through a sieve. Mix this with some

creamy Béchamel sauce flavoured with curry powder. Half-fill the
two shells with rice *à l'indienne* (page 37) with which you have mixed
the lobster flesh from the claws and legs. Arrange on it the tail slices,
cover them with the sauce, and dispose them on a long dish. Hand
the rest of the sauce separately.

Homard en coquilles. Put a layer of whatever sauce you are using in
the bottom of the scallop shells, garnish them with sliced or diced
cooked lobster flesh, chopped mushrooms, slices or dice of truffle,
tomato, etc. Cover with the sauce, and glaze in the oven or not, as
you prefer.

NOTE: It is understood that the garnish must be hot when it is
put into the shells. If the shells have to be glazed it is advisable to put
a border of Duchesse potatoes (page 36) round the edge, so as to
prevent the sauce from overflowing.

à la bretonne. The shells are filled with a mixture of lobster,
prawns or shrimps, and mushrooms, the sauce used being a white
wine sauce strongly flavoured with onion. The shells are sprinkled
with grated cheese before being browned.

à la crème. Slices of lobster in a border of Duchesse potatoes.
Cover with cream sauce, and brown quickly.

à la Nantua. The shells are garnished with a *salpicon* of lobster
flesh and truffles, and masked with a *sauce Nantua* (page 48).

Thermidor. The shells are garnished with lobster flesh, mushrooms, and truffles. Cover with a mustard-flavoured *sauce Bercy*
(page 45), and brown quickly.

Homard à la nage. Make a *nage* or *court-bouillon* as follows: mince a
large carrot and two onions, and stew them in butter. Add a pint and
three quarters of white wine and the same of water, with a bouquet of
chervil, parsley, thyme, and bayleaf tied together. Bring to the boil,
and simmer for half an hour. Plunge the lobster in this *nage* as it boils,
and for a lobster weighing about a pound let it boil for about twenty
minutes. When cooked, it can be served hot or cold, just as it is. If
cold, it can be left in the *nage* to get cold, and served in it, or with a
mayonnaise. If it is served hot, melted butter is the proper accompaniment.

Homard rôti au whisky. Cut the lobster in two lengthways, and break the claws. Put it into a baking dish shell side down. Season with salt and pepper, and on each half put two tablespoonfuls of melted butter mixed with Colman's mustard. Then sprinkle over a few white breadcrumbs browned in the oven, and roast the lobster, basting it well, for a quarter of an hour or a very little longer. To serve, dish the lobster, and pour over it the butter from the baking dish. Add a glass of whisky, set it alight, and finish by basting with the butter. Serve very hot.

Coupe de homard Polignac. Make a *court-bouillon* with very dry Pommery, a *bouquet garni* reinforced with a piece of celery, mushroom stalks, a little onion, and some very coarsely broken pepper. Salt it moderately. Quickly cut in pieces across three live lobsters weighing about a pound each, take out the little pouch and the creamy parts from the heads, plunge them and the pieces in the rapidly boiling *court-bouillon*, and boil for twenty minutes. Drain and shell the pieces, cut the flesh in slices, remove the flesh from the claws and legs, and put it all in a timbale or a glass dish. Add some fine grapes, skinned and with their pips removed. Pass the stock through a cloth, and with it make a fine jelly, which should be a light rose in colour, completing it by a little more Pommery. When this jelly is cold, or nearly cold, pour it over the lobster, and keep the dish on ice until it is wanted.

Côtelettes de homard. Make a *salpicon* in the proper proportions (see cutlets, under *Hors-d'œuvre*, page 64) with lobster flesh, mushroom, truffles, and very much reduced fish *velouté.* Shape the mixture when cold into cutlets, egg-and-breadcrumb them, and fry them in the usual manner. Serve separately whatever sauce is chosen.

Côtelettes de homard Arkangel. Cook a lobster, and cut its flesh into dice; mix this with an equal amount of large-grained caviar, and bind with *Mousse de homard* (page 194). When the mixture is set, shape into little cutlets, or, simpler still, put the mixture to set in little cutlet-shaped oiled moulds, and let it set there. Cover them with *chaudfroid* sauce flavoured with a lobster broth, and then with jelly. Arrange on a dish garnished round the edge with slices of jelly, and hand separately a *sauce russe* (page 52).

Homard à la crème. Cut the lobster in pieces across, and fry them in butter. Moisten with thin seasoned cream, and cook for a quarter of an hour. Take out the pieces, shell them, remove the flesh from the claws and legs, and put it all in a timbale. Add to the cooking liquor a certain amount of thick cream, reduce it until it reaches the right thickness, finish with a little good burnt brandy and a few drops of lemon juice, and pour over the lobster.

Homard diablé, ou grillé. Cut a live lobster in half lengthwise, and lay the two halves shell down on a metal dish. Season the flesh, sprinkle it with melted butter flavoured with mustard, sprinkle with browned breadcrumbs, and cook in a hot oven. Serve separately a rather highly seasoned *maître-d'hôtel* butter flavoured with mustard.

Homard à la française. Fry in butter some small lobster cut in pieces across and seasoned with salt and cayenne pepper. Moisten with white wine and fish *fumet*, add some very thin *julienne* shreds of onion and carrot stewed in butter, and cook for a quarter of an hour. Arrange the pieces in a timbale, bind the stock lightly with blended butter (page 42), finish with more butter, and pour over the lobster.

Homard froid en aspic. Line a border mould with white jelly, and decorate it as you will. Put a layer of jelly in the bottom, and on this arrange thin slices of lobster tail cooked in *court-bouillon*, so that they slightly overlap each other. Cover with more jelly, and so on in alternate layers until the mould is full, finishing with a layer of jelly. Leave to set, and turn out when wanted.

NOTE: If desired, slices of truffle may be laid between the slices.

Homard froid en aspic à la russe. Cut the lobster tail into even rounds, put on each a slice of truffle cut with a scalloped cutter, cover with jelly, and let them set. Lightly line a border mould with white jelly. Arrange in it the slices of lobster tails, so that the decorated side touches the side of the mould. Fill up the hollow space inside with a thick *salade russe*, cover with a thin layer of jelly, and leave it to set. Turn out only when wanted.

Homard Grammont. Cook a lobster in *court-bouillon*, and cut it in half lengthways. Take out the flesh from the tail, and cut it in slices. Garnish the halves of the shell with lobster mousse seasoned with paprika pepper, arrange on it the slices (which you have previously covered with jelly), alternating them with some fine poached oysters also covered with jelly. Put the shells on a long dish, and surround them with the oyster shells garnished with a *salpicon* of oysters and the flesh from the claws and legs of the lobster, bound with mayonnaise sauce. Hand separately a mayonnaise flavoured with lemon juice and finished with whipped cream.

Homard à la hambourgeoise. Cook the lobster in *court-bouillon*, remove the flesh from the tail, and cut it in slices. Arrange these slices in a little sauté pan, add Madeira and meat glaze, bring to the boil and bind with breadcrumbs blended with butter. Dilute with a little cream, then finish with chopped parsley and a few drops of lemon juice. Arrange the slices in a timbale, cover them with the sauce, and serve very hot.

NOTE: The sauce should be thick enough to coat the slices. The centre may be garnished with the flesh from the claws and legs and sprinkled with lobster butter or simply with plain melted butter.

Homard à la hongroise. This is made in the same way as *Homard à la crème* (page 191), with the addition of a broth of onion and a flavouring of paprika pepper.

Homard à la mâconnaise. Proceed in the same manner as for *Matelote* of Eel *à la batelière* (page 38). For this method of preparation choose small lobsters weighing round about half a pound, cut them in pieces across, and cook them *à l'etouffée*, that is to say, with butter in a covered pan. Bind the cooking liquor of the *matelote* with the soft roe and the creamy parts mixed with butter. This dish should be rather highly seasoned.

Mayonnaise de homard. Cut the lobster tail flesh in slices, and with this and the flesh from the claws and legs make a mayonnaise in the same way as described in the recipe for Salmon mayonnaise (page 130). The lobster should be cooked in a *court-bouillon*.

Homard Mephisto. Cut a live lobster in half lengthways, take out the flesh and pound it in a mortar with seasoning, mustard, and a little cream. Garnish the shells with this mixture, sprinkle it with breadcrumbs, sprinkle with melted butter, and cook in the oven. Serve at the same time a mustard-flavoured *maître-d'hôtel* butter.

Mousse froide de homard. Proceed exactly as under *Mousse froide d'Écrevisses* (page 186).

Homard à la Newburg. (1) Cut the live lobster in pieces across, and fry these in butter. Swill the pan with sherry, add enough cream nearly to cover the pieces. Cook for twenty minutes, and then arrange the pieces in a timbale. Bind the stock with egg yolks, and pour it over the pieces.

Homard à la Newburg. (2) Cook the lobster in *court-bouillon*, and cut the tail flesh in slices. Arrange them in a sauté pan and cook them gently in butter. Sprinkle them well with sherry, reduce this, and then moisten them with enough cream to cover them. Boil for a few minutes, then bind with cream and egg yolks, and pour into a timbale. Add a few slices of truffles.

Homard à la Palestine. Cut the lobster in pieces across, and fry it in butter with a *mirepoix* (page 33). Pour over a glass of brandy, set it alight, then moisten with white wine and fish *fumet*. Cook for a quarter of an hour, then take the flesh from the pieces and keep it warm in a covered sauté pan. Now pound up the head and the tail shells, fry them lightly in oil with an ordinary *mirepoix*, moisten with the stock of the lobster, and cook for another quarter of an hour. Now add a little fish *velouté* and the creamy parts and the soft roe of the lobster crushed with a little butter and a pinch of curry powder. Cook on for a few seconds longer, then pass through a sieve, and finish with cream and butter. Have ready on a dish a moulded border of rice *à l'indienne* (page 37). Put the pieces of lobster in the middle of this; cover them with some of the sauce and hand the rest in a sauceboat.

Homard à la parisienne: see *Langouste à la parisienne* (page 182).

Homard phocéenne. Prepare the lobster as if for *à l'américaine* (page 188), increasing the amount of garlic and adding a seasoning of saffron. Add to the sauce a *julienne* of red sweet peppers, and serve on a dish bordered with saffron-flavoured rice *à l'indienne* (page 37).

Homard au porto. For this you will want a lobster of about a pound in weight, which must be stewed whole in butter and seasoned with salt and paprika pepper. Moisten it liberally with port wine, cook for thirty minutes, and drain it. Strain the stock and reduce it by three quarters. Bind it with two egg yolks and a few spoonfuls of cream, and finish off the fire with a few drops of port. Keep hot in the *bain-marie*. Meanwhile shell the lobster, cut the tail in slices, and leave the flesh of the claws whole. Arrange in a timbale, and cover with the sauce.

Homard à la russe: see *Langouste à la russe* (page 184).

Homard Saint-Honorat. Cut in half lengthways a lobster weighing about a pound. Prepare it in the same way as *Homard à l'américaine* (page 188). When it is cooked, take it out, remove the tail flesh, and cut it in slices. Half-fill the shells with pilaff rice, lay the slices on this, and cover them with the sauce. Garnish with mussels *à la crème* (served in sea-urchin shells, if you can get them, the spikes of which have been flattened), with fried oysters on top.

Salade de homard. This is made with the same ingredients as lobster mayonnaise, but they are seasoned with an ordinary salad dressing: oil, vinegar, salt, and pepper.

Soufflé de homard. (1) Half-cook a lobster in a *nage* (page 34), and cut it in half lengthways. Take out the flesh and pound it with the necessary seasoning. Pass it through a tammy, and add to it some Béchamel sauce to which two raw egg yolks have been added. Bring to the boil, take off the fire, and let the mixture get cold slowly, adding a little white of egg stiffly whisked. Garnish the half shells with this mixture, sprinkle them with a little grated cheese, and cook them for twenty minutes in a moderate oven. Serve a sauce separately: *américaine*, *Newburg*, white wine, *Bercy*, and so on.

NOTE: You can add to the mixture, if you like, some thin slices of the lobster tail, or truffle in dice, or poached soft roes, shelled shrimps, minced cooked mushrooms, etc.

Soufflé de homard. (2) Cut a live lobster in half lengthways, remove the flesh, and pound it with the necessary seasonings and a few breadcrumbs soaked in milk and then pressed dry. Pass it through a tammy, put it into a bowl over ice, and work into it a reasonable amount of thick cream. Meanwhile cook the shells in water, being careful not to break them. See that they are well drained. Now garnish them with the soufflé mixture and sprinkle the surface with breadcrumbs. Cook on a baking-sheet in a moderate oven for fifteen to twenty minutes, and serve them on a napkin. Serve at the same time, if you like, one of the sauces mentioned in the previous recipe, especially if the soufflé mixture contains any of the ingredients of the sauce.

Homard thermidor. Cut the lobster in half lengthways after it has been cooked. Remove and cut in slices the flesh from the tail. Cover the bottom of each half shell with mustard-flavoured *Bercy* sauce mixed with Béchamel sauce. Arrange the slices on top, and cover them with the same sauce. Brown lightly.

NOTE: The lobster slices may be alternated with mushrooms cooked in butter.

Homard Tourville. Make a risotto (page 37). Cut in large dice a cooked lobster tail, mix with it some mushroom dice cooked in butter and some poached mussels and oysters. The lobster flesh should make quite half of this *salpicon.* Bind with a fish *velouté* flavoured with a *fumet* of shellfish, heat it up, and serve it in the middle of the risotto. The lobster, etc., is then covered with *mornay* sauce, sprinkled with grated cheese, and quickly browned.

NOTE: The risotto border can be moulded or simply arranged on the dish with a spoon.

Homard Vanderbilt. Cut a live lobster in half lengthways and prepare it *à l'américaine.* Remove the flesh from the tail and cut it in slices. Mask the bottom of the half shells with a creamy *sauce américaine,* and add crayfish tails and truffle dice; or you can mix these with the sauce itself. Arrange the lobster slices on this bed, putting slices of truffle between. Cover with *sauce américaine* thickened with egg yolks, and brown lightly in the oven.

Homard flambé du vieux moine. Cut a live lobster in half lengthwise, and lay the two halves shell down on a metal dish. Season the flesh; sprinkle it with melted butter and browned breadcrumbs. Cook in a hot oven. Five minutes before end of cooking, sprinkle with a small glass of Trappistine liqueur on each half lobster before singeing it with a mixture made of Trappistine and brandy in equal parts. Light by pouring over the lobster and basting it all the time until the flame is extinguished. Serve with *beurre au fenouil,* as follows.

Beurre au fenouil. Put in saucepan some not too finely crushed peppercorns, star-aniseed, and fennel, half a glass of dry white wine, a tablespoonful of vinegar. Cook until it is reduced to the quantity of a coffee spoon. When the liquid boils, put in three ounces of butter in small pieces, boil it once rapidly, then take it off the fire.

Finish with two tablespoonfuls of *hollandaise* sauce. Season with salt to taste, and strain before serving.

Homard Winthertur. The same as *Homard cardinal* (page 190), except that the *salpicon* of lobster is replaced by peeled shrimps. Mask with *cardinal* sauce and sprinkle with chopped truffles.

Demoiselles de Caen chez elles. Cook some very small lobsters, weighing about half a pound each, in *court-bouillon*. Remove the claws and legs, and empty the tails without breaking the top shell. Cut this flesh in slices. Cut some mushrooms in thin slices and cook them slowly in butter. When they are done, take them out and keep them warm on a plate. In the same butter put the slices of lobster. Cover the pan and heat them through gently. Then swill the pan with a small glass of brandy. Prepare a light and unctuous *cardinal* sauce (page 46). Heighten the seasoning with a touch of cayenne, and finish the sauce with a few drops of brandy. Make a base of pilaff rice (which will serve as a garnish as well), and on it arrange the lobsters, on their backs. Mask the bottom of their shells with the *cardinal* sauce, and in them, overlapping each other, arrange the slices of lobster and slices of truffle. Cover with the same sauce, and brown lightly. Some slices of truffle should be placed on each lobster as they come from the oven, and the dish should be served at once.

Paëlla de homard. Toss in butter, as if you were making a pilaff, some chopped onion, a touch of garlic, and Carolina rice. Add peeled, pressed, and roughly chopped tomatoes, some sweet red pepper cut in little dice, some very small green peas (*petits pois*), and a pinch of saffron. Moisten the rice to half its height again with fish *fumet* or white stock, add a *bouquet garni* and the usual seasoning, and cook for a quarter of an hour. When the rice is cooked, separate it with a fork, and mix with it slices of lobster or *langouste* as the principal ingredient, accompanied by shelled mussels; crab flesh or crayfish tails are auxiliaries. Moisten again very slightly, give it another seven or eight minutes in the oven, and send it to table in a timbale.

NOTE: If the rice is put into an earthenware casserole for serving at table, the mixture with the fish can be done in this. It is then only necessary to add the moistening, cover the casserole, put it into the oven for the final heating, and serve it as it is.

Pâté de homard. Cut up a live lobster: keep aside the creamy parts and the hard and soft roes, if there are any. Season the pieces, fry them in butter long enough to stiffen the flesh, pour in a glass of brandy and set it alight, and then add an equal quantity of tarragon vinegar, and a little cream. After a few minutes' cooking, take out the pieces of lobster, and put into the stock as many breadcrumbs as will completely absorb it. Meanwhile take the meat out of the pieces of the tail, leaving it intact, and especially the flesh from the claws. Pound the creamy parts and the soft and hard roes, add the same amount of fresh butter, the soaked breadcrumbs, a little anchovy essence, and the yolks of several hard-boiled eggs. Pass through a tammy, correct the seasoning, and heighten it with a little cayenne. Now roll out some short-crust, put it in a long buttered dish, and raise the edges with a band of pastry about three quarters of an inch high. Mask the middle of the pastry with a layer of the forcemeat, and on this arrange the pieces of lobster so as to reconstitute its shape, putting the claws on each side. Cover with the rest of the forcemeat, and then with a cover of pastry, which must be well joined on to the bottom layer. Brush with egg yolk, and put it into a hot oven just long enough to cook the pastry. Serve at once.

NOTE: The lobster must be soft to eat, and the consistency of the forcemeat should be that of a purée, neither too firm nor too soft. Indeed, this dish should be unlike any other.

MUSSELS (*MOULES*)

To whatever use they are to be put, the mussels, scraped and brushed in several waters, must first be 'opened' with a little white wine, chopped onion and shallot, and freshly ground pepper. To serve them, one of the shells is usually discarded. To 'open' them, you proceed as follows: for three and a half pints of mussels, add a medium-sized onion and a shallot finely chopped, five or six parsley stalks, a sprig of thyme, the third of a bayleaf, a pinch of freshly ground pepper, and eight tablespoonfuls of white wine. Cover the pan tightly, put it on a quick fire, and at the end of two minutes shake the mussels. Do this two or three times more during their cooking, which should take only five or six minutes in all. The mussels should then be cooked and their shells wide open.

Brochettes de moules amiral. Egg-and-breadcrumb some poached and wiped mussels, and skewer them, a dozen on a skewer. Wrap each skewer in a very thin rasher of bacon, sprinkle with butter, cook them for a few minutes in the oven, and serve them with a tomato sauce handed separately.

Moules bonne femme. 'Open' the mussels in the manner described above, adding a thin *julienne* of mushrooms and the white part of celery. Put the mussels in the serving dish, reduce the stock by half, add some blended butter (page 42) and a little cream, and pour this over the mussels.

Coquilles de moules au currie. 'Open' the mussels as for *Moules bonne femme*, but with the mushrooms and celery cut in large dice instead of in *julienne* shreds. Add, too, a pinch of curry powder. When they are cooked, remove them from their shells. Reduce the stock by three quarters, add, off the fire, egg yolks and cream, and mix the mussels with this sauce. Garnish scallop shells with it, sprinkle with coarse browned breadcrumbs, and brown in the oven.

Moules à la dinardaise. 'Open' the mussels, and from each remove one shell. Arrange them in a shallow fireproof dish, and cover them with a creamy *gratin* sauce, rather highly seasoned and with chopped chives added to it. Brown at the last moment.

Moules frites. Take large 'opened' mussels, poach them, shell them, and wipe them dry. Season them lightly, dip them in fritter batter, and plunge them into very hot fat. Serve on a napkin with fried parsley. Hand separately the sauce chosen.

NOTE: Instead of being coated with batter, the mussels may be egg-and-breadcrumbed.

Moules à la marinière. (1) 'Open' the mussels in the usual way, adding an ounce and a half of butter for each three and a half pints of mussels. Serve as they are.

Moules à la marinière. (2) 'Open' the mussels as above, and put them into a timbale after taking off one of the shells from each. Reduce the stock by half, bind it lightly with blended butter (page 42) or a little fish *velouté*, and pour it over the mussels.

Moules pêcheur. Prepare the mussels as for *Marinière*, adding the heart of a head of celery finely chopped.

Moules en pilaff. Bind the poached and shelled mussels with a sauce of some kind, for example curry, *américaine*, and so on. Butter a bowl or a timbale and line it with a fairly thick layer of pilaff rice (page 37). Garnish the middle with the ragoût of mussels, cover the top with rice, turn out on to a round dish, and surround the pilaff with some of the sauce used to bind the mussels.

Moules à la poulette. Prepare as for *Marinière* (2), and put them in a timbale. Reduce the stock to half, bind it with *velouté*, egg yolks, and cream, and finish with a few drops of lemon juice. Pour over the mussels, and scatter over it a little roughly chopped parsley.

Moules à la provençale. 'Open' the mussels, take off one of the shells from each, and put them in a dish. Sprinkle them with melted *beurre d'escargots*, sprinkle them with breadcrumbs, and brown the top in the oven.

NOTE: *Beurre d'escargots* is made by mixing and well blending a pound of butter, two ounces of finely chopped shallot, two cloves of garlic crushed to a paste, and a good dessertspoonful of chopped parsley, salt, pepper, and mixed spice.

Moules à la rochelaise. 'Open' some large mussels with white wine, shallot, celery, chives, and mushrooms, all chopped. Add butter, pepper, and a touch of nutmeg. Arrange them on a dish, having removed one shell from each. Reduce the stock by three quarters, bind it with fresh breadcrumbs, and pour it over the mussels. Brown lightly at the last minute.

Moules Saint-Michel. Prepare the mussels as for *Marinière* (2). Finish the sauce at the last minute with chopped parsley and chervil, and a spot of mustard.

NOTE: If mussels have to be kept until the next day, it is better to take them from their shells and keep them in a cool place wrapped in a napkin. The stock may be decanted and kept in a cool place in a porcelain bowl, uncovered. It can be used for a *velouté* or a *Soupe aux moules* (page 76).

OYSTERS (*HUÎTRES*)

There is no doubt that the best way of eating oysters is *au naturel*: that is to say, raw from their shells. Nevertheless, certain ways of cooking them are in demand. These preparations are usually served in the deep shells, which are of course well cleaned beforehand.

Huîtres à l'américaine. Take the oysters from their shells and wipe them. Put in the bottom of the deep shells a little coarsely ground pepper and a pinch of fried breadcrumbs. Add the oysters, sprinkle them with grated Gruyère cheese and a few breadcrumbs, put a dab of butter on each, and brown quickly in the oven.

Anges à cheval (sometimes called *Brochettes d'huîtres*). The best savoury in the world. Wrap the raw oysters in a thin rasher of bacon, and skewer them in half dozens on small skewers. Grill them and arrange them on pieces of toast sprinkled with fried breadcrumbs seasoned with a little cayenne.

Bouchées aux huîtres. Poach the oysters in their own liquor, drain them and remove their beards. Mix them with a Béchamel sauce to which have been added some anchovy butter, the reduced liquor of the oysters, a touch of cayenne, and a binding of egg yolks. Garnish small bouchées with these oysters.

Coquilles d'huîtres au currie. Poach the oysters, drain them, and remove their beards. Make a light sauce with the liquor from the oysters and some cream flavoured with curry powder. Put the oysters in the scallop shells, cover them with this sauce, sprinkle with fine browned breadcrumbs, and put in the oven for five or six minutes before serving.

Cromesquis d'huîtres. Make a mixture as described below for *Cro-quettes*. Divide it into pieces about the size of a pigeon's egg, and roll them into balls. Wrap up each in a very thin piece of unsweetened pancake, dip them in frying batter, and fry them in deep fat. Serve them on a napkin with fried parsley.

Croquettes d'huîtres. Poach the oysters, drain them, and cut them in dice. Mix them with a Béchamel sauce to which you have added the reduced liquor from the oysters and bound with egg yolks. The final sauce should be very thick: that is to say, eight tablespoonfuls would be enough to bind half a pound of shelled oysters. Spread this mixture on a dish, and let it get cold. Then divide it into whatever sized pieces you want for your croquettes, shape them as you will, egg-and-breadcrumb them, and at the last moment fry them in very hot fat. Serve them on a napkin with fried parsley.

Huîtres en brochettes. Open the oysters, drain them, dry them, and season them. Put them on skewers and into a dish with a little butter. Stiffen them quickly in the oven, and finish them on the grill at the last moment. Serve with them either *maître-d'hôtel* butter or a raw *Bercy* butter: that is, a *maître-d'hôtel* with lemon juice and very finely cut shallots.

Huîtres sur croûtons. Shell some oysters and wipe them. Cook some butter in a frying pan until it is a light brown and smells of nuts, then fry the oysters in this. Arrange them on little round *croûtons* of fried bread, and sprinkle them with the *beurre noisette*.

Croustades d'huîtres Montglas. Line some small brioche or dariole moulds with short-crust pastry and bake them 'blind'. Fill them with the same garnish as that suggested for *Bouchées* opposite, put on each a slice of truffle, and cover with a circle of puff pastry.

NOTE: The cooking of croustades 'blind', or *à blanc*, is done thus: When they have been lined, you must again line the inside of the paste with greaseproof or thin kitchen paper and fill this with rice or dried peas. After the croustades have been baked, this filling is taken out, and the croustades are kept in a cool oven for a few minutes to dry them.

Huîtres à la diable. Poach several dozen oysters in their own liquor, drain them, and remove their beards. With the oyster liquor and some fresh cream make a Béchamel sauce; season it with salt, grated nutmeg, and a suspicion of paprika pepper. Mix the oysters with this sauce, and garnish the hollow shells with the mixture. Sprinkle with a few fried breadcrumbs, arrange the shells on a baking-sheet, and put them in the oven for a few minutes before serving them. Be careful not to let them boil.

Huîtres à la florentine. Put in the bottom of scallop shells some leaf spinach stewed in butter. Add the oysters, cover with *mornay* sauce, and sprinkle with grated cheese before browning in the oven.

Huîtres frites (or *à l'Orly*). Wipe some raw oysters and egg-and-breadcrumb them. Cook them in clarified butter, serve them on a napkin, and accompany them by a sauceboat of tomato sauce.

Huîtres frites à la Villeroy. Poach the oysters, remove their beards, and wipe them. Dip them in a nearly cold *sauce Villeroy* (page 49) so that they are thickly coated with it. Put them on a dish as you do them, and let them get cold. Then egg-and-breadcrumb them, and fry them in deep fat just before you want them. Serve on a napkin with fried parsley.

Huîtres maréchal. Poach the oysters, wipe them, dip them in fritter batter, and fry them in deep fat. Arrange them in threes on slices of lemon, and surround them with a little fried parsley.

Huîtres mornay. Proceed exactly as for oysters *à la florentine*, omitting the spinach.

Pannequets d'huîtres. Make some very thin pancakes with unsweetened batter. Spread on each a layer of the mixture for croquettes (page 202), roll them up, cut them in lozenge-shape, and put them in the oven for a few minutes before serving.

Petits pâtés d'huîtres. Roll out some puff pastry, and cut out of it with a plain or fluted cutter as many rounds as you want patties. Put these out on a baking dish or tin, and put in the middle of each a piece of the croquette mixture (page 202) as big as a small nut. Wet the edges, cover with another round of pastry of the same size but a little thicker, join well together, brush with egg yolk, and bake in a hot oven for twelve minutes.

Huîtres Prunier (or *Croustades Prunier*). Poach some oysters and remove their beards; also cook some mushrooms. Mix these with a fish *fumet* flavoured with oysters and mixed with an equal amount of *hollandaise* sauce. Garnish the croustades with this mixture, and put a slice of truffle on top of each.

Rissoles d'huîtres. With a *salpicon* of oysters, or oysters coated with Villeroy sauce, proceed as directed for Crab rissoles (page 182). Egg-and-breadcrumb these rissoles, and fry them in deep fat. Serve on a napkin with fried parsley.

Soufflé aux huîtres. Poach three dozen oysters; remove their beards, and cut them in two or three according to their size. Meanwhile make a white *roux* (page 37) with three dessertspoonfuls of flour, moisten it with the liquor from the oysters and with milk, season it with salt, pepper, and a touch of cayenne, bring to the boil, and boil for a few minutes. It should have the appearance of a thick mash. Add two ounces of butter, three egg yolks, the oysters, and six stiffly whisked

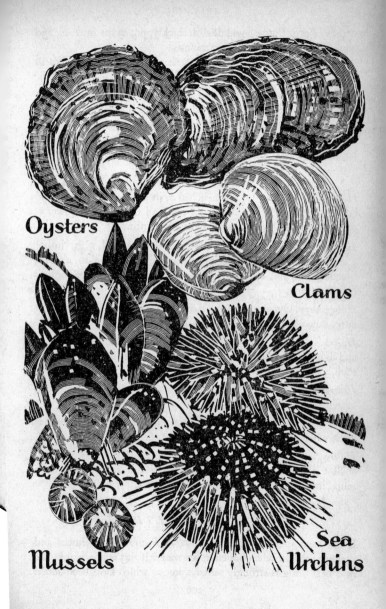

Oysters

Clams

Mussels

Sea
Urchins

whites of egg. Butter a soufflé dish thickly, put in the mixture, and cook in a slow oven for twenty minutes.

NOTE: With the same mixture you can make small soufflés in small fluted cases.

Huîtres à la tartare. Take the best hollow shells, as nearly as possible of the same size, and in the bottom of each put some watercress leaves. On these put a few cold poached oysters, with their beards removed, and cover them with a *sauce tartare* seasoned with a little paprika pepper.

Variété à la Prunier

Huître saintongeaise. Oyster poached in its own juice, drained, and replaced in its shell, which has been well cleaned. *Bercy* sauce, decorated with slice of sausage, lightly browned.

Huître rochelaise. Uncooked oyster, served in its shell, with a butter composed of very finely chopped parsley, shallot, onion, chervil, breadcrumbs, and lemon juice. The whole is warmed very slightly before serving.

Huître curry. Oyster poached, placed on rice mould with a thin light curry sauce.

Huître sautée tomate. Cover oyster with crushed cracker biscuits, and lightly fry in butter. Place a spoonful of tomato ketchup in the shell, warm, and place oyster on top.

Huître mornay. Poached oysters with *mornay* sauce, covered with grated cheese and lightly baked.

Huître au poivre rose. Poached oyster with Boston sauce which is made with the sauce coloured slightly with paprika.

Huître poulette. Oyster poached in stock seasoned with onion and shallot. Reduce stock, add double cream and a little *hollandaise* sauce, minced parsley, and minced mushroom.

PRAWNS (*CREVETTES ROSES*)

It has been stated before (under *Hors-d'œuvre*) that prawns and shrimps are best when boiled in sea water. If this is impossible, the next best thing is strongly salted water to which have been added thyme, bayleaf, peppercorns, and a *bouquet garni*. Bring the water to the boil, and throw in the prawns alive. Cook for two or three minutes according to size. Let them get cold, but do not hasten their cooling by plunging them in cold water.

Crevettes en aspic. Bind with thick jellied mayonnaise some small prawns, or large ones cut in small dice. Make some little balls of this mixture, and keep them on ice until set. Line a border mould with white fish jelly, decorate the bottom as you like, and set the decoration with a little jelly. When it has set, add more jelly to form a thin layer. When this has set, arrange the prawn balls on it, alternating them with small black truffles, and fine prawns placed upside down so as to be right way up when the mould is turned out. Finish by filling up the mould with these three ingredients and the jelly. Leave to set, and turn out when wanted.

Crevettes en barquettes. Garnish the boats with shrimps or little prawns bound with the sauce indicated by the title of the dish: for example, *Crevettes en barquettes à l'américaine* with *sauce américaine*; with *sauce au currie*, or *cardinal, hollandaise, Nantua, normande, soubise, vénitienne*, white wine, and so on. You can add to the shrimps a *salpicon* of truffles and mushrooms, or you can top off the boats by a slice of truffle, a fried mussel, and so on.

Croquettes de crevettes. Make a *salpicon* with prawns or shrimps, mushrooms, and truffles, bound with the sauce chosen. Proceed as in all other croquettes.

Pilaff de crevettes. The preparation of this pilaff is always the same. It consists of an outside of pilaff rice (page 37) with an inside of prawns or shrimps bound with a sauce. You prepare it by lining the bottom and sides of a buttered pudding basin or timbale with a fairly thick layer of pilaff rice; the garnish is put in the middle, it is covered in with rice and turned out on the serving dish. It is surrounded by some of the same sauce which has been used in the garnish. Here, briefly, are a few different kinds of pilaff:

Américaine. Prawns bound with *sauce américaine*, in an ordinary pilaff rice.

Cardinal: Prawns bound with *sauce cardinal*; diced truffles added to the rice.

Currie: Prawns bound with curry sauce; the rice flavoured with curry powder.

Hongroise: Prawns bound with a white wine sauce flavoured with paprika pepper; the pilaff rice also flavoured with paprika.

Joinville: Prawns bound with *sauce Joinville*; a *julienne* of mushrooms added to the rice.

Nantua: Prawns bound with *sauce Nantua*; plain pilaff rice.

Newburg: Prawns bound with Newburg sauce; ordinary pilaff rice, and prawns stuck over the pilaff after it is turned out.

Orientale: Prawns bound with white wine sauce flavoured with saffron; dice of tomatoes added to the pilaff rice.

Valenciennes: Prawns bound with creamy *sauce américaine*; dice of sweet red peppers added to the pilaff rice.

SCALLOP or ESCALLOP
(*COQUILLES SAINT-JACQUES*)

The scallop, which was worn by pilgrims to the shrine of Saint James of Compostella, owes its French name, *Coquille Saint-Jacques*, to the following legend:

When the body of St James was being miraculously conveyed in a ship without sails or oars from Joppa to Galicia, it passed the village of Bonzas, on the coast of Portugal, on the day that a marriage had been celebrated there. The bridegroom with his friends were amusing themselves on horseback on the sands, when his horse became unmanageable and plunged into the sea; whereupon the miraculous ship stopped in its voyage, and presently the bridegroom emerged, horse and man, close beside it. A conversation ensued between the knight and the saint's disciples on board, in which they apprised him that it was the saint who had saved him from a watery grave, and explained the Christian religion to him. He believed, and was baptized there and then; immediately the ship resumed its voyage, and the knight came galloping back over the sea to rejoin his astonished friends. He told them all that had happened, and they too were converted, and the knight baptized his bride with his own hand. Now when the knight emerged from the sea, both his dress and the trappings of his horse were covered with scallop shells; and therefore the Galicians took the scallop shell as the sign of St James.

These are the simpler fashions of preparing this delicious shellfish. It must be remembered that (1) the scallops should be placed on the top of a stove to make them open – when the top shell rises slightly, take it off with a knife; (2) slip the end of a palette knife under the scallop, so as to remove it from the shell with the soft roe and the beard; (3) wash and brush the hollow scallop shell, as it will be used not only for serving the scallops themselves, but for other purposes afterwards.

In fairness to English fishmongers, it must be stated that these operations will be performed for you without the asking. This reminds me of a dictum I saw recently, and a very true one: 'In a fishmonger's shop more is done to save the customer trouble, after the purchase is made, than in any other food shop.'

Coquille Saint-Jacques à l'américaine. Stew the scallops lightly in butter, pour over a glass of brandy, and set it alight. Moisten with the stock of *Homard à l'américaine* (page 188), cook for ten minutes, and take out the scallops. Thicken the stock with butter, and put the scallops back. Serve separately some rice *à l'indienne* (page 37).

Coquille Saint-Jacques à l'armoricaine. Lightly fry the scallops with a fine *mirepoix bordelaise* (page 34), moisten with white wine, add roughly chopped tomatoes, a *bouquet garni*, and the usual seasoning, and cook for ten minutes. Remove the scallops, strain the stock and reduce it by half, add a little cream, and finish it with chopped chervil and tarragon.

Coquille Saint-Jacques à la bordelaise. Fry lightly in butter a *mirepoix bordelaise* (page 34). Add the white and the red parts of the scallops, put on the lid and let them stew very gently, then pour in a glass of brandy, and set it alight. Moisten with white wine, add some roughly chopped tomatoes, and cook for ten minutes. Remove the scallops, reduce the cooking liquor, thicken it with butter, and correct the seasoning.

NOTE: The process translated above as 'stewing gently' is in the original French *faire suer*, or in plain English 'let it sweat', which is what they really should do. The phrase is really untranslatable, but the process will be familiar to all cooks, who constantly use it in the preliminaries to braising.

Scallops

Dublin
Bay
Prawn

Sardines

Coquilles Saint-Jacques à la Bretonne. Fry lightly in butter the white and red part of the scallops cut in dice, with chopped onion and shallot. Moisten lightly with white wine, add a little chopped parsley and some breadcrumbs, and boil for seven or eight minutes. By then the mixture should have the appearance of a light sauce. Remove the pan from the fire, butter the mixture slightly, and put it into the scallop shells. Sprinkle with coarsely grated browned breadcrumbs, then with melted butter, and brown quickly.

Coquilles Saint-Jacques en brochettes. Poach some scallops and cut the white part in rounds. Wrap each of these in a very thin piece of bacon rasher, and stick them on skewers, alternately with the red part, egg-and-breadcrumbed. Grill them slowly, and serve with the sauce chosen, handed separately.

Coquilles Saint-Jacques au currie. Stew the scallops gently (*faire suer*, page 209) with chopped onion in butter; moisten with white wine, add a *bouquet garni* and a pinch of curry powder, and cook for a few minutes. Take out the scallops, reduce the stock, strain it, and add a little cream. Rice *à l'indienne* (page 37) should be handed with this.

Coquilles Saint-Jacques au gratin. Cook the scallops with white wine and *Duxelles* (page 31). Reduce the stock and add it to a *gratin* sauce (page 47). Put some of the sauce in the bottom of the shells, lay the scallops on it, cover with more sauce, sprinkle with browned bread-crumbs, and brown in the oven.

Coquilles Saint-Jacques frites. Cut the white part of the scallops, raw, in rounds. Season them, egg-and-breadcrumb them, and fry them in clarified butter. The red parts, whole, should be treated in the same way. Hand a tomato sauce.

Coquilles Saint-Jacques marinière. Using both the red and the white parts, proceed exactly as for *Moules marinière* (2) (page 200).

Coquilles Saint-Jacques à la meunière. Cut up the white parts in fairly thick slices, season them with salt and pepper, dip them in milk and then in flour, and fry them in clarified butter. Arrange on a dish, sprinkle them with nutbrown butter, and scatter a little chopped parsley over them.

Coquilles Saint-Jacques mornay. Cut the white part in rounds, season them, and poach them and the red parts with white wine. Cover the bottom of the scallop shells with *mornay* sauce (page 48), and lay on it the well-drained pieces of scallop. Cover with more sauce, sprinkle with grated cheese, and brown lightly.

Coquilles Saint-Jacques à la nantaise. Cut the white part in rounds, and poach them with the red part with a little white wine. Arrange them on the serving dish, surround them with slices of cooked mushrooms, cover them with a fine white wine sauce (page 49), and brown lightly.

Coquilles Saint-Jacques Newburg. Toss the white and the red parts in butter, add enough sherry to cover them, and cook for ten minutes. Arrange them in a timbale and add a few spoonfuls of cream. Reduce the sauce and bind it with a little Béchamel sauce, finish with lobster butter, and pour over the scallops in the timbale.

Coquilles Saint-Jacques à la poulette. Poach the scallops, white and red parts, with mushroom stock (page 36) and white wine. Drain them. Reduce the stock and add the necessary amount of fish *velouté*. Bind with egg yolks and cream, butter lightly, and add a few drops of lemon juice. Mix the scallops with this sauce, and serve them in a timbale sprinkled with chopped parsley.

Coquilles Saint-Jacques provençale. Fry the white part of the scallops in butter and olive oil. Slice up a few *cèpes*, or mushrooms, season them, and add, with shallots and garlic. Also add some breadcrumbs and chopped parsley. Serve very hot.

Coquilles Saint-Jacques Prunier. Poach the white and red parts with white wine and a *bouquet garni*. Reduce the cooking liquor, add the proper amount of fish *velouté*, bind with egg yolks, and thicken with butter. Cover the bottoms of the shells with some of this sauce, add the white parts cut in slices and the red parts minced up with some cooked mushrooms, cover with more sauce, and brown lightly.

SHRIMPS (*CREVETTES GRISES*): See PRAWNS

CHAPTER NINE

*

Turtle – Frogs – Snails

IT is unlikely that most of us will ever have to deal with a turtle, or even to cook frogs or snails. But in case we do, here are the ways to prepare them. Frog's legs are delicious fare, something like very tiny chicken, and we shall help to remove a long-standing and popular reproach that the French eat nothing but frogs, if we come to like them ourselves! As for snails, they have to be eaten to be believed, and to those who like them they are ambrosial.

TURTLE (*TORTUE*)

It is not very likely that private houses or indeed many establishments will ever want, or be in a position, to make turtle soup, but, for the curious, here are details of the way to make it. They are taken, with acknowledgements, from Escoffier's *Guide to Modern Cookery*.

Potage de tortue clair (Turtle Soup)

Slaughtering: For soup, take a turtle weighing from 120 to 180 pounds, and let it be very fleshy and full of life. To slaughter it, lay it on its back on a table, with its head hanging over the side. By means of a double butcher's hook, one spike of which is thrust into the turtle's lower jaw, while the other suspends an adequately heavy weight, make the animal hold its head back; then, with all possible despatch, sever the head from the body. Hang the body over a receptacle immediately, so that the blood may be collected, and leave it thus for one and a half to two hours.

Dismemberment: Thrust a strong knife between the carapace or upper shell and the plastron or lower shell, exactly where the two meet, and separate the one from the other. The turtle being on its back, cut all the adhering flesh from the plastron and put the latter aside. Now cut off the flippers; remove and throw away the intestines, and carefully collect all the green fat. Then cut away the flesh adhering to the carapace; once more remove all fat, and keep both in reserve.

Treatment of carapace, plastron, and flippers: The carapace and the plastron, which are the outside bony framework of the turtle, constitute the only portions from which the gelatinous flesh used as the garnish of the soup is obtained. Saw the carapace into six or eight pieces, and the plastron into four. Put these pieces, with the flippers, into boiling water or into steam, to blanch. Withdraw the flippers as soon as they are sufficiently stiff for their skin to be removed; leave the pieces of carapace and plastron to blanch for five minutes more, in order that they may admit of being scraped. Now cool the pieces of carapace and plastron, and the flippers, and put them into a stewpan containing enough water to cover them abundantly. Set to boil, garnish with vegetables, as in the case of an ordinary broth, and add a small quantity of turtle herbs (see below). Five or six hours should be allowed for the cooking of the carapace and plastron, but the flippers, which are put to further uses in other culinary preparations, should be withdrawn at the end of five hours. When the pieces are taken from the stock, remove all the flesh from the bones and cool it; then trim it carefully, and cut into small squares one and a half inches across. These squares, with the green fat, poached in salted water and sliced, constitute the garnish of the soup.

Preparation of the soup: There are two modes of procedure, though their respective results are almost identical.

(1) Make a broth of the flesh of the turtle alone, and then add a very gelatinous beef consommé to it, in pursuance of the method employed when the turtle soup is bought ready-made. This procedure is in practice the best, more particularly if the soup has to be kept some time.

(2) Make an ordinary broth of shin of beef, using the same quantity of this as of turtle. Also include half a calf's foot, and one half pound of calf's shin per three pounds of beef. Add the flesh of the turtle, or, in the event of its being thought necessary to clarify — an operation I do not in the least advise — reserve it for that purpose. The condiments and herbs being the same for both methods, I shall now describe the procedure for Method No. 1.

Ingredients: Put into a stewpan of convenient size the flesh of the turtle, and its head and bones. Partly moisten with the stock of the carapace, and complete the moistening, in the case of a turtle weighing 120 pounds, with enough water to bring the whole to 50 quarts. By this means a soup of about thirty to thirty-five quarts will be obtained at the end of the operation. Add salt in the proportion of one ounce to every five quarts; set to boil, skim, and garnish with twelve carrots, a bunch of leeks (about ten, bound with a head of celery), one pound of parsley stalks, eight onions with ten cloves stuck into them, two pounds of shallots, and one head of garlic. Set to boil gently for eight hours. An hour before straining the soup, add to the garnish four strips of lemon peel, and a bunch of turtle herbs, comprising sweet basil, sweet marjoram, sage, rosemary, savory and thyme, and a bag containing four ounces of coriander and two ounces of peppercorns. Finally, strain the soup through a napkin, add the pieces of flesh from the carapace and plastron which were put aside for the garnish, and keep it until wanted in specially made sandstone jars.

Serving: When about to serve this soup, heat it, test and rectify its seasoning, and finish it off by means of a portwine glass of very old Madeira for every quart. Very often a milk punch is served with turtle soup (see below).

Milk punch. Prepare a syrup from half a pint of water and three and a half ounces of sugar, the consistency being 17 (Baumé's Hydrometer). Set to infuse in this syrup two orange and two lemon rinds (*zestes*), that is, only the coloured part of the peel. Strain at the end of ten minutes, and add half a pint of rum, a fifth of a pint of Kirsch, two thirds of a pint of milk, and the juice of three oranges and three lemons. Mix thoroughly. Let it stand for three hours; filter, and serve cold.

Potage tortue lié. This soup is the same as that described above, except that it is thickened either with three ounces of *roux blond* (page 37) or with an ounce of arrowroot mixed with a little cold consommé for every quart of the soup.

Potage à la tortue de conserve. When this is of a good brand, it only needs double its quantity of very strong consommé to make the soup.

Seasoning should be corrected, and the final touch of old Madeira added in the proportion and manner given above.

Potage à la tortue sèche. For the preparation of this soup the dried turtle must be soaked in cold water for at least twenty-four hours. It is cooked in the same way as the carapace and plastron described above. Once cooked, it is treated in exactly the same manner as fresh turtle. The stock serves to moisten the meat with which the special consommé is made very rich and gelatinous, and to which are added, at the last minute, the flesh cut in dice and the old Madeira.

Potage à la tortue verte de conserve. Put in a little stewpan a very small chicken, first lightly coloured in the oven, half a pound of knuckle of veal cut in rounds, a small onion stuck with half a clove, half a parsley root, half an ounce of mushroom peelings, and a bouquet composed of a leek, a small stick of celery, a small piece of thyme and bayleaf, a touch of mace, and a little basil and marjoram. Moisten with two quarts of ordinary consommé, bring to the boil, and cook gently for two hours. Then strain it through a cloth, add to it half an ounce of arrowroot or potato flour mixed with a little cold consommé, mix quickly with a whisk, season with as much salt as you need, and let it boil gently, skimming it, for a quarter of an hour. Warm in the *bain-marie* enough green turtle to make a pint and three quarters, drain the pieces, cut them into one-inch squares, and add them to the soup. Finally season this with a touch of cayenne, and finish it, at the last minute, with a touch of Worcestershire sauce and four tablespoonfuls of sherry.

TERRAPIN (*TORTUE TERRAPINE*)

Here again is an animal which the ordinary housewife is unlikely to see alive. But this, nevertheless, is how they are served in America.

To Cook the Terrapin. Plunge the terrapin into boiling water, let them cook for fifty minutes, then plunge them into cold water. Now put them on their backs, removing the intestines, heart, and lungs, and skin the legs, removing the claws. Cut up the flesh in pieces, season it with salt and pepper, put it into a stewpan with just enough water to cover the pieces, and let them cook gently for an hour. Then turn them out and keep in a cool place until wanted.

Terrapine Club. Two cooked terrapin, two tablespoonfuls of butter, a cup of cream, a teaspoonful of salt, three egg yolks, and a glass of sherry. Toss the prepared terrapin in the butter, having first drained them well. Add the cream, let it boil and reduce a little, then add the beaten egg yolks, stirring, and lastly the sherry.

Terrapine Maryland. Two cooked terrapin, two tablespoonfuls of Madeira, half a teaspoonful of salt, one tablespoonful of butter, a cup of cream, two truffles, two egg yolks, a touch of cayenne. Toss the well-drained terrapin flesh in the butter, and add salt, cayenne, truffles, and Madeira. Mix the cream with the beaten egg yolks, mix it gently with the other ingredients in the pan, and heat up without allowing to come to the boil.

SNAILS (*ESCARGOTS*)

Snails are in season from November to March.

Escargots dits de Bourgogne. Brush the snails in several waters, and remove the chalky partition which closes them. Put them to scour, the day before they are wanted, in a little water salted with two handfuls of coarse salt for every hundred snails. The next day wash them well again in plenty of water to remove the slime, put them into a stewpan, cover them with plenty of water, and boil for eight minutes. Drain, plunge into cold water, and put them back into the pan with white wine, salt, pepper, a large *bouquet garni*, an onion stuck with four cloves, a head of garlic, and a glass of old brandy. Cook gently for three to three and a half hours, according to the size of the snails. Let it get cold in the stock. Then drain them, take them out of their shells, and remove the black end from each. Put them back in their shells, which you have meanwhile washed, drained, and dried, and finish by filling up the shells with *Beurre d'escargots* (page 201). To serve, arrange on a baking dish, and put in the oven for a few minutes before they are wanted. Serve very hot.

NOTE: Recognizing the difficulties which snail-lovers may encounter in the initial preparation of their favourites, Prunier's can supply them ready stuffed in their shells. They have then only to be heated up before serving.

Escargots petits gris au vin rouge. Scour and blanch the snails as described above. When they have been plunged into cold water,

Snails

Frog

Turtle

take them out of their shells, wash in several waters, and drain well. Meanwhile put into an earthenware pan some dice of blanched streaky bacon or pickled pork, button onions, crushed garlic, and good red wine in proportion to the number of snails. Then add the snails themselves, salt, pepper, and a *bouquet garni*. Bring to the boil, cover, and cook in the oven, very slowly, for two hours. When they are cooked and quite tender, finish with a light blended butter (page 42) and a liqueur glassful of old brandy. Serve in the dish they were cooked in, very hot.

FROGS (*GRENOUILLES*)

Grenouilles à la bordelaise. Fry the frogs' legs *à la meunière* (page 24) with chopped shallots and breadcrumbs. Add roughly chopped parsley, and serve.

Grenouilles à l'espagnole. Season the frogs' legs with salt, pepper, and a touch of mixed spice. Sprinkle them with brandy and let them marinate for two hours. Then wipe them and fry in a little butter in the frying pan until golden. At once add thin slices of mushroom and fresh sweet peppers, chopped parsley and lemon juice.

Grenouilles aux fines herbes. Fry the frogs' legs *à la meunière*, and finish with *fines herbes* (page 32).

Grenouilles frites. Season the frogs' legs and let them marinate for an hour with the juice of a lemon, olive oil, a touch of garlic and chopped parsley. Then dip them in frying batter and fry in deep fat. Serve on a napkin with fried parsley.

Grenouilles frites, sauce américaine. Egg-and-breadcrumb the frogs' legs and fry in deep oil. Hand a *sauce américaine* (page 44) with them.

Grenouilles parmentier. Season the frogs' legs, roll them in flour, and fry in very hot butter. Add some small potato dice fried in butter, and toss them together to mix well. Serve in a timbale, sprinkled with chopped parsley.

Pompadour de nymphes (or *grenouilles*).

The Editor is not sure whether it was Escoffier or someone else who, in order not to offend the susceptibilities of his *clientèle*, first called frogs *nymphes*. From the evidence of the almost lyrical

'*Nymphes à l'Aurore*', which appears in his *Modern Cookery*, Escoffier is strongly suspected.

(1) Cook the frogs' legs in a light *blanc* (see below), with a *bouquet garni* and lemon. Twenty-five minutes should see them done. Drain, bone, and keep the best parts of the meat for the garnish. Add to the rest of the frogs' flesh an equal amount of sole or pike, and make of this a forcemeat in the usual manner (page 31), adding for each pound of flesh the same amount of panada (page 34), four ounces of butter, four egg yolks and one whole egg, and a seasoning of salt and pepper. At the last, add four dessertspoonfuls of tomato purée, and pass the whole thing through a tammy. With part of this forcemeat make a few small *quenelles* in the shape of olives, poach them in salted water, plunge them when cooked into cold water, and keep them by. (2) Make a *velouté* with the stock of the frogs, and prepare a garnish with minced mushrooms, shelled shrimps, the *quenelles*, the pieces of frogs' flesh already reserved for the purpose, and some slices of truffle. Bind this garnish with part of the *velouté*. (3) Butter a charlotte mould, decorate it with rounds of truffle, and then line the bottom and sides with a layer of the forcemeat about half an inch thick. Fill up the middle with the garnish, cover the top with more forcemeat, and poach the mould in a *bain-marie* for about forty minutes. When it is cooked, take the *Pompadour* from the *bain-marie* and let it stand for six to seven minutes before you turn it out. At the time of serving, turn it out and surround it with the rest of the *velouté*, to which you have added a little truffle juice, mushroom stock, and cream. Serve very hot.

NOTE: An ordinary *blanc*, which is used a great deal in French cookery for boiling white vegetables, is made as follows: put a heaped tablespoonful of flour in a little water, and when it is mixed quite smooth, add two quarts of water with two tablespoonfuls of vinegar and a little salt; stir until it boils, then add whatever has to be cooked in it — in this instance, *a bouquet garni* and the frogs' legs, substituting lemon for vinegar — and finally three tablespoonfuls of clarified veal or beef dripping. This last forms a covering to keep out the air, and the food will cook quite gently underneath and preserve its whiteness and a better flavour.

Grenouilles à la poulette. Poach the frogs' legs with mushroom stock (page 36) and white wine: drain and mix them with a *poulette* sauce to which you have added some cooked button mushrooms. Add the reduced stock of the frogs to the sauce. Serve in a timbale, sprinkled with chopped parsley.

Grenouilles à la provençale. Fry the frogs' legs *à a meunière* (page 24), with a tiny bit of garlic.

Rizotto de Grenouilles à l'indienne. Prepare a risotto (page 37), and mould it in a border mould. Stew the frogs' legs in butter, sprinkle them with a pinch of curry powder, moisten with cream, and finish cooking them. Drain the legs, and after removing the bones, mix them with the reduced stock. Serve in the risotto border.

Grenouilles à la saintongeaise. Egg-and-breadcrumb the frogs' legs and fry them in clarified butter. On serving, sprinkle them with nut-brown butter with chopped shallot added.

Grenouilles à la vendéenne. For four or five people you will want fifty frogs' legs. Beat up two whole eggs as if for an omelette, with salt, pepper, and grated nutmeg, and mix in two dessertspoonfuls of cream. Dip the legs in this mixture, then in fine fresh breadcrumbs. Fry them in very hot oil so that they are nice and crisp. Serve separately a light tomato sauce rather strongly flavoured with lemon.

CHAPTER TEN

*

Some Prunier Specialities

WHILE this is, strictly speaking, a fish book, it has been thought advisable to include in it a few recipes of dishes other than fish which are specialities of Prunier's in London. These are given because guests so often ask for the recipes that it is felt there is some special merit in them for English people. They are all grouped together, therefore, in this chapter.

Œufs Lucullus. Hard-boil the required number of eggs: cut into halves, place on small squares of toast. Crown with creamed *foie gras* flavoured with port and seasoning, which should be piped on top of the half eggs which have been allowed to cool off, and cover the whole with meat jelly (made of bone stock with gelatine).

Omelettes with fish. Three eggs, half a pinch of salt, very little pepper, and half an ounce of butter. Break the eggs, season them, and beat them very slightly. Put the butter in a very clean hot frying-pan, pour in the eggs, and stir briskly until there is a slight thickening. Now let the eggs spread over the bottom of the pan, and remove the pan from the centre of the fire. Put the garnish in the middle of the omelette, and start folding the omelette over, beginning with the side nearest to the handle of the pan, tilting the pan as you do so. Omelettes may be garnished with shrimps or prawns, mussels, sea-urchins, the flesh of crab, lobster, Dublin Bay prawns (*langoustines*), smoked haddock, caviar, etc. When using prawns (*langoustines*), mussels, lobsters, etc., first toss the meat in butter, and add two spoonfuls of cream for each person.

Banderille flambée à l'espagnole (for four persons). Take one pound of fillet steak cut in large dice, a quarter of a pound of mushrooms cut in slices, salt, pepper. Slightly brown in butter. Take a quarter of a pound of ham, cut in small slices to match the size of the meat and mushrooms, so as to put them on skewers alternately – one piece meat, one mushroom, one piece of ham, etc. – to finish on the grill. Serve with four tomatoes *provençale*, i.e. tomatoes cooked in oven with breadcrumbs, parsley, and garlic. The skewers are to be served on a separate dish, so as to be singed with brandy when ready to serve, which is with a sauce made as follows: reduce a glass of red wine with one minced shallot and thicken with a teaspoonful of flour, butter, and small pieces of marrow, to which add some pimentoes cut in dice.

Tournedos Boston. Poach six flat oysters for each tournedos. Reduce their stock, and add to it half a dessertspoonful of Béchamel sauce and two of *hollandaise* sauce. Grill the tournedos, garnish with the oysters, and coat thickly with the sauce.

Tournedos grillé, beurre anchois. Grill the tournedos carefully, and serve with a butter made with one ounce of salted anchovy fillets, washed and skinned, an ounce and a half of butter, and a pinch of pepper. Pass the butter through a fine sieve. When finished, it should be like creamed butter.

Pieds de mouton à la poulette. Make a *blanc* (page 220) with two quarts of cold water, two dessertspoonfuls of flour, half an ounce of salt, a large onion stuck with a clove, three dessertspoonfuls of vinegar, and a bouquet of parsley, chervil, thyme, and bayleaf. When the *blanc* is boiling and the sheep's trotters are ready to go in, add two ounces of finely minced beef kidney suet. Singe the trotters with spirit or on a gas flame, then remove the bone, either by disjointing it or by cutting through the skin on the inside of the trotter, and take out the small woolly bit between the two bones. Then scald the trotters again for eight to ten minutes. Put them into the boiling *blanc* and cook them very gently for about an hour and a half, according to the age of the sheep.

Make the *sauce poulette* as follows: melt an ounce of butter, add an ounce of flour, brown it lightly, and moisten with a pint of white stock and three tablespoonfuls of mushroom stock (page 36). Season with a pinch of white pepper and a pinch of nutmeg, bring to the boil, stirring all the time, then add an ounce of mushroom parings and a small bunch of parsley, and cook gently for twenty-five minutes. Then strain into a saucepan, stir on a brisk fire for a few

minutes, add three egg yolks to thicken it, and finish with two ounces
of butter and the juice of half a lemon. A few minutes before serving
add to the sauce a dozen small cooked mushrooms and twelve trotters
(two for each person). Dress in a timbale or deep dish, and sprinkle
with chopped parsley.

Poires 'Belle Angevine'. Poach the pears in a syrup flavoured with
vanilla. Cook slowly in a saucepan with the lid on, so as to keep the
pears not too firm, but what we call in French *fondantes*, which means
melting, and let them cool in this syrup. Then drain and core with an
apple corer: replace what has been taken out by a filling made of
salpicon (an assortment of glacé fruit, cut in small dice, macerated in
Cointreau liqueur). The pears thus prepared should be put in a
small saucepan-shaped 'bed' made of nougat. Coat the pears in
apricot syrup flavoured with Cointreau, or raspberry syrup if in
season. Then decorate with a little cream Chantilly and crystallized
Parma violets. This sweet should be served cool.

Pots de crème au chocolat. Dissolve seventeen ounces of chocolate
in a pint and three quarters of milk, bring to the boil, and add three
and a half ounces of sugar. Let it cool, and add nine egg yolks, but do
not work the mixture too much. Put in small pots in a dish containing
water, and cover. Put into a gentle oven, and let them cook slowly.
Take them out when the cream is not quite firm and still shakes a
little, and leave them to cool in the dish.

Mousse au Kirsch. Mix half a pound of caster sugar with eight egg
yolks. Heat a pint of milk with vanilla, and pour in the eggs. Bring
almost to the boil, but not quite, or it will spoil. Allow to cool, stirring frequently, and when cold add a pint of double cream. Put the
mixture into a freezer and mix thoroughly. Allow to freeze for about
two hours. When it is a good creamy consistency, add a large wineglassful of Kirsch, and stir again until thoroughly mixed. Serve in
deep glasses.

Mousse au chocolat (for ten people). One pound of *ganache* (see
below), a quarter pound of *pâte à bombe* (see below), half a pound of
whipped cream. To make the *ganache*, melt one pound of chocolate
in a little milk on a slow fire, and leave to cool. The ingredients
required for the *pâte à bombe* are one and a half pints of syrup at
30°C. (86° F.) and eight egg yolks. To make the *pâte à bombe* mix the

syrup and the egg yolks and cook in a *bain-marie*. Strain while still hot, and then whip until cool. Add the *pâte à bombe* to the *ganache* and place the container in a *bain-marie*. Whip in half a pound of cream until sufficiently thick, taking care not to let it boil. Take the container out of the *bain-marie* and let the contents finish thickening off the fire. When quite cold, put in the refrigerator.

Crêpes à l'orange. Make some batter as for ordinary pancakes, and cook some. Place in the centre of each pancake the following mixture: grate the rind of an orange, and add this to caramel with a little orange Curaçao.

Crêpes Prunier. These are thin pancakes stuffed with a *Crème patissière* (custard made with a little flour, *not* custard powder). Mix with one third of whipped cream flavoured with Trappistine liqueur. Roll the pancakes and put them on a buttered dish, as for an omelette, and warm them in the oven. Serve them very hot; at the last moment pour on a little Trappistine liqueur and set alight.

Lindy's cheesecake

2½ lb. cream cheese	1¾ cups sugar
3 tablespoons flour	5 eggs
1½ teaspoons grated orange rind	2 egg yolks
1 teaspoon grated lemon rind	¼ cup heavy cream
pinch of vanilla pod (inside pulp), or ¼ teaspoonful vanilla extract	

Combine cheese, sugar, flour, grated orange and lemon rind, and vanilla. Add eggs and egg yolks, one at a time, stirring lightly after each addition. Stir in cream.

Cookie dough mixture

1 cup sifted plain flour	1 teaspoon grated lemon rind
pinch of vanilla pod (inside pulp)	¼ cup sugar
1 egg yolk	¼ cup butter

Combine flour, sugar, lemon rind, and vanilla, make a well in the centre, and add egg yolk and butter. Work together quickly with the hands until well blended. Wrap in waxed paper and chill thoroughly in the refrigerator for about one hour. Roll out one-eighth of an inch thick and place on the greased bottom of a nine-inch loose-bottom cake tin. Trim off the dough by running a rolling pin over the sharp edge. Bake in a hot oven (400° F., gas Regulo 5) for twenty minutes, or until a light gold. Cool. Butter sides of cake tin and place over base. Roll remaining dough one-eighth of an inch thick, and cut to fit the sides of the greased ring. Fill with cheese mixture. Bake in a very hot oven (550° F., gas Regulo 9) for twelve to fifteen minutes. Reduce temperature to slow (200° F., Regulo 1–4), and continue baking for one hour. Cool before cutting.

MICHEL BOUZY'S MENUS FOR HOLY WEEK

DÉJEUNER
(six persons)

Petits Bouchées aux Crevettes
Sole grillée Béarnaise
(Pomme de Terre en Robe)
Pâté de Saumon aux Pistaches
Nouilles fraîches à la Crème
Poires au Rubis

DÉJEUNER
(eighteen persons)

Les Huîtres de Belon sur Toast
La Barbue saumonée braisée
(garnie de barquettes d'Épinards à la Crème)
Les Homards à la Nage
Pommes de Terre Croquettes
Les Abricots au Riz

DÉJEUNER
(twelve persons)

Crevettes – Palourdes – Oursins
Les Merlans au Gratin
Le Homard rôti
Le Bar en Gelée
Les Beignets de Reinettes

DÉJEUNER
(sixteen persons)

Les Crevettes Bouquet
Les Moules frites
Le Saumon au Fumet
La Brandade de Morue
Le Haddock au Beurre fondu
Le Rizotto de Clams
Les Poires Figaro

DÎNER
(twelve persons)

La Bouillabaisse
Le Turbotin aux Champignons
Le Pilaff de Crabe sauce Currie
Les Écrevisses en Buisson
Les Crêpes au sucre

DÎNER
(fifteen persons)

Soupe aux Moules
Les Filets de Sole Carême
Fricandeau d'Esturgeon
(garni de Jardinière)
Le Pâté d'Anguille
Les Céleris et Fonds d'Artichauts
au Velouté
L'Ananas Chantilly

CHAPTER ELEVEN

*

A Note on Wine and Fish

IF one were to be asked off hand what wines should be drunk with fish, I suppose the answer would be this:

With caviar. Nothing, or perhaps vodka.

With oysters. Muscadet, Chablis, or a good white Burgundy such as Pouilly, Meursault, etc. or champagne.

With fish soups. A young Hock or Moselle, or a dryish white Burgundy, the choice depending on whether a white or red wine is to follow.

With turtle soup. Punch (page 215). An authority has rightly remarked that Madeira is better *in* the soup than with it.

With lobsters and crustacés. Chablis or white Burgundy; or, if you are not following with a fine red wine, champagne.

With fish in general. White French or German wines, dry or dryish. Some like Sauternes, if nothing dryer is to follow.

This list needs some qualifications. Let us begin at the beginning. Caviar speaks for itself. Its strong flavour naturally precludes any wine, which would be killed at once. If anything must be drunk (and this would not be at a serious meal), the Russian vodka is the only possible thing. With oysters, a real Chablis is the one and only wine, I think. Champagne *mousseux* is lost on them; but there is much to be said for a glass of the still Champagne which has been coming into fashion again, with a dozen oysters – and if they are to be a meal in themselves, a word must be said for stout. Some of the less dry French wines, like Anjou, are quite good with them, too. The advice given above for fish soups is a sound one, I think, for the days of a universal glass of sherry with the soup seem a little *vieux jeu* nowadays, when our palates are so much more sophisticated. In the same way, lobster and the other *crustacés* should be treated in much the same way as the *bisques* of which they are composed, but everyone will agree that if the lobster is the *clou* of a meal, such as an after-the-theatre supper, nothing could be better than Champagne, and plenty of it.

We now come to the whole question of drinking wine with the ordinary fish. In the first place, it is safe to say that it should always be white. There are a few cases where red wine may be drunk with fish, but only when the fish has been cooked in that wine. Red mullet lends itself particularly to red wine, and so to a certain extent does salmon. In Escoffier's *Guide to Modern Cookery* there will be found a section on *Soles aux grands vins*, where recipes are given for poaching sole in Volnay, Pommard, Romanée, Clos-de-Vougeot, and so on. But I do not think that these dishes, or the drinking of red wine with them, will appeal to us now. When we think of white wine with fish, we think according to our palates. Fifty or sixty years ago it used to be popular to drink Sauternes with fish, and there is an apocryphal story about King Edward VII which is difficult for us moderns to believe. A certain chef had prepared a wonderful fish dish for the King, and after the dinner was over was found to be in an ecstasy of delight. 'But,' they said, 'the King never said anything about your dish at all!' 'Didn't you hear?' asked the chef. 'He said that his Château Yquem had never tasted so delicious. Was not that a tribute to my dish?' But then, I have never been able to forgive King Edward for his liking salmon with curry! But this is told simply to show that not only a sweet wine like a Sauterne was drunk with this course, but even a liqueur-like wine of the type of Château Yquem, which nowadays no one would dream of drinking before the sweet.

So when I read here and there that the white wine accompanying fish should always be dry, I sometimes have my doubts. In the usual way I have what is called a dry palate: that is, I am inclined to prefer the dryer sorts of wine, but in the case of fish I find that just a little sweetness is desirable, or the wine may taste a little acid. But as I have said, this is a matter of taste, and the best way to discover your own palate is to try it out – preferably at Prunier's!

André Simon, in his *Art of Good Living*, makes the point that at an informal luncheon it would be as well to serve a light wine, Graves or Anjou, with a simple dish, whereas if our meal is more elaborate we go to the extent of a good Moselle or a Chablis, and for an even great occasion Champagne or a high-class hock or white Burgundy;

and there is of course sound common sense in this. If we suit our wines to our meals, we also suit our meals to our purses, and this is a wise way of doing it. There are a great many cheaper and very delicious French wines now to be found in the English market, and most of these can be tried at Prunier's. I have already mentioned still Champagne (*Champagne nature*); there are also Anjou, Vouvray, Sancerre, and others, which are not only excellent in themselves, but offer an original thought for the hostess planning a luncheon at home and wishing to give a wine which is a little out of the ordinary and impressive as well.

And I must just add a note here, that when I was writing of red wines I had quite forgotten a delicious bottle of *vin rosé* from Anjou which I drank not long ago with a trout cooked a little elaborately *à la meunière*. It was admirable! But then you cannot call *vin rosé* red wine, nor the divine trout an ordinary fish!

CHAPTER TWELVE

*

A Short Glossary of Terms used in Cooking

THIS short glossary has been prepared for the use of those whose knowledge of culinary French is limited.

Ail. Garlic

Aïoli. A kind of garlicky mayonnaise popular in the south of France

Alose. Shad

Anchois. Anchovy

Anguille. Eel

Anguille de mer. Conger

Attereaux. Skewers

Bain-marie. A large receptacle containing hot water in which various foods can be poached, sauces kept hot, etc.

Bar. Bass

Barbeau. Barbel

Barbillon. Small barbel

Barbue. Brill

Barquette. A boat-shaped pastry case, pastry boat

Baudroie. Monk, or angler fish: rockfish

Beignet. Fritter

Beurre. Butter

Bigorneau. Winkle

Bisque. A rich creamy soup, e.g. *Bisque de homard*

Blanc. A special preparation for boiling whitemeat or vegetables

Blanchaille. Whitebait

Blanchailles en. Fish cut in strips the size of whitebait

Bleu au. Fish cooked in a special manner with vinegar and water, so that it is bright blue when done

Bouchée. A small puff-pastry case

Bouillabaisse. A savoury stew of fish

Bouillon. Stock

Bouquet. Prawns

Bouquet garni. A bunch of herbs used for flavouring, usually consisting of parsley stalks, thyme and bayleaf

Brandade. A special dish made with salt cod

Brème. Bream (freshwater)

Brochet. Pike

Brocheton. Small pike, jack

Brochette, en. On skewers

Brunoise. Fine *salpicon*

Cabillaud. Cod, fresh

Cadgery. Kedgeree

Canapé. A slice of fried or toasted bread for holding savouries

Câpres. Capers

Carpe. Carp

Carpillon. Small carp

Carolines. Savoury small éclairs

Carrelet. Flounder, or plaice

Chowder. An American fish soup

Ciseler. To score before cooking

Colin. Saithe, coalfish, hake

Congre. Conger eel

Coquille, en. On a scallop shell

Coquilles Saint-Jacques. Scallops

Côtelette. Cutlet

Coulibiac. A rich Russian pastry made with salmon

Court-bouillon. A mixture of water, herbs, vegetables, and either wine or vinegar, used for cooking fish

Crabe. Crab

Crêpe. Pancake

Cresson. Watercress

Crevettes grises. Shrimps

Crevettes roses. Prawns

Cromesquis. A kind of fritter

Croquettes. A mixture of fish shaped like a cork, rolled in egg-and-breadcrumbs, and fried

Croûtes. Bread shaped and fried, for containing some garnish or other

Croûtons. Small dice of fried bread

Currie. Curry

Darne. A slice cut across the fish; steak or cutlet of fish

Daurade. Sea bream

Diablé. Devilled

Duchesses. Small savoury buns stuffed with various fillings

Écrevisse. Crayfish (freshwater)

Églefin. Haddock

Églefin fumé. Smoked haddock

Éperlan. Smelt

Équille. Sand-eel

Escabèche. A kind of 'souse' for smelt and other fish

Escalope. A thin slice

Escargot. Snail

Espadon. Swordfish

Esturgeon. Sturgeon

Farci, farcie. Stuffed

Fines herbes. Chervil, chives, parsley, and tarragon finely chopped and mixed in equal parts

Flétan. Halibut

Four, au. Baked (*lit.* 'in the oven')

Frit, frite. Fried

Fritot, en. Fried in batter

Fruits de mer. Any small shellfish, oysters

Fumet. A highly concentrated stock

Gardon. Roach

Gelée. Jelly

Glace. Ice

Glace (de viande, de poisson). Glaze, meat or fish

Glacé, glacée. (1) Iced; (2) glazed, with glaze; (3) quickly browned in the oven

Gratin, au Gratiné, gratinée. Generally, sprinkled with breadcrumbs and butter, and sometimes cheese, and browned in the oven. But see pages 27–9

Goujon. Gudgeon

Goujons, en. Fish cut to the size of gudgeon before cooking

Grenouille. Frog

Grondin. Gurnet

Hareng. Herring, fresh

Hareng, fumé. Kipper

Hareng, salé. Bloater

Hareng, saur. Red herring, smoked herring

Homard. Lobster

Huîtres. Oysters

Julienne, en. Cut in thin match-like shreds

Kadgiory. Kedgeree

Kari. Curry

Laitance. Soft roe

Lamproie. Lamprey

Langouste. Crawfish (sea-water)

Langoustine. Dublin Bay prawn

Lard. Bacon

Limande. Lemon sole, sometimes dab

Lotte. Eel-pout

Loup de mer. Bass

Maquereau. Mackerel

Marinade. A mixture used for steeping fish before cooking

Matelote. A savoury fish ragout

Merlan. Whiting

Morue. Salt cod

Moule. Mussel

Muge, Mulet. Grey mullet

Nage. A special *court-bouillon* for shellfish

Nephrops. Dublin Bay prawns

Noisette (when cooking butter (e.g. page 43))

Nymphes. Frogs

Œufs (de poisson). Hard roe

Ombre. Grayling

Oursin. Sea urchin

Palourde. Cockle

Paupiette. A rolled fillet of fish

Perche. Perch

Pilaff. A rice dish

Piroguis. A small fish pastry from Russia

Plie. Plaice

Poisson. Fish

Poutargue. An oriental preparation of dried tunny or mullet eggs

Quenelles. A kind of savoury dumpling

Raie. Skate

Rastegaïs. A sort of small coulibiac or Russian fish pastry

Riz. Rice

Rizotto. An Italian dish of rice and meat or fish, risotto

Roll-mops. Soused bloater fillets

Rôti. Roasted

Rouget. Red mullet or red gurnard

Roux. The initial preparation of flour and butter, cooked to varying degrees of browning, used as a thickening agent

Royan. A kind of sardine

Saint-Pierre. John Dory

Salé. Salted

Salpicon. Dice, about a quarter of an inch, of any ingredient used for the preparation of a dish; if cut very finely, the preparation becomes a *Brunoise*

Saumon. Salmon

Saumon fumé. Smoked salmon

Suprêmes. The best fillets

Tanche. Tench

Thon. Tunnyfish, tuna

Tortue. Turtle

Tourte. Tart, pie

Truite. Trout

Truite saumonée. Salmon trout

Turbotin. Chicken turbot

Velouté. A thick fish sauce or soup

Vin. Wine

Vive. Weever

Vol-au-vent. A fine puff pastry case filled with fish or meat

INDEX

Four more Penguin Handbooks are described on the following pages

WINES AND SPIRITS

L. W. Marrison

PH 87

The world produces over four thousand millions of gallons of wine each year, equivalent to nearly two gallons for each human being. Although it is all made in much the same way as was the wine that Noah and the Pharaohs drank, a great many refinements of the old methods have been introduced during the last century or two. Much also has been discovered in the last few decades of how the fermentation process is carried on by the wine-yeasts. The process of making spirits was discovered, perhaps by the Arabs, some twelve centuries ago, possibly in an effort to temper the rigours of the Dark Ages.

Wines and Spirits attempts to give a factual account (with 32 illustrations and 18 maps) of the making of these alcoholic drinks, and when the author deviates from purely factual description it is only in order to offer some guidance on the selection of good wines.

A BOOK OF MEDITERRANEAN FOOD

Elizabeth David

PH 27

This book is based on a collection of recipes made by the author when she lived in France, Italy, the Greek Islands, and Egypt, doing her own cooking and obtaining her information at first hand. In these pages will be found recipes, and practical ones, evoking all the colour and sun of the Mediterranean; dishes with such exciting and unfamiliar names as the *Soupe au Pislou*, the *Pebronata* of Corsica, or the *Skordalia* of the Greeks. The book includes recipes from Spain, Provence, Greece, Italy, and the Middle East, making use of ingredients from all over the Mediterranean now available in England. The majority of the dishes however do not require exotic ingredients, being made with everyday vegetables, herbs, fish, and poultry, but treated in unfamiliar ways.

'In *Mediterranean Food* Mrs David proves herself a gastronome of rare integrity. . . . She refuses to make ignoble compromises with expediency. And in this, surely, she is very right. . . . Above all, she has the happy knack of giving just as much detail as the average cook finds desirable; she presumes neither on our knowledge nor our ignorance' – Elizabeth Nicholas in the *Sunday Times*